REVIEWS OF UNITED KINGDOM

STATISTICAL SOURCES

Volume VI

Wealth
and
Personal Incomes

Reviews of United Kingdom Statistical Sources

Editor W. F. Maunder

Vol I 1. *Personal Social Services*, B. P. Davies

2. *Voluntary Organizations in the Personal Social Service Field*, G. J. Murray

Vol II 3. *Central Government Routine Health Statistics*, Michael Alderson

4. *Social Security Statistics*, Frank Whitehead

Vol III 5. *Housing in Great Britain*, Stuart Farthing

6. *Housing in Northern Ireland*, Michael Fleming

Vol IV 7. *Leisure*, F. M. M. Lewes and S. R. Parker

8. *Tourism*, L. J. Lickorish

Vol V 9. *General Sources of Statistics*, G. F. Lock

Vol VI 10. *Wealth*, A. B. Atkinson and A. J. Harrison

11. *Personal Incomes*, T. Stark

Vol VII 12. *Road Passenger Tranport*, D. L. Munby

13. *Road Goods Transport*, A. H. Watson

Vol VIII 14. *Land Use*, J. T. Coppock

15. *Town and Country Planning*, L. F. Gebbett

REVIEWS OF UNITED KINGDOM STATISTICAL SOURCES

Edited by W. F. MAUNDER

Professor of Economic and Social Statistics
University of Exeter

VOLUME VI

WEALTH

by

A. B. ATKINSON
Professor of Political Economy,
University College, London

and

A. J. HARRISON
Lecturer in Economics,
McMaster University, Hamilton, Ontario

and

PERSONAL INCOMES

by

T. STARK
Lecturer in Economics,
The New University of Ulster

Published for The Royal Statistical Society
and the Social Science Research Council
by

PERGAMON PRESS

OXFORD · NEW YORK · TORONTO · SYDNEY · PARIS · FRANKFURT

U.K.	Pergamon Press Ltd., Headington Hill Hall, Oxford OX3 0BW, England
U.S.A.	Pergamon Press Inc., Maxwell House, Fairview Park, Elmsford, New York 10523, U.S.A.
CANADA	Pergamon of Canada Ltd., 75 The East Mall, Toronto, Ontario, Canada
AUSTRALIA	Pergamon Press (Aust.) Pty. Ltd., 19a Boundary Street, Rushcutters Bay, N.S.W. 2011, Australia
FRANCE	Pergamon Press SARL, 24 rue des Ecoles, 75240 Paris, Cedex 05, France
FEDERAL REPUBLIC OF GERMANY	Pergamon Press GmbH, 6242 Kronberg-Taunus, Pferdstrasse 1, Federal Republic of Germany

First Published 1978

For bibliographic purposes this volume should be cited as:
Atkinson, A. B. Harrison, A. J. & Stark, T. *Wealth and Personal Incomes*, Pergamon Press Ltd on behalf of The Royal Statistical Society and the Social Science Research Council, 1978

British Library Cataloguing in Publication Data

Reviews of United Kingdom statistical sources.
Vol. 6: Wealth; and, Personal incomes.
1. Great Britain – Statistical services
I. Maunder, Wynne Frederick II. Atkinson, Anthony Barnes III. Harrison, Anthony John
IV. Stark, Thomas V. Royal Statistical Society
VI. Social Science Research Council (Great Britain)
314. 1 HA37. G7 77–30556

ISBN 0–08–022450–4

Printed in Great Britain by Cox & Wyman Ltd, London, Fakenham and Reading

Contents

Foreword

The Sources and Nature of the Statistics of the United Kingdom produced under the auspices of the Royal Statistical Society and edited by Maurice Kendall, filled a notable gap on the library shelves when it made its appearance in the early post-war years. Through a series of critical reviews by many of the foremost national experts, it constituted a valuable contemporary guide to statisticians working in many fields as well as a benchmark to which historians of the development of Statistics in this country are likely to return again and again. The Social Science Research Council and the Society were both delighted when Professor Maunder came forward with the proposal that a revised version should be produced, indicating as well his willingness to take on the onerous task of editor. The two bodies were more than happy to act as co-sponsors of the project and to help in its planning through a joint steering committee. The result, we are confident, will be adjudged a worthy successor to the previous volumes by the very much larger 'statistics public' that has come into being in the intervening years.

Dr C. S. Smith
Secretary
Social Science Research Council
May 1977

E. M. L. Beale
Honorary Secretary
Royal Statistical Society
May 1977

MEMBERSHIP OF THE JOINT STEERING COMMITTEE

(May 1977)

Chairman: Professor Sir Roy Allen

Representing the Royal Statistical Society:

Dr W. R. Buckland
Miss S. V. Cunliffe
Dr S. Rosenbaum

Representing the Social Science Research Council:

Mr A. Noble
Mr T. S. Pilling
Dr W. Taylor

Secretary: Mr D. E. Allen

Although the late T. S. Pilling was not especially involved with this particular volume, as it is the first to appear since his death the opportunity must be taken to place on record the great indebtedness of the series as a whole to his interest and wise guidance. He was a member of the Joint Steering Committee (representing the SSRC) from its inception until 1975 and as such was involved in all the problems and difficulties of the early planning phase. In many ways he was a king-pin at this stage as he was the main source of liaison with official developments thus enabling purposeless duplication of effort to be avoided. It had been my personal hope that he might soon return to the Committee and, indeed, in a recent personal letter he had expressed his willingness to consider the idea. Alas, this is not now to be.—W.F.M.

Introduction

It is tempting to believe that the subject matter of this volume (the sixth in the series) is of particular current interest in that it relates to a topic which is receiving close scrutiny at the present time. The standing *Royal Commission on the Distribution of Income and Wealth* is one indicator which testifies to this state of affairs, but, in a more general sense, there is a pervasive climate of contemporary political and economic debate which revolves round the issue of what are fair shares for whom. This latter line of thought opens up a very wide horizon and clearly it would be unrealistic to assume that a dispassionate study of statistics is ever going to influence political persuasion in any immediate sense; it is not anticipated that this volume is likely to become essential reading for party workers.

For the medium and longer term the outlook is more open and if reason rules at all in human affairs it is at least a legitimate hope that there may be a connection between the valid interpretation of the evidence and the formulation of policy. However, with this view of things the current preoccupation with the topic takes on a new dimension and the present concern is less a matter of some passing fashion rather than the intensification of a continuing theme. The Royal Statistical Society, of course, itself can point to a long history of investigation and reporting on many aspects of income and wealth, as testimony to which it is sufficient to recall that Charles Booth's first results on his momentous London survey were published in two papers appearing in its *Journal* in 1887 and 1888. Issues of concern now extend much further than any straightforward idea of poverty and it would seem a fairly safe prediction that interest in the future will continue to grow and expand likewise.

In case these opening remarks should suggest an exclusive concentration on aspects of political philosophy, it may be as well to stress that throughout the preparation of these reviews the needs of all kinds of users have been borne in mind as closely as possible. If the sources themselves are more relevant to some users than to others, then that, of course, is not the responsibility of the authors who have tried to net everything within their brief. In fact, a glance at either of the two subject indexes discloses that while aggregative distributions may have pride of place, there is still a considerable amount of information available at a disaggregated level.

The primary aim of this series is to act as a work of reference to the sources of statistical material of all kinds, both official and unofficial. It seeks to enable the user to discover what data are available on the subject in which he is interested, from where they may be obtained, and what the limitations are to their use. Data are regarded as available not only if published in the normal printed format but also if they are likely to be released to a *bona fide* enquirer in any other form, such as duplicated documents, computer print-out or even magnetic tape. On the other hand, no reference is made to material which, even if it is known to exist, is not accessible to the general run of potential users. The distinction, of course, is not clear-cut and mention of a source is not to be regarded as a guarantee that data will be released; in particular cases it may very well be a matter for negotiation. The latter caution applies with particular force to the question of obtaining computer print-outs of custom specified tabulations. Where original records are held on magnetic tape it might appear that there should be no insuperable problem, apart from confidentiality, in obtaining any feasible analysis at a cost; in practice, it may well turn out that there are capacity restraints which override any simple cost calculation. Thus, what is requested might make demands on computer and programming resources to the extent that the routine work of the agency concerned would be intolerably affected.

The intention is that the sources for each topic should be reviewed in detail, and the brief supplied to authors has called for comprehensive coverage at the level of 'national interest'. This term does not denote any necessary restriction to statistics collected on a national basis (still less, of course, to national aggregates) but it means that sources of a purely local character, without wider interest in either content or methodology, are excluded. Indeed, the mere task of identifying all material of this latter kind is an impossibility. The interpretation of the brief has obviously involved discretion and it is up to the users of these reviews to say what unreasonable gaps become apparent to them. They are cordially invited to do so by communicating with me.

To facilitate the use of the series as a work of reference, certain features have been incorporated which are worth a word or two of explanation.

First, the text of each review is designed, in so far as varying subject matter permits, to follow a standard form of arrangement so that users may expect a similar pattern to be followed throughout the series. The starting point is a brief summary of the activity concerned and its organization, in order to give a clear background understanding of how data are collected, what is being measured, the stage at which measurements are made, what the reporting units are, the channels through which returns are routed and where they are processed. As a further part of this introductory material, there is a discussion of the specific problems of definition and measurement to which the topic gives rise. The core sections on available sources which follow are arranged at the author's discretion – by origin, by subject subdivision, or by type of data; there is too much heterogeneity between topics to permit any imposition of complete uniformity on all authors. The final section is devoted to a discussion of general shortcomings and possibly desirable improvements. In case a contrary expectation should be aroused, it should be said that authors have not been asked to produce a comprehensive plan for the reform of statistical reporting in the whole of their field. However, a review of existing sources is a natural opportunity to make some suggestions for future policy on the collection and publication of statistics within the scope concerned.

Secondly, detailed factual information about statistical series and other data are given in a Quick Reference List (QRL). The exact nature of the entries is best seen by glancing at the list and accordingly they are not described here. Again, the ordering is not prescribed except that entries are not classified by publication source since it is presumed that it is this which is unknown to the reader. In general, the routine type of information which is given in the QRL is not repeated verbally in the text; the former, however, serves as a search route to the latter in that a reference (by section number) is shown against a QRL entry when there is a related discussion in the text.

Third, a subject index to each review acts as a more or less conventional line of enquiry on textual references; however, it is a computerized system and, for an individual review, the only peculiarity which it introduces is the possibility of easily permuting entries. Thus an entry in the index to the first review in this volume is:

Net worth of industrial and commercial companies

which is shown also as:

Industrial and commercial companies, net worth of

as well as:

Commercial companies, net worth of industrial and

The object at this level is merely to facilitate search by giving as many variants as possible. In addition, individual review subject indexes are merged into a cumulative index which is held on magnetic tape and may possibly be used to produce a printed version from time to time if that seems desirable. Computer print-outs of the cumulative index to date are available on application to me at the Department of Economics, University of Exeter. In addition, selective searches of this index may be made by the input of key-words; the result is a print-out of all entries in which the key-word appears in the initial position in the subject index of any review. Like the cumulative index itself, this is a facility which may be of increasing help as the number of reviews in print grows.

Fourth, each review contains two listings of publications. The QRL Key gives full details of the publications shown as sources and text references to them are made in the form [QRL serial number]; this list is confined essentially to data publications. The other listing is a general bibliography of works discussing wider aspects; text references in this case are made in the form [B serial number].

Finally, an attempt is made to reproduce the more important returns or forms used in data collection so that it may be seen what tabulations it is possible to make as well as helping to clarify the basis of those actually available. Unfortunately, there are severe practical limitations on the number of such forms that it is possible to append to a review and authors perforce have to be highly selective.

If all or any of these features succeed in their intention of increasing the value of the series in its basic function as a work of reference it will be gratifying; the extent to which the purpose is achieved, however, will be difficult to assess without 'feedback' from the readership. Users, therefore, will be rendering an essential service if they will send me a note of specific instance where, in consulting a review, they have failed to find the information sought.

As editor, I must express my very grateful thanks to all the members of the Joint Steering Committee of the Royal Statistical Society and the Social Science Research Council. It would be unfair to saddle them with any responsibility for shortcomings in execution but they have directed the overall strategy with as admirable a mixture of guidance and forbearance as any editor of such a series could desire. Especial thanks are due to the Secretary of the Committee who is an unfailing source of help even when sorely pressed by the more urgent demands of his other offices.

The authors join me in thanking all those who gave up their time to attend the seminar held to discuss the first drafts of their reviews and which contributed materially to improving the final versions. We are most grateful also to Philippa Stratton, of Heinemann Educational Books, for all her help, particularly during the vital production stages. The subject index entries for the Review of Wealth were compiled by Mrs Marion Reed and those for the Review of Personal Incomes by Mrs Juliet Horwood who has also been responsible for many other aspects of the work. Our thanks go also to Mrs Gill Skinner, of the Social Studies Data Processing Unit at the University of Exeter, who has written the computer programs for the production of the subject indexes. Finally, we also wish to record our appreciation of the permission granted to us by the Controller of Her Majesty's Stationery Office to reproduce Crown copyright material.

University of Exeter W. F. MAUNDER
May 1977

10 Wealth

by

A. B. ATKINSON
University College, London

and

A. J. HARRISON
McMaster University, Canada

Acknowledgements

In writing this review we have received a great deal of assistance, and it is not possible to mention by name all those to whom we are indebted. We should however make three particular acknowledgments. Firstly, the Inland Revenue Statistics Division, and in particular J. Astin, A. T. Dunn, and W. Gonzalez, have been extremely patient in answering our questions and in correcting our misapprehensions. Without their aid, the review would never have been completed. Secondly, the comments made at the seminar held in February 1975 have been most helpful in preparing the revised version. Finally, we should like to thank the editor for his guidance at all stages, and Mrs Juliet Horwood for her assistance with the publication.

Reference Date of Sources Reviewed

This review is believed to represent the position, broadly speaking, as it obtained at July 1975. Later revisions have been inserted up to the proof-reading stage [February 1977] taking account, as far as possible, of any major changes in the situation.

List of Abbreviations

AR	Annual Report of the Commissioners of the Inland Revenue
DS	Registrar General's Decennial Supplement
E	England
ED	Estate Duty
FA	Finance Act
G	Gini Coefficient
GMR	General Mortality Rate
IRS	Inland Revenue Statistics
NI	Northern Ireland
S	Scotland
SMR	Social Class Mortality Rate
W	Wales

Contents

I Introduction

1.1 Importance of Statistics on Wealth

The distribution of wealth in Britain is an important aspect of our society; at the same time it has until recently received relatively little attention from economists and other social scientists. The statistical information at present available—from either official or other sources—is far more limited than that, say, on the pattern of consumer expenditure or the structure of industrial production. Similarly, the published estimates have been subject to much less careful scrutiny. The aim of this review is to describe the main sources of statistical information about the distribution of wealth, to provide an assessment of their reliability and to suggest areas where improvements seem necessary.*

The paucity of statistical information about the distribution of wealth in virtually all advanced countries (there being even less information in most than in Britain) may possibly be explained by the fact that it is not of immediate importance for the management of the economy. The developments which made national income accounting a necessity did not generate the same demand for statistics about the concentration of wealth. This does not mean, however, that a better understanding of the distribution of wealth is without value. Successive governments have tried through taxation, and other measures, to reduce the concentration of wealth. In order to investigate the effect of such measures, we need information about personal holdings of wealth, and how they have changed over time. Proposals have been made for changes in the methods of taxation, for example the introduction of wealth taxation. The implications of such changes can only be measured with the aid of a reliable body of data on the distribution of wealth. More generally, we need information about personal wealth-holdings if we are to understand the role played by the concentration of wealth and the way in which it is created. Without evidence on the size distribution of wealth it is difficult to test theories put forward to explain inequality, and to isolate the importance of factors such as inheritance, thrift and luck.

The need for further statistical information in this field was recognized in the establishment in 1974 of the Royal Commission on the Distribution of Income and Wealth. The Commission's standing reference on the distribution stated that 'there is a need for a thorough and comprehensive enquiry into the existing distribution of income and wealth. There is also a need for a study of past trends in that distribution and for regular assessments of the subsequent changes.' This review was in its final stages when the Commission's first report was published, and it has only been possible to make limited reference to its work [B 39].

1.2 Definition of Field

1.2.1 In this review we are concerned with the *distribution of wealth in the personal sector*. The precise definition of the *personal sector* is that adopted by Revell [B 24]: 'households, unincorporated businesses and personal trusts (including undistributed estates of deceased persons)'. It may be noted that this is a narrower definition than that employed in the national income accounts (see the discussion by Stark in his companion survey). In particular, the personal sector as defined here

* This review is primarily concerned with methods and sources. A discussion of the findings concerning the distribution of wealth in Great Britain is contained in Atkinson and Harrison [B 3].

excludes all non-profit bodies, as well as life assurance and superannuation funds.

The restriction of attention to the personal sector of the economy precludes consideration of certain aspects of wealth-holding. If we are concerned with the concentration of wealth on account of the differences in investment income to which it may give rise, then a study of the personal distribution may be quite adequate; if, however, we are concerned about the control over the economy which wealth may convey, then we should clearly need to consider the distribution among other sectors (the holdings of banks versus non-financial companies, etc.). A related problem is the treatment of those sectors apart from the personal sector, and the external sector, which have a positive net worth. In Britain the public sector has in recent years had a positive net worth. Should this be ignored or allocated in some way to persons? Also important in quantitative terms according to the estimates of Revell [B 24] is the positive net worth for the company sector (the excess of the net value of assets over the stock exchange valuation). If this were allocated to the shareholders, it would make a substantial difference to the size distribution. These problems are discussed briefly in subsection 6.2 and should be borne in mind by the reader.

1.2.2 The definition of *wealth* and the method of valuation raise a number of problems, and a variety of definitions could be adopted. (The terms *wealth* and *net worth* will be used interchangeably throughout the review to denote the net value of assets minus liabilities.) Following the precedent set in the literature on the definition of income (e.g. Simons [B 31]), we should define wealth in a comprehensive manner, including all assets (and liabilities) which could convey command over resources. This, even more here than in the case of income, introduces the problem of valuation. In this review, we shall consider two different bases which, although they do not exhaust the possibilities, provide some means of assessing the sensitivity of the results to the choice of definition. The first is a valuation on a 'realization' basis, or the value obtained in a sale on the open market at the date in question. The second is a valuation on a 'going concern' basis, or the value to a person or household on the assumption that the asset is retained. These valuations can clearly differ. The market value of second-hand furniture, for example, is very likely to be considerably below its value to a household as a going concern. In certain cases, such as occupational pensions, the realization value may well be zero (even in the case of an insured scheme it is not in general possible to borrow on the strength of the accumulated rights). The difference between these arises in part because of market imperfections* and the consequent gap between buying and selling prices. The difference also reflects the fact that the value of assets to intra-marginal holders may exceed the market price. This latter factor is probably important in the case of real property and of shareholdings, where a controlling interest typically commands a higher price than quoted for transactions on the stock exchange. This may indeed be one reason for the observed positive net worth of the company sector. The definition also raises the issue of 'social property' and the rights to state benefits. If the rights to occupational pensions are included, it might be considered reasonable to extend this to cover National Insurance pensions, sickness, unemployment, maternity and other benefits, all of which have an actuarial value to the individual (on a going concern basis). The sources described in this review do not extend the concept of wealth in this way, but again these issues should be borne in mind.

There are two further definitional questions which should be mentioned at this stage:

* Compare Simons, 'The precise, objective measurement of income implies the existence of perfect markets from which one . . . may obtain the prices necessary for routine valuation of all possible inventories of commodities, services, and property rights. In actuality there are few approximately perfect markets and few collections of goods or properties which can be valued accurately by recourse to market prices' ([B 31], p. 56).

1.2.3 *Geographical Coverage*

The official estimates published by the Inland Revenue at the time of writing relate to the distribution of wealth in Great Britain, and this will be the main concern of this review, but the basic estate data for Northern Ireland are described in subsection 2.4 and the unofficial estimates are discussed in subsection 4.3. (The Inland Revenue plans to include Northern Ireland in estimates for 1974 onwards.) As explained in the *Second Report on the Standing Reference* of the Royal Commission on the Distribution of Income and Wealth (published October 1976), the Inland Revenue assumed responsibility for the administration of estate duty in Northern Ireland from 1 January 1974, and the department are undertaking an examination of the figures with a view to preparing estimates for Northern Ireland.

1.2.4 *Definition of Unit*

We shall consider two main units of analysis: the *nuclear family* (man, wife and dependent children) and the *individual*. In the latter case attention is in general focused on the distribution among *adults* (defined as aged 18 and over).

1.2.5 The subject of the review is clearly closely related to the companion-piece by Stark on the distribution of income. The pattern of wealth-holding is directly linked to the distribution of investment income, and indeed this is one method by which estimates of the wealth distribution have been made. The main difference lies in the distribution of earned incomes, and even here it could be argued that the present study should consider human capital—or the amounts invested by individuals in the acquisition of skills or educational qualifications. If we are to include the capitalized value of future occupational pensions (on a going concern basis), then there appears to be no reason to exclude the capitalized value of future earnings. However, even apart from the problems of estimation involved, this would lead us to trespass too far into the territory covered by other surveys in the series. We shall therefore confine ourselves to a discussion in subsection 7.5 of the relationship between the distributions of income and wealth, and the need for estimates of the joint distribution.

1.3 Methods of Estimation

There are generally acknowledged to be three main methods which can be used to estimate the distribution of wealth, all of which have been employed at different times. The official estimates produced by the Inland Revenue are derived using the *estate method*. Other authors have made unofficial estimates using this method, but in addition have followed two alternative approaches, the *investment income method* and the *sample survey method*. In this section we provide a brief explanation of the theory underlying each of the methods, leaving detailed comments to the later sections.

1.3.1 *The Estate Method*

Under the present system of taxation (in July 1975), the only occasion when a person's total assets and liabilities are revealed to the fiscal authorities is when he dies, and the returns of wealth made for this purpose are an important source of information about the distribution of wealth. The Inland Revenue has for many years published the details of estates based on a sample drawn from the estate duty records held by the Estate Duty Office and the Scottish Estate Duty Office. This information, which is classified by the size of the estate and the age and sex of the deceased, provides in turn the basis for the estimates of the distribution of wealth.

The method of estimating the distribution of wealth from this source is in essence straightforward. If it is assumed that those of a particular age and sex dying in a given year are representative of the living population, the overall distribution may be obtained by 'blowing up' the estate data by a mortality multiplier equal to the reciprocal of the mortality rate. In other words, if the mortality rate for a particular male age group is 1 in 1,000, we assume that for every man who died at this age in a given year, there are 999 alive in similar circumstances and we multiply the numbers and values of estates in this age group by 1,000. In effect, the estate method uses the dead as a sample of the living population, with due allowance for the differences in the 'sampling fractions'.

The estate duty approach has a long history, although it has become more refined over the years. In the earliest studies a single multiplier was applied to all capital wealth, so that early estimates of total personal wealth on the basis of the revenue from the Probate Duties, used a multiplier of thirty, taken to be 'the cycle for each devolution of property'. Later writers used multipliers ranging from twenty-nine to fifty-five, which led to what Sir Bernard Mallet described as 'the most disquieting discrepancies' ([B17], p. 66). Mallet was in fact, the first to employ the method of taking multipliers related to the age of the deceased, a method which was at once accepted as clearly more accurate. In the discussion of Mallet's paper it was suggested that the mortality rates used

> should not be that of the general mortality of the whole country, but some such table as that of the mortality amongst the families of the peerage; or, perhaps, the mortality tables derived from the life assurance companies ([B 17], p. 85).

In the subsequent paper by Mallet and Strutt [B 18] such social class multipliers were applied, and the method thus amended has been used by nearly all subsequent investigators employing the estate duty approach, including the Inland Revenue.

1.3.2 *Investment Income (Giffen) Method*

Although the estate duty method has been that most commonly employed in the past fifty years, the investment income approach was much used by early writers. It is particularly associated with Sir Robert Giffen, who described it as follows ([B 9], pp. 346–7):

> It becomes possible by means of the income tax assessments to apply a certain number of years' purchase, according to the best estimate that can be formed, to the different descriptions of income from property, and by this means an estimate of the capital yielding income can be arrived at. There is, no doubt, some difficulty in establishing what the multiplier in each case should be [but] great masses of the property are in such a form, for instance railway shares and stocks, that anyone with a knowledge of market conditions can easily apply an approximate figure by which the total income may be multiplied so as to show the capital represented at its market value.

The essence of the investment income approach is to apply a 'yield multiplier' to work back from the distribution of investment income to the distribution of wealth: if, for example, the yield is thought to be 5%, the multiplier is 20, so that an investment income of £5,000 would be assumed to correspond to wealth of £100,000. The yield multiplier clearly depends on the form in which wealth is held and the normal procedure has been to calculate a weighted average yield based on the composition of wealth indicated by the estate duty statistics. In this calculation it is clearly important to allow for the fact that the composition of wealth varies with the size of the holding: e.g. that cash and bank deposits tend to be held more by those at the lower end of the distribution and company shares more by the rich. The method may be illustrated by the following hypothetical example:

		Proportion of Wealth of that Type (%)	
Asset	*Yield*	*Wealth of £10,000*	*Wealth of £1 million*
Cash	0	20	0
National Savings	2	40	0
Land and buildings	3	40	50
Company shares	5	0	50
Average yield		2·0	4·0

Since a large part of the wealth of the man worth £10,000 is held in cash and National Savings, the weighted average yield is considerably lower than that for the millionaire. As a result the yield multiplier applied to the investment income of the first man would be higher than that applied to that of the second. An investment income of £200 would be assumed to correspond to wealth of £200/0·02 = £10,000, and an investment income of £40,000 would be assumed to correspond to £1 million. (It should be noted that since the statistics relate to income as assessed for income tax, the yield does not include capital gains or other non-taxable income such as imputed rent.)

1.3.3 *Sample Survey Method*

The third approach is to use data specially collected for the purpose in a sample survey. From a representative sample of families or individuals it is possible to estimate the holdings among the population as a whole. This approach has the merit of giving direct evidence about wealth-holding, rather than the indirect evidence provided by the investment income method, and of relating to living population rather than estates at death. On the other hand, for reliable results the survey has to meet a number of stringent criteria. It has to secure a satisfactory response at all levels of wealth, it has to ensure a complete statement of assets and liabilities by those taking part, and it must overcome the problems associated with obtaining a reasonably accurate valuation of all holdings.

1.4 Plan of the Review

The review begins with the estate duty statistics collected by the Inland Revenue, which are the main primary source of data. The method by which these statistics are obtained, and the form in which they are published, are described in Section 2. The use of the estate duty returns by the Inland Revenue to produce official estimates of the distribution of wealth is set out in Section 3, together with a review of their main shortcomings. The same source has been employed by academic investigators, and the resulting 'unofficial' estimates are covered in Section 4. This section takes up the problem of obtaining a consistent series of figures over the course of this century. The alternative methods of estimation, via the investment income approach and sample surveys, are treated in Section 5. The data available for the personal sector as a whole are the subject of Section 6, which also covers information about the holding of individual assets. Finally, Section 7 discusses briefly some of the desirable improvements in statistics in this area.

2 The Estate Duty Returns

2.1 Estate Returns

2.1.1 The primary data used for the estate method are obtained by the Inland Revenue from a sample drawn from the estate duty records. By their nature the estate data relate to *individuals* and not to families or tax units. In this respect the wealth estimates based on the estate data should be contrasted with those obtained by other methods, such as the investment income method and sample surveys. The implications of this are discussed by Atkinson and Harrison [B 3].

The estate data relate to individuals dying in a given financial year. They do not however cover all deaths. In 1971, for example, there were only 293,000 estates, compared with 657,000 adult deaths (*Inland Revenue Statistics 1974* [QRL 31], p. 175). In general in recent years only about half of all estates have come to the attention of the Estate Duty Offices. The estates covered are those where duty is payable and (since the data for 1960–1) those estates not liable to duty where the grant of representation (grant of confirmation in Scotland) comes to the notice of the Estate Duty Offices. The estate duty exemption limit has been changed in the post-Second World War period as follows (*Inland Revenue Statistics 1973* [QRL 31], p. 161):

Deaths occurring on or after	*Exemption level*
10 April 1946	£2,000
30 July 1954	£3,000
10 April 1962	£4,000
4 April 1963	£5,000
16 April 1969	£10,000
31 March 1971	£12,500
22 March 1972	£15,000

The estates not covered by the statistics are basically, therefore, those which are *both* not subject to duty *and* consist entirely of items for which a grant of representation is not required. A grant, or probate, is in general required to establish the right to recover or reserve any part of the personal estate of a deceased person—see Tristram and Coote ([B 34], p. 7). There are a number of exceptions (including the estate of a deceased British sovereign), among them the following:

(i) property to which title can pass by delivery (e.g. cash or household goods),

(ii) property where the owner can nominate a person (or persons) to whom the asset should be transferred (e.g. industrial life assurance policies),

(iii) jointly owned property (such as a house) passing by survivorship to the other joint tenant,

(iv) property covered by the Administration of Estates (Small Payments) Act 1965.

The last of these allows sums up to £500 held in certain forms to be transferred without a grant of representation having to be obtained.* The main assets affected are National Savings Certificates, building society deposits, Post Office (National) Savings Bank and Trustee Savings Bank deposits and Premium Bonds.

It is likely that in most cases the estates missing from the statistics involve relatively small amounts. This needs to be qualified for the most recent years in view of the increase in the threshold and the introduction in the Finance Act 1972 of additional exemptions for transfers to surviving spouses, charities and national heritage bodies. The non-aggregation provisions (see below) also need

* Prior to 1965, the limit was £100 for most types of asset covered by these provisions. Just as the review was completed, it was announced that the limit is to be £1,500 from 10 August 1975.

to be taken into account, but these are unlikely to affect the bulk of the estates missing from the statistics. It should be emphasized that we are concerned here with estates which are *totally* missing, cases where the estate statistics cover only *part* of the value of the property left at death are discussed later in Section 3.

2.1.2 From the estates coming to the notice of the Inland Revenue a sample is drawn, with sampling fractions which vary with the size of the estate and age of the deceased (those used in 1972–3 are shown in Table 2.1). The fractions range from 1% for cells where there were relatively large numbers (e.g. solvent estates below £3,000 where the deceased was aged 55 or over) to 100% for cells where there were small numbers of estates (e.g. those over £50,000). Where the sampling fraction is less than 100%, there may be some variation from the desired random sample in view of the temptation to pass over bulky, and therefore probably 'difficult', files, but the Statistics Division are confident that the procedure is satisfactory.* No estimates of sampling errors are published.

Table 2.1 Sampling Fractions for Estate Returns—1972–3

<table>
<tr><th>Lower limit of net capital value</th><th>Under 45 Sampling Fraction</th><th>45–54 Sampling Fraction</th><th>55 and over Sampling Fraction</th></tr>
<tr><td>Insolvent</td><td>100</td><td>100</td><td>100</td></tr>
<tr><td>Nil</td><td>10</td><td>1</td><td>1</td></tr>
<tr><td>3,000</td><td rowspan="6">100</td><td>2</td><td>2</td></tr>
<tr><td>5,000</td><td>5</td><td>5</td></tr>
<tr><td>10,000</td><td rowspan="4">100</td><td>10</td></tr>
<tr><td>12,500</td><td>20</td></tr>
<tr><td>20,000</td><td>50</td></tr>
<tr><td>50,000</td><td>100</td></tr>
</table>

Source: *Inland Revenue Statistics*, 1974 [QRL 31], p. 102

The data collected by the Inland Revenue inevitably reflect the form of the estate duty (now capital transfer tax) legislation. Some of the main implications with respect to the coverage of property are considered in Section 3. Here it is only noted that the estate duty provisions for non-aggregation may affect the nature of the sample drawn. In some cases (for example, where both settled and unsettled property pass on death, and the latter does not exceed a certain limit) the estate may be counted twice in the statistics.

2.1.3 The reporting document completed by the Estate Duty Offices (Form Stat. No. 4) is reproduced in the Appendix. The details of the form have varied from year to year,* but in general the first side shows the date of death, sex, domicile, and residence of deceased, the type of document (discussed below), the total capital and particulars of the duty paid. The reverse side gives (* denotes classified by asset type):

*Gross personalty
*Gross realty
*Deductions
Net Total Estate
Free and Not Free Estate
Estate by Disposition
Gifts—by year before death
Capital and duty at reduced rate

This information is supplied when the original affidavit or account is examined, but may later be amended. The amendments are given on a separate form (referred to as a corrective affidavit or account).

The completed forms are sent to the central computer unit at Worthing. When received, they are vetted by a computer programme. This checking is not complete, but includes the duty paid, the addition of totals, and a test that holdings of certain assets (e.g. national savings certificates) do not exceed legal maxima. The vetted returns are then added to a standing file, which is held by year of account. This file then provides the basis

* 'Difficult' cases tend to involve large estates, where the sampling fraction is much higher, and above £50,000 the sample is complete.

* The Appendix reproduces two versions of the form. One relates to 1970–1 and the other to 1975–6 (incorporating the change to Capital Transfer Tax).

for the published data described in subsection 2.2.

2.1.4 The date at which estates are recorded and the treatment of alterations to the original returns should be described, as they have been a cause of confusion (the Inland Revenue's notes on this subject were made more transparent in *Inland Revenue Statistics 1973* [QRL 31], p. 170). In general, the principle is that estates are recorded when duty is first paid* (or for estates not liable to duty, when the grant of representation comes to the notice of the Estate Duty Offices), and that corrective returns are reported in the year in which they are received, with (to date) no attempt being made to adjust the statistics for earlier years. The effect of the treatment of corrective returns is that:

Numbers. No addition is made to the total number of estates. On the other hand, in the tables showing the numbers of estates with particular types of property, new items of particular types of property are counted whenever they first appear (even if they belong to earlier estates). For example, a corrective return showing unquoted securities for an estate where no previous amounts had been given under this heading would lead to a further item being added to the number of estates with this particular kind of property. Similarly, if as a consequence of a change in the net value of an estate in a subsequent year the estate is transferred to another range, the number of estates in the new range is increased by one in this subsequent year and the number in the original range diminished by one.

Value. The adjustments to the value are reported in the year in which they are notified. Where the addition, or subtraction, leaves the estate within the same capital range, the amount of the change is simply included in this range for the later year. Where the change moves an estate between classes, the *total* capital is added to the new range, and the previous total is subtracted from the old range, both applying to the later year.

To illustrate the way in which this works, suppose an estate of £11,500 is reported in 1969–70, and a further £2,000 is reported in 1970–1. No change would be made to the 1969–70 figures, but for 1970–1 the numbers in the range £10,000–£12,500 would be reduced by 1 (and the amount reduced by £11,500), whereas the numbers in the range £12,500–£15,000 would be increased by 1 (and the amount increased by £13,500).

As is noted by the Inland Revenue, this procedure leads to 'some blurring of the figures'. This is illustrated by the fact that it may on occasion lead to negative totals appearing in the upper estate classes, and to the average estate size lying outside the class interval. For example, the estate returns for 1966–7 show minus 2 for the number of estates in the range £100,000–£200,000 owned by men aged 25–34, and the average size of estates in the range £50,000–£100,000 owned by women of the same age was £177,000 (*Inland Revenue Statistics 1970* [QRL 31], Table 114).

2.2 Published Classifications

The range of published tabulations may be illustrated by reference to the 1974 *Inland Revenue Statistics* [QRL 31]:

(a) *Tables 90–1*. Number of estates by ranges based on comprehensive data available from administrative records 1963–4 to 1972–3 (GB) and 1968–9 to 1972–3 (EW and Scotland).*

(b) *Tables 92–4*. Net capital value of estates and duty paid by ranges (GB, EW and Scotland)

* A change recorded in *Inland Revenue Statistics 1974* ([QRL 31], p. 102) is that since 'April 1972 in England and Wales, estates have been counted when duty is first assessed, unless some duty has already been paid, and in some cases this will bring them into the year preceding first payment of duty'.

* The division between EW and Scotland is according to where the estate is dealt with, which depends broadly upon the domicile of the deceased and not upon where the property is situated.

based on sample drawn as described in subsection 2.1, from 1968–9 to 1972–3.

(c) *Table 95*. Amounts of net personalty and net realty by range of estate, 1968–9 to 1972–3 (GB), based on sample.

(d) *Tables 96–7*. Analyses of estates by asset type of all property (by amount) above the exemption limit from 1963–4 to 1972–3 (GB) and 1968–9 to 1972–3 (EW and Scotland), based on sample.

(e) *Table 98*. Analysis of estates by asset type of all property (number of cases and amount) on a more detailed basis from 1970–1 to 1972–3 (GB), based on sample.

(f) *Table 99*. Analysis of estates by ranges and by asset type (number of cases and amount), 1972–3 (GB), based on sample.

(g) *Table 100*. Numbers and net capital of estates by age and sex of the deceased for 1972–3 (GB), based on sample.

(h) *Table 101*. Analysis of net capital of estates over £15,000 by title and mode of disposition for 1972–3 (GB), based on sample.

(i) *Table 102*. Analysis of gifts *inter vivos* included in estates over £15,000 by period before death, for 1972–3 (GB) based on sample.

The main tables published since 1960 are described in the Quick Reference List. It may be noted that the tables relate to Great Britain; for discussion of the statistics for Northern Ireland, see subsection 2.4. In each case location is defined in terms of *domicile*, although the statistics do not follow this strictly, since liability to estate duty extends to property situated in the United Kingdom but owned by those domiciled elsewhere (with certain exceptions). This leads to some overstatement (see Revell [B 24], pp. 130–2).

2.3 Changes in Estate Duty and the Introduction of Capital Transfer Tax

We describe below some of the changes in the estate duty legislation which should be taken into account when using the data for different years. They are listed chronologically and cover the period since 1911 (the first year for which estate data were published in a form suitable for the application of the mortality multiplier method—see below). The list is intended to be illustrative and not comprehensive.* It should be noted that the continuity of the statistics is affected not only by changes in legislation but also by changes in administrative practice and in the form of compilation which are not listed. An example of the former is the administrative concession in force until 1958, under which the Inland Revenue valued an owner-occupied house at less than its market value where occupied by a near relative of the deceased who remained resident in the house. An example of the latter is the change in 1920 in the basis of compilation from 'capital brought to our notice' to 'capital on which duty is paid in the year', and the change back to a 'notice' basis in 1965.

1914 Abolition of Exemption for Settled Property. The Finance Act (FA) 1914 abolished the Settlement Estate Duty and at the same time the relief for settled property passing a second time. The consequence was the increase in the value of settled property appearing in the estate statistics.

1921–3. Establishment of Northern Ireland and Eire as Separate Jurisdictions. From 22 November 1921, and 1 April 1923, respectively, Northern Ireland and Eire were established as independent taxing jurisdictions. According to the Annual Report [QRL 20] this 'slightly affected the comparability of statistics for Great Britain' (p. 17). After these dates moveable property situated in GB but forming part of an Irish estate was included in the GB statistics, whereas this had not previously been the case.

* We should stress that the list does not cover all major changes in estate duty; it covers only those likely to affect the comparability of the estate statistics. Many important amendments to the estate duty (e.g. the reduced rates on certain business assets) have no effect on the statistics.

1940. Extension of Property Covered. The FA (No. 1) 1940 extended the definition of property deemed to pass on death to include for example certain life interests, and introduced a charge on the benefits received by the deceased from a controlled company.

1946. Gifts. Under the FA 1946 the period of charge for gifts was extended from three to five years.

1954. Aggregation Provisions. The FA 1954 made changes in the non-aggregation provisions, concerning settled versus 'other' properties and life policies in which the deceased never had an interest. This affected the number of items appearing as separate estates.

1962. Inclusion of Immovable Property Situated Abroad. The FA 1962 removed the exemption for immovable property situated out of Great Britain. This led to property being included in the estate statistics which had previously been excluded.

1968. Aggregation and Gifts. The FA 1968 modified the provisions for the non-aggregation, so that the proceeds of insurance policies dutiable as gifts made by the deceased were made aggregable with the rest of the estate, subject to relief for policies effected before 20 March 1968. The period of charge for gifts was extended from five to seven years.

1969. Settled Property. The FA 1969 made major changes to the law governing the estate duty treatment of settled property and imposed new charges, in particular on the death of a beneficiary from a discretionary trust.

Introduction of Capital Transfer Tax. In the March 1974 Budget it was announced that the estate duty was to be replaced by the Capital Transfer Tax and this was enacted in the FA 1975. At the time of writing the full consequences of this change for the estate statistics are not clear. There appears to be no reason in principle why the same general format could not be maintained using data on estates (sampling the returns made at death and excluding those relating to gifts *inter vivos*), and we understand that the Inland Revenue intend in broad terms to continue their present practice.* At the same time, there will inevitably be changes in some of the details of the published statistics, and their coverage is likely to be affected by the exemption for property transferred to a surviving spouse.

2.4 Northern Ireland

On 1 January 1974 the collection of estate duty in Northern Ireland was taken over from the Department of Finance by the Inland Revenue. As a result the Estate Duty Office in Northern Ireland now follows the procedures described above as used by the Inland Revenue in the collection of information on estates. Prior to the change the only important difference in procedure between the two offices was that the published statistics of estates for Northern Ireland were based on different sampling percentages. These were as follows:

0–£5,000	10%
£5,000–£10,000	20%
Above £10,000	100%

with no variation according to age. It must also be noted that until 1974 gifts *inter vivos* in Northern Ireland were exempt from duty if made more than four years before death, compared with a seven-year period for gifts in Britain.

The last separate statistics on estates relating to Northern Ireland were prepared for the year ended 31 March 1974. These, and the statistics for earlier years, are published in the September edition of the bi-annual *Digest of Statistics for Northern Ireland* [QRL 23]. The following analyses are published (references to table numbers are to the

* The Royal Commission on the Distribution of Income and Wealth recommended that 'statistics derived from the administration of both taxes (the capital transfer tax and the prospective wealth tax) can be linked to those of estate duty so that trends can continue to be measured' ([B 39], p. 147).

September 1974 Digest, the last one to contain estate statistics):

(a) *Tables 127 and 129*. Numbers and net capital values of estates 1963/4 to 1973/4.
(b) *Tables 128 and 130*. Numbers and net capital values of estates 1973/4 by range of estate and age and sex of deceased.
(c) *Table 131*. Classification of all property 1973/4 by range of net capital value of estate.
(e) *Table 132*. Analysis of property 1963/4 to 1973/4.

Earlier Digests cover equivalent earlier ten-year periods.

3 The Inland Revenue Estimates of the Distribution of Wealth

The most important development in recent years has been the publication since 1960 of estimates of the distribution of wealth in Great Britain, initially in the annual reports of the Inland Revenue [QRL 20] and more recently in *Inland Revenue Statistics* [QRL 31]. (A summary of the published tables is given in Table 3.1 below.) As a result, we now have an 'official' series covering the years since 1960. These estimates are derived from the estate duty returns using mortality multipliers adjusted for social class (the method and the adjustments made are described in more detail later). The results are presented showing the number of people with net wealth in different ranges together with the total amount of wealth owned. In addition the Gini coefficient of concentration for each year is given as an aid to comparisons over time,* although it should be noted that the coefficient published in the text tables only takes account of wealth-holders covered by the estate returns (see subsections 3.1.5–6 below). In this section we describe the method of estimation in more detail and discuss the reliability of the resulting estimates.

3.1 The Method of Estimation

3.1.1 Once the estate duty returns for any year have been tabulated, mortality multipliers are applied to yield the Inland Revenue's estimate of the distribution of wealth. This method was outlined in principle above and involves the multiplication of the total number and value of estates in each cell by the appropriate mortality multiplier (which is the reciprocal of the mortality rate). The cells are classified by the age and sex of the deceased to allow for differing mortality experience. A further classification by estate size is introduced in order that the multipliers applied at different sizes of estate can be adjusted for variations in mortality with economic status. Since no mortality data are available by wealth or income group, the Inland Revenue, following earlier writers, assume that wealth is correlated with social class (as defined by the Registrar-General's occupational categories), and adopt the following mortality multipliers:

(i) for estates over £5,000 those relating to social classes I and II (broadly the managerial and professional classes),
(ii) for estates under £5,000, rates midway between those for social classes I and II and those for the population as a whole (the division was made at £3,000 before 1970/1).

3.1.2 The social class differentials are derived from the Registrar General's Decennial study of occupational mortality [B 37] which, in turn, is based on matching the deaths registered for a five-year period (most recently 1959–63) to the population at risk as enumerated in the Census of Population (in 1961). This procedure suffers from a number of drawbacks, and in particular there are serious discrepancies between the occupational statements at death registration and those at the census, leading to systematic bias in the occupational mortality rates. In view of this, we need to apply certain corrections to the Registrar General's social class rates (these are described in more detail in subsection 3.2.3). The social class differentials thus obtained are then applied to the

* The Gini coefficient is one half the mean difference divided by the mean. Geometrically, it is the proportion of the triangular area on a Lorenz diagram which falls between the Lorenz curve and diagonal.

mortality rate for the general population to give the required multipliers. For example, suppose that the adjusted Decennial Supplement data show that the mortality rate for social classes I and II is 80% of that for the general population. If the overall mortality rate for a given group in 1970 was 1 in 1,000, then the social class multiplier for estates over £5,000 would have been (1,000/0·8) = 1,250. The social class differentials are taken as constant between census years. (For the estimates of the wealth distribution prior to the 110th annual report the Inland Revenue estimated the social class differentials on the basis of the results of the 1951 Census of Population.) The mortality multipliers employed for 1970–3 are published in the report of the Royal Commission on the Distribution of Income and Wealth [B 39] and further details are available from the Inland Revenue on request.

In applying the multipliers to the estate data, the problem occurs that for certain classes, particularly the largest estates and the youngest age groups, the number of estates is extremely small: in 1969–70, for example, only one man died between the ages of 35 and 45, leaving an estate of over £200,000. The Inland Revenue have attempted to reduce the error involved by:

(i) combining the observations partly across age groups and partly across estate classes and applying a combined multiplier,
(ii) in the case of the largest wealth groups, averaging the multiplied-up data over a number of years.

The first of these adjustments means that in particular estate classes the multiplier applied is not that appropriate to the particular age-group but is instead a weighted average of a number of different age-groups' multipliers. (It may be noted that a further, exceptional adjustment was made to the data for 1972–3 'owing to the co-incidental occurrence of the deaths of several millionaires in the younger age-groups', *Inland Revenue Statistics 1974* [QRL 31], p. 175.)

3.1.3 The estate duty statistics relate to the financial year ending 31 March. On the basis of the average interval between death and payment of first duty or grant of representation where no duty is payable (between 3 and 4 months), the Inland Revenue estimate that the statistics may be taken as representing those of the preceding calendar year, and the mortality rates used are those for the calendar year. The procedure for the treatment of corrective affidavits, or accounts, described in the previous section means that in effect the Inland Revenue estimate that the adjustments which will be made in the future to current deaths are equal to those made in that year to past deaths. For example, if the estate of a person dying in 1968 is valued initially at £1 million and then in 1969 an extra £½ million is added, it is effectively assumed that an estate of £1 million in 1969 would be later adjusted by that amount.

3.1.4 The definition of wealth follows that in the estate returns, and the only adjustments made are those for funeral expenses and capital gains tax liability payable as a result of death (which are added back to the estate). The rationale for these adjustments is that the liabilities would not have arisen if the person had not died. For this reason the capital gains tax liability involved is only that payable as a result of death being deemed to be realization, in the years in which that applied. (Other ways in which the value of the estate differs from the wealth of the living—e.g. in the case of life assurance—are discussed below.)

The main components of total net wealth are:

British government securities
\+ Other government and municipal securities
\+ Quoted and unquoted shares and debentures (including unit trusts)
\+ Money on mortgage or bonds
\+ Cash
\+ Deposits in building societies and banks
\+ Household goods, pictures, china, etc.
\+ Policies of life assurance

+ Trade, business and professional assets	
= Total gross personalty	
— Debts owing	
= Total net personalty	
+ Land and buildings (gross realty)	
— Mortgages	
= Total net wealth	

asset, and (iii) the numbers of holdings of particular items or groups of items analysed by size. As well as covering the most recent year, the Inland Revenue's publications typically reproduce the results from certain previous years. A full list of published tables up to *Inland Revenue Statistics 1974* is given in Table 3.1. In 1975, in a welcome new development, the Inland Revenue brought out the main wealth estimates in a separate booklet

Table 3.1 Estimates of Personal Wealth by Inland Revenue

Source	*Total wealth by asset type (number of cases and amount)*	*Distribution of wealth by ranges (and Gini coefficient G)*	*Number of holdings of selected items by range of wealth*
Inland Revenue Statistics			
1974*	Table 103, 1968–72 (1972 MF)	Table 104, 1968–72 (1972 MF) G	Table 105, 1968–72
1973*	Table 91, 1962–71 (1971 MF)	Table 92, 1961–71 (1971 MF) G	Table 93, 1967–71
1972	Table 85, 1961–70 (1970 MF)	Table 86, 1961–70 (1970 MF) G	Table 87, 1966–70
1971	Table 129, 1960–9 (1969 MF)	Table 130, 1960–9 (1969 MF) G	Table 131, 1965–9
1970	Table 120–1, 1960–8 (1968 MF)	Table 122–3, 1960–8 (1968 MF) G	Table 124, 1965–8
Annual Reports			
1968 (No. 111)	Table 138, 1964–7 (1967 MF)	Table 139, 1964–7 (1967 MF)	Table 140, 1964–7
1967 (No. 110)	Table 184, 1964–6 (all MF)	Table 185, 1964-66 (1966 MF)	Table 186, 1964–6
1966 (No. 109)	Table 165, 1960, 1964–5 (all MF)	Table 166, 1960–5 (1965 MF)	Table 167, 1964–5
1965 (No. 108)	Table 134, 1960, 1963–4 (all MF)	Table 135, 1960, 1963–4 (all MF)	—
1964 (No. 107)	Table 144, 1960, 1962–3 (all MF)	Table 145, 1960, 1962–3 (all MF)	—
1963 (No. 106)	Table 143, 1960–2 (all MF)	Table 144, 1960–2 (all MF)	—
1962 (No. 105)	Table 192, 1960–1 (all MF)	Table 193, 1960–1 (all MF)	—
1961 (No. 104)	Table 126, 1960 (MF)	—	—

Notes: Abbreviations: MF male and female separately; G Gini coefficient

*The *Inland Revenue Statistics* 1973 and 1974 also contain a new table giving the classification of property by range of wealth (Table 94 in 1973 and Table 106 in 1974).

The estate data, multiplied up and adjusted in the manner described above, provide estimates of the distribution of wealth by age, sex, country (England and Wales, Scotland) and type of property (a total of forty-four composite categories of assets and liabilities is distinguished, the precise classification varying slightly from year to year). The data published in the Inland Revenue reports [QRL 20] and in *Inland Revenue Statistics* [QRL 31] cover (i) the distribution of total wealth for Great Britain by range of net wealth, where the number of classes is rather smaller than in the basic estate statistics (e.g. the top size category is £200,000+), (ii) the breakdown of total wealth by type of

Estimated Wealth of Individuals in Great Britain 1973 [QRL 24], which was available ahead of the publication of *Inland Revenue Statistics*. The three tables in this booklet give:

Table 1. Classification of property by asset type (number of cases and amount) by range of wealth 1973 (corresponds to a combination of Tables 103, 104 and 106 in *Inland Revenue Statistics 1974*).

Table 2. Number of holdings of selected items analysed by size 1973 (corresponds to Table 105 in *Inland Revenue Statistics 1974*).

Table 3. Distribution of wealth and Gini coefficients 1961, 1965, 1966, 1971–3 (male and female separately for 1973) (corresponds to table published in *Social Trends*—see below).

3.1.5 Figures derived from the official estimates are published in *Social Trends* [QRL 35] where the results are expressed in terms of the percentage share owned by 'the most wealthy 1 per cent, 2 per cent, etc.'. It is important to note that these percentages relate only to that part of the population covered by the estate returns and not to the *whole* population. In 1975 a new table was introduced in *Social Trends* showing the distribution among the whole adult population (Table 5.11 in [QRL 35] 1975). A number of users have clearly been confused on this point: for example the Hudson Report [B 41]. The percentage shares of the top 1%, etc. of the whole population are higher than those indicated in the *Social Trends* tables. This point is recognized in the appendix (to both *Social Trends* and *Inland Revenue Statistics*) where two series of Gini coefficients are presented. Series A does not take into account wealth-holders not covered by the estate returns; Series B is calculated for the whole population aged 15 and over, making the assumption that those not covered by the returns have zero wealth. The difference between the two series is very substantial: for example, for 1973 the Series A Gini coefficient is 0·65, whereas the Series B coefficient is 0·84.

3.1.6 It may also be noted that the Green Paper on the Wealth Tax [B 42] contained an appendix providing estimates of the shares of wealth owned by the top 1% and 5% of the whole population aged 15 and over for 1960, 1965 and 1970. These estimates also made allowance for the wealth of those not covered by the estate duty returns and for non-dutiable settlements. An updated version of this table covering 1972–4 is included in a memorandum submitted to the Select Committee on a Wealth Tax (minutes of evidence, 23 April 1975).

3.1.7 In evidence to the Select Committee on a Wealth Tax (Minutes of Evidence, Appendix 118), the Inland Revenue summarized information available about changes in the concentration of wealth since 1920. The summary consisted of tables for the shares of the top 1%, 5%, and 10%, together with a brief account of the sources. The Inland Revenue also described their internal enquiries into the extent of settled property and the increase in discretionary and accumulating trusts in the period 1960–1972.

3.2 Assessment of the Inland Revenue Estimates

The Inland Revenue themselves in presenting the results described above refer to a number of major qualifications and recognize that their estimates are 'subject to fairly wide margins of error and are in some respects incomplete'. In what follows our aim is to present a detailed critique of the Inland Revenue statistics, and to assess how far different factors are likely to bias the official estimates of the degree of concentration and the trends over time.

3.2.1 *Coverage of Estates and 'Missing People'*

As pointed out in subsection 2.2, the estate duty statistics cover those estates on which duty was paid in a given year or for which grants of representations were issued, and those estates which do not come to the notice of the Estate Duty Office are excluded. Since the estates omitted are typically those where no property has been left, or where the assets consist only of those which may be transferred without probate and on which estate duty is not payable, it seems reasonable to suppose that few of the people excluded from the Inland Revenue estimates are likely to own large amounts of wealth. The wealth-holders who are missing from the official estimates, therefore, are likely to belong to the lowest ranges. It follows that if the existence of these wealth-holders is simply ignored—as it is in the Series A Gini coefficients—then the degree of concentration is understated. On the other hand, the alternative assumption that those omitted have zero wealth (Series B) leads to coefficients which are overstated.

This point is recognized by the Inland Revenue, who regard the Gini coefficient as primarily an indicator of the *trend* in the degree of concentration: 'the main value of the coefficients is thought to lie in the trend over time of their movement, rather than their absolute values in a particular year' [QRL 31]. However, this assumes that the extent to which estates are omitted has remained constant over time, whereas there are reasons to believe that it has changed. Most important is the fact that the Administration of Estates (Small Payments) Act of 1965 increased the limit below which small amounts could be transferred without probate. As a result the coverage of small estates was less adequate after September 1965, when the Act took effect, than before. This is largely responsible for the decline in the total number of wealth-holders appearing in the Inland Revenue statistics, which fell from 19·5 million in 1964 to 17·3 million in 1967. Estimates which ignore those not covered by the estate duty statistics (Series A) give an exaggerated impression of reduced concentration over time,* whereas the alternative estimates (Series B) understate the trend.

Neither of the extreme assumptions described above is, however, really adequate. To ignore the existence of half the adult population is clearly wrong. At the same time it is not reasonable to suppose that they own no wealth at all and it is necessary to investigate in more detail the likely wealth of those who do not appear in the Inland Revenue's tables. This is discussed further in Section 4.

* In effect a number of small wealth-holdings were simply removed from the estimates. The Inland Revenue's notes were incorrect in this respect until *Inland Revenue Statistics 1972*. (Compare *Inland Revenue Statistics 1971*, p. 228 which is incorrect on this point, with *Inland Revenue Statistics 1972*, pp. 156–7 where the position is clearly set out.)

3.2.2 *'Missing' Wealth and Estate Duty Avoidance*

The reliance on statistics derived from the estate duty returns is open to the criticism that even for those estates covered the returns provide an incomplete picture of wealth-holding on account of the provisions in the estate duty law which allow wealth to be transferred without duty being paid or at a reduced rate of duty. While it is not true that all these provisions lead to wealth disappearing from the returns,* there can be little doubt that substantial amounts are 'missing' from the estate duty statistics, or, as it is expressed by the Inland Revenue, 'certain elements are omitted because no duty is payable on them either because of special exemption or because they fall outside the scope of estate duty law'.

In some cases these provisions mean that the estate does not appear in the statistics at all. As we saw in Section 2, this happens where it is non-dutiable and consists entirely of items for which probate is not required. Examples of the kind of property for which probate is not necessary were given in subsection 2.1.1. Here we are concerned with cases where the estate is recorded but certain types of property are excluded. These may be classified under two headings:

Exclusions Subject to Specified Limits

For example:

(i) gifts, joint property, and property settled by the deceased where their total value together with the free estate does not exceed the point at which duty becomes payable,
(ii) items treated as estates by themselves which do not appear if they do not exceed the exemption limit: for example, certain life policies and property settled otherwise than by the deceased when the rest of the property does not exceed a certain level.

* A person may, for example, purchase agricultural property; because of the lower rates of duty, this reduces his estate duty liability, but the full value of the assets is still shown in the return.

Exclusions with No Limit

For example:

(i) property settled on a surviving spouse (with no power to dispose of the capital) which bore estate duty, or would have borne it but for the exemption limit, and which is exempt on the death of this spouse,
(ii) property held under discretionary trusts (before the 1969 Finance Act),*
(iii) objects of national, scientific, historic or artistic interest which are exempt from duty,
(iv) growing timber, which is not aggregated with the rest of the estate and on which duty is not paid unless and until the timber is sold,
(v) annuities for life and rights to occupational pensions,
(vi) death benefits under certain pension schemes.

Finally, reference should also be made to the problems of evasion of estate duty, which clearly leads to property being missing. However, as is pointed out by Revell, 'most people would probably agree that this is at a low level in Britain—if only because the legal methods of avoidance are so many' ([B 24], p. 112).

3.2.3 *Mortality Multipliers*

The method of deriving multipliers employed by the Inland Revenue closely follows the pattern set by earlier academic investigators; it does, however, suffer from a number of drawbacks. Some of these were referred to earlier, but a fuller list is given below:

(a) The mortality rates are obtained by combining information from two sources and there are serious discrepancies between the occupational statements at death registration and those at the census. This is reflected first in the numbers recorded as 'unoccupied' because of lack of information. Although the Census schedule asks retired respondents to record their previous occupations, many fail to follow this instruction. This problem may also arise at death registration but the evidence shows that it is much less prevalent. As a result, the size of the population is relatively understated, and hence the mortality rate overstated, for the occupied population.
(b) These discrepancies also arise between occupational categories and 'there is a tendency for the death registrations to give a somewhat more rosy view of the social class distribution of the deceased than the Census' (Lydall and Tipping [QRL 12]). This has been demonstrated at successive censuses by special matching exercises carried out by the Registrar General who concluded that 'for males aged 20–64, there is evidence of a strong tendency to report occupations assignable to Social Classes I and II more often at death registration than on the census schedules' ([B 36], p. 7).
(c) The Registrar General's analysis of female mortality does not include widows. More generally, no allowance has so far been made for differing mortality experience by marital status, which the American data suggest to be of considerable importance, see Smith [B 32].
(d) The Inland Revenue's use of a cut-off level (applying the average multiplier for class I and II combined above this level, and lower multipliers below) makes inadequate allowance for the social class gradient. As Revell has pointed out, the £3,000 plus group ranges 'from the man of 45 who has just finished paying off the mortgage on his house and has few other possessions at one

* Under the Finance Act 1969, estate duty is, in broad terms, payable on the death of a beneficiary under a discretionary trust on the same proportion of the trust property as the proportion of trust income received by the deceased in the preceding seven years. Depending on the policy followed by the trustees, it is clearly possible for property held in this form still not to appear in the statistics.

end to the man whose total wealth is £3 million or more at the other' ([B 24], p. 114). There are therefore good reasons for graduating the multiplier with wealth above this level. More generally, the assumption that wealth is correlated with social class as measured in the census is open to question. As is pointed out by Revell ([B 24], p. 116), it is probably a better approximation to a hierarchy of earned income than to a hierarchy of wealth.

(e) The Inland Revenue make no adequate allowance for differential trends in mortality over time. The social class mortality rates are assumed to remain the same percentage of the general mortality rate for long periods, whereas mortality in the upper social classes may steadily improve more (or less) rapidly than for the remainder of the population. The only adjustment made has been the switch to use of results based on the 1961 Census. In the 110th annual report, estimates were presented for the first time on this basis (from 1964 on). Comparing the estimates for two overlapping years (1964 and 1965) in the 109th report, Table 166, and the 110th report, Table 185, it appears that this adjustment led to a discrete jump in the series, increasing the total numbers and amounts of wealth by about 5%.

The first of these, problem (a), is dealt with by the Inland Revenue in the same way as Lydall and Tipping [QRL 12], who simply allocate the unoccupied proportionately over all social classes at the census and at death registration. This assumption is described by the Registrar General as one 'which is almost certainly untenable in fact; but which allows a clearer indication of the main tendencies' ([B 36], p. 7). Lydall and Tipping also made an adjustment for the problem (b). They estimated from the matching study of the 1951 Census that 'it would appear that the "upper class" mortality rates for males are over-estimated by 8·3 per cent' [QRL 12], and therefore adjusted by this amount the rates for men. (This argument was assumed also to hold for males in Scotland.) The Inland Revenue made the same adjustment for multipliers based on the results of the 1951 Census, but has not made any adjustment to more recent data. The third problem (c) is under consideration by the Inland Revenue, although no analysis has yet been published. Problems (d) and (e) remain.

3.2.4 *Sampling Problems*

There are four main types of problem which arise from the use by the Inland Revenue of the estate duty statistics as a sample of wealth-holding. Firstly, there are the problems which arise from the employment of estate data in any form. The fundamental assumption underlying the estate method is that those in a particular age group dying in a given year may be regarded as a representative sample of the living population in that age group, but this is clearly open to question. In particular those dying in a particular age group are likely to have had below-average health and this may well have affected their asset level. Those with poor health may have retired earlier and hence been less able to accumulate savings; they may have had nursing and other medical expenses which have caused them to draw on their savings. Perhaps, more importantly, those with a shorter life expectancy are more likely to have taken steps to avoid estate duty. The effect of such action depends on the form which avoidance takes. In certain cases, such as the deathbed purchase of agricultural property, we have seen that the full value is still reported; in other cases, such as that of non-dutiable settled property, the wealth disappears completely. In the case of gifts *inter vivos*, which were under Estate Duty probably the single most important form of avoidance, the effect is less straightforward.

The implications of gifts *inter vivos* for the estate duty method have been the subject of controversy since it was argued that such gifts render the approach invalid.* As pointed out by Mallet and Strutt [B 18] the recipients are subject to the same laws of mortality and the wealth appears in the estates of those in this group who die in a given period. If a person aged 65 transfers part of his wealth to his son aged 40 this wealth is still represented in the estate duty estimates since some of those aged 40 will die and the lower mortality rate will be offset by the higher mortality multiplier in estimating total wealth. If both donors and recipients had the same life expectancy as others in their age/sex groups, this refutation of the above mentioned argument would clearly be correct. However, as we have seen, there are reasons to doubt whether this is likely to be so; to quote Lampman: 'it might seem reasonable to assume that persons, particularly at older ages, with shorter than average life expectancy for their age group, would be more likely to be donors than those with longer expectancies' ([B 15], p. 68n). If this view is correct, and if gifts are made largely by the wealthy (to avoid duty), then the degree of concentration is understated. At the same time, a factor working in the opposite direction is that where the donor dies within seven years, the gift is included both in his estate and (applying the Mallet/Strutt argument) in the wealth of the recipient.† This double-counting causes the degree of concentration to be overstated.

The second set of problems is that arising from the size of the sample. As described in Section 2, the present procedure followed by the Inland Revenue is to take a complete census of large estates and of estates over £3,000 left by younger persons. But even this is not sufficient. Because of the small numbers in particular cells, the Inland Revenue applies combined multipliers across certain combinations of age groups and estate classes and smoothes the data for the largest estate classes as described earlier. In our view, this 'smoothing' procedure is not entirely satisfactory. The reason for concern is not that errors may be introduced through variation in the total number of deaths in a particular age group, since this would be reflected in an exactly offsetting variation in the mortality multipliers. The problem arises with the distribution of estates among wealth classes. This suggests that any combination of observations before applying the multipliers should be *not* between age groups (which would introduce errors arising from variation in the overall mortality rate for each group) but solely between estate classes.

The third group of problems concerns the form in which the estate duty statistics are collected. We described earlier the way in which the Inland Revenue deal with such matters as the time lag in recording estates. These adjustments are only approximate and may affect the accuracy of the final estimates. For example, while three to four months is the average interval between death and payment of first duty, the time lag may be very much longer for some large estates. The quantitative importance of this and the other problems of recording estates depends on the stability over time of the mortality multipliers and the changes taking place in asset prices. If there is an upward trend in the mortality multipliers (a downward trend in mortality rates), the number of current deaths is smaller than those appearing (with a delay) in the estate duty figures, and the number of wealth-holdings is overstated. Similarly, the adjustments made relating to earlier estates overstate those likely to be made on current estates. On the other hand, an upward trend in asset prices causes wealth (and the adjustments) to be understated, and in a time of substantial capital gains this could be an important factor.

Finally, there is the problem of errors in the recording of estates below the estate duty exemption limit. As is explained by the Inland Revenue:

* Under the estate duty if the donor lived for a specified period (seven years until 1974) after the gift is made, it was not counted as part of his estate.

† As pointed out by Lampman ([B 15], p. 69) this does not all represent double-counting since gifts made in the year of death are unlikely to show up fully in the estates of the recipients.

> The figures obtained from estates below the exemption limit for estate duty . . . are less reliable than those from estates paying duty because in general they do not have to be examined so thoroughly. (*Inland Revenue Statistics 1974* [QRL 31], p. 174.)

The fact that small estates are checked less thoroughly may lead one to expect that the average wealth will be understated; however, it is likely that liabilities also are understated. Revell notes that: 'when an estate is clearly not liable to duty, nobody has any incentive to do elaborate sums to compute the debts owing by the deceased and they will almost certainly be under-stated' ([B 24], pp. 158–9).

3.2.5 *Methods of Valuation*

The valuation of assets in the estate data was discussed by Revell in the context of national balance sheets, and he concluded that 'in general the valuation of items for estate duty is just what we need—a valuation at market prices' ([B 24], p. 112). However, as we have seen, given that many markets are characterized by imperfections, market value may be an ambiguous concept. A contrast was drawn earlier between the value obtainable on realization (a 'sell up' value) and the value to the person or household as a 'going concern'. The Inland Revenue method of valuation is closer to the former. In the case of household goods, for example, the valuation is based on second-hand market prices, and, as Revell points out, with the exception of cars, these values 'are usually derisory' and would not be applicable if the household was viewed as a going concern. Similarly, in the case of the assets of unincorporated businesses, these may be valued for estate duty purposes on a second-hand basis, which may be quite different from the value to the owner on the assumption that he continues in business.

The choice between different bases for valuation clearly depends on the purpose at hand, and no general conclusion may be reached about the appropriateness of the Inland Revenue method. There are however certain classes of asset which raise particular valuation problems, and some of the more important are discussed below:

(a) *Life Policies*. For this class of assets the estate duty valuation is clearly inappropriate on both approaches. In the estate duty statistics, life assurance policies on the deceased's own life are valued at the sum assured (plus any bonus), whereas in the hands of the living they are worth less than this amount. Campion [QRL 3] felt in fact that wealth should be estimated without any additions due to death and therefore excluded life policies altogether. However, as Langley has pointed out,

> The possession of a policy puts a person in a similar position to a man of capital in many ways. He may, for example, assume risks and obligations which he would otherwise hesitate to assume and may raise a loan on the policy ([QRL 9], p. 34).

She goes on to suggest that the policies have a surrender value which could be employed. This, or the market sale price of a policy, might be a more appropriate one for valuation on a 'sell-up' basis. On the other hand, in the case of the going concern valuation Revell has argued that

> Surrender value is always computed so as to impose a penalty on surrender, and it is therefore inappropriate for the holder viewed as a 'going concern' . . . For this there is no alternative but the present value of the income stream or capital payment ([B 24], p. 31).

He assumes that this latter value is equal to the actuarial reserves or fund held against the policy and uses this as the basis for his estimates.

(b) *Pension Rights*. This class of assets brings out very clearly the difference between the two different methods of valuation. On a 'sell up' basis, no value would in general be attached to these assets, since the holder cannot realize the asset or borrow on the strength of it (even in the case of insured pension schemes it is not usually possible to pledge them against a loan). The Inland Revenue treatment may therefore be appropriate in this case. On the other hand, these rights are worth something to the holder as a going concern, and on this alternative basis some allowance should be made for their value.

(c) *Settled Property*. It has been argued that the estate duty valuation of settled property may be inappropriate in certain circumstances. For example, the formula introduced in the Finance Act 1969 to allocate the capital held in discretionary trusts based on income received may not correspond at all accurately to the value of the deceased's interest. Settled property is again an example where different bases for valuation are likely to lead to rather different results. It also illustrates the fact that the sum of separate interests in a property may fall short of the value of the property as a whole.

3.2.6 *Individual and Family Wealth*

The Inland Revenue estimates relate to the distribution among individuals, but for many purposes we might be more interested in the distribution among nuclear families. By their nature, the estate data do not allow the estimates to be converted; at the same time, it is possible to place upper and lower bounds on the extent of concentration by making extreme assumptions about the correlation between wealth of family members. This procedure has been followed by Lyons [B 16], and Atkinson and Harrison [B 3]. It should be noted that estimates can be presented either treating a family as a single unit or adopting a *per capita* basis, with the total wealth (w) of each family being divided by the number of members (n) to given units with wealth w/n. This is discussed further in [B3].

3.3 The Inland Revenue Statistics—A Summing Up

We have described above some of the principal difficulties with using the Inland Revenue statistics. It is clear that the estate method must be treated with care and that in certain respects the official estimates present an incomplete picture. It must be remembered that the Inland Revenue's work is linked to the administration of capital taxation and that they do not set out to cover the entire distribution of wealth nor to make adjustments for missing wealth and differing methods of valuation. At the same time, despite these shortcomings, the Inland Revenue statistics are of considerable value. While the methods need refinement to provide a more complete picture, the estate data must in our view form the essential nucleus of any estimate of the upper part of the wealth distribution, particularly when we bear in mind the substantial problems which arise with other approaches (see Section 5).

4 The Estate Method—Unofficial Estimates

We have already noted the contribution which Mallet [B 17] made to the development of the multiplier technique, a contribution which was later extended by Mallet and Strutt [B 18]. These studies were concerned with the estimation of total personal wealth, and the first application of the technique to the size distribution of wealth was that by Sir Henry Clay [QRL 5] in 1925. Since that date interest in the subject has followed a cyclical pattern with major studies following at approximately ten-year intervals. Table 4.1 summarizes the main features of these studies, as well as a number of others where the distribution of wealth was not the primary concern, such as Barna [QRL 2] and Cartter [QRL 4]. Subsection 4.1 discusses certain aspects of these studies in more detail, while subsection 4.2 examines how far these studies may be used to give a consistent series over time. Estimates for Northern Ireland are described in subsection 4.3.

4.1 Studies Using Estate Method

4.1.1 *Mortality Multipliers*

The basic data in all these studies were the estate duty returns. (In some cases the authors had access to unpublished data; in other cases they relied on the published tables.) They differed, however, in a number of respects. The first important question concerns the multipliers employed. Clay [QRL 5] applied to estates over £500 the multiplier appropriate to occupations of a clerical and professional character, and the general multiplier to estates below £500. Wedgwood [QRL 19] followed Clay in using these death rates, arguing that they were applicable to the bulk of the upper and middle classes. The next writers to adopt the estate method were Daniels and Campion [QRL 7] and Campion [QRL 3]. These studies made estimates using both general mortality rates and social class mortality rates, although the authors felt that the latter were more relevant. The social class multipliers used by them were derived from the Registrar General's report on occupational mortality. These data on occupational mortality have only been published with considerable delay. In particular, the later studies by Langley [QRL 9] and Cartter [QRL 4] could draw on no more recent data than 1931 and they applied the same class mortality differentials as Campion. Since the Second World War, two further reports by the Registrar General have become available. That for 1951 was employed by Lydall and Tipping [QRL 12], who first made adjustments for the unoccupied and for errors in occupational statements, and that for 1961 by Atkinson and Harrison [B 3]. The estimate by Revell [QRL 15] for 1960 was intended to be compared with those of earlier investigators and for this purpose he felt that the general mortality rate was adequate (the 1960 figure being compared with those obtained by Daniels and Campion and Langley using general mortality rates). Atkinson and Harrison have also made estimates [QRL 1 and B 3] using social class mortality multipliers based on life office data. This is derived from the Continuous Mortality Investigation which draws on the mortality experience of life offices in the United Kingdom, covering those accepted for ordinary life and endowment policies at standard rates of premium. (They give in addition estimates derived using the general mortality multipliers and try to assess the sensitivity of the estimates to the choice of multipliers.)

4.1.2 *Treatment of Small Wealth-Holdings*

The second way in which the studies have differed

Table 4.1 Studies Using Estate Method

Author	Year(s)	Coverage: Area	Coverage: Age	Types of Multipliers	Treatment of small wealth-holdings	Other adjustments (see text for details)
Clay [QRL 5]	1911–13 1920	EW	Over 15 and occupied	GMR for estates under £500; over £500 mortality rates of occupations of a clerical and professional nature	Estimates value of furniture, tools, effects, etc. of exempt persons plus collective savings of this same group	None
Wedgwood [QRL 19]	1923–4	EW	Over 25	SMR for males, based on Clay. GMR for females	Takes Clay's figure for 1920 as still applicable to 1924	None
Daniels and Campion [QRL 7]	1911–13 1924–30	EW	25 and over	GMR and SMR based on 1911 DS (intermediate class I and II as then defined). GMR and SMR based on 1921 DS and preliminary results of 1931 DS (intermediate Class I–II (average) and III).	Follows Clay's technique adjusting downwards on grounds that the unadjusted extrapolated figure was too high	None
Campion [QRL 3]	1911–13 1926–8 1936	EW	25 and over	As Daniels and Campion	As Daniels and Campion	None
Barna [QRL 2]	1937	UK (Merely % adjustment for NI)	No control total for population used	GMR	None	Settled property
Langley [QRL 9]	1936–8 1946–7	EW and GB	25 and over	GMR and SMR based on Campion	Takes a range based on estimates of Clay and Daniels and Campion for earlier years and extrapolation of ED figures	None
Cartter [QRL 4]	1947–9	GB	Over 25	SMR based on Campion	Assumes average holding below £100 of £45	None
Langley [QRL 10]	1950–1	GB	25 and over	GMR	As earlier study for less than £100; extrapolates ED figure below £2,000	None
Lydall and Tipping [QRL 12]	1951–6	GB	20 and over	SMR based on 1951 DS for classes I and II (average) adjusted for errors in occupational statements and for unoccupied	Uses results of Oxford Savings Survey, and extrapolates ED figures	Settled property and pension funds
Revell [QRL 15]	1954 1960	EW	Over 25	GMR	None	None
Atkinson [QRL 1]	1968	GB	18 and over	Range of assumptions including SMR based on 1961 DS and on life office data	Estimates based on balance sheet totals	Adjustments for missing wealth using balance sheet totals

has been in their treatment of the wealth of people missing from the estate duty returns. In 1925 Clay [QRL 5] made an estimate of the wealth in the hands of people with less than £100 (the estate duty limit at that date) based on the funds of savings banks and other 'working-class' savings, and the value of household goods and personal effects. In the following investigations, Wedgwood [QRL 19], Daniels and Campion [QRL 7], Campion [QRL 3] and Langley [QRL 9] all based their estimates on extrapolations of Clay's original figures, although in some cases they had reservations about their use. Daniels and Campion, for example, felt that 'an estimate prepared on similar lines to that of Professor Clay suggests that the total might be over £1,000 million for 1929–30 but it is thought that such a total is too high' ([QRL 7], p. 48). As a result they adjusted the figures downwards. The increase in the estate duty threshold to £2,000 in 1946 meant that the problems of allowing for small wealth-holdings became more serious but no very satisfactory solution was proposed until the study by Lydall and Tipping [QRL 12]. They based their estimates of those below the estate duty exemption level on three main sources and techniques:

> (1) extrapolation of cumulative frequency curves, (2) evidence gleaned from the 1954 savings survey about the relative holdings of particular assets by those above and below this level, and (3) information about total assets of persons (e.g. life funds) available from independent sources ([QRL 12], p. 86).

Atkinson and Harrison [QRL 1 and B 3] developed the third of these approaches using the balance sheet data of Revell [B 24] and Roe [B 29]. A fuller description of the data is given in Section 6, but the important feature for present purposes is that these authors gave estimates of total personal holdings of wealth classified by asset type. In essence the approach adopted by Atkinson and Harrison is to adjust the estate duty estimates of the distribution to bring them in line with the control totals. (The same approach has subsequently been followed by official statisticians in the Appendix to the Green Paper on the Wealth Tax [B 42] and in the first report of the Royal Commission on the Distribution of Income and Wealth [B 39].) The procedure is first to estimate the amount in each asset category which is covered by the estate duty-based estimates. This is obtained by applying the data on asset composition of wealth for different wealth ranges to the total wealth in each range.* Summing over all wealth ranges then yields an estimate of the total holdings of that asset, which can be compared with the control total for the personal sector from the national balance sheet.

The relationship between estate duty estimates and national balance sheet totals was discussed by Revell with particular reference to 1961. In that year, the estimate of total personal wealth made by him on the basis of estate data was £63·9 billion, whereas the corresponding balance sheet total was £77·6 billion. In some cases, Revell's balance sheet figures were based on the estate duty estimates, and the discrepancy arises from those assets where independent information gave a different total holding. The main sources of this discrepancy are shown in Table 4.2 (although the assets and liabilities listed there do not exhaust those for which they were discrepancies, they account for a major part of the difference). The existence of a discrepancy does not imply that adjustments are necessary. The discrepancies may arise as much through errors in the balance sheet totals as through inadequacies of the estate duty estimates. In certain cases, the balance sheet totals for the personal sector are obtained as residuals and the divergence from the estate estimates may simply reflect errors in the totals for other sectors. In view of this, the policy adopted by Atkinson and Harrison is to make adjustments only to those assets

* The Inland Revenue were able to provide for 1968 estimates of the asset composition of wealth-holdings based on the unpublished estate returns classified by age and asset structure. This information was first published in 1973 (see subsection 2.2).

where there is an *a priori* reason to expect wealth to be missing from the estate duty estimates. In the case of quoted company shares, for example, there is no clear reason for the discrepancy between the estate duty estimates and Revell's figures obtained from register surveys, and no adjustment is made.*

Table 4.2 Discrepancy Between Estate Duty Estimates and National Balance Sheet, 1961

	(£ billion) Estate Duty	Balance Sheet
Assets:		
Unquoted UK Government	3·4	4·2
Savings bank deposits	2·9	3·2
Building society deposits	3·6	3·1
Household goods, etc.	2·1	4·0
Trade assets	2·2	4·4
Exempt settled property	0	1·4
Expectant interests	2·5	0
Quoted UK shares	12·1	13·9
Unquoted UK Shares	3·1	5·4
Life policies and pension rights	7·2	13·5
Land and buildings*	13·0	20·2
Liabilities:		
House mortgages	1·2	4·9
Debts	2·9	4·9
Net worth	63·9	77·6

Source: Revell [B 24], Table 7.1. This excludes holdings by overseas residents

* The liability 'other deductions from landed property' is subtracted from this item.

The discrepancy may reflect differences in the method of valuation. Revell's approach is closest to that described earlier as a 'going concern' basis. In view of this, Atkinson and Harrison give figures both on a realization basis and on a 'going concern' basis.

The final stage involves the allocation of the additional wealth by ranges. In this allocation, two main factors are taken into account. First in some cases the nature of the asset suggests that it is likely to be held in certain wealth ranges: for example, those types of property covered by the Administration of Estates (Small Payments) Act 1965. Secondly, where the discrepancy arises through differences in the method of valuation, the procedure followed is to increase the holding in each range by an appropriate multiple. Even allowing for these two factors, however, it is necessary to make a number of assumptions, and the procedure followed is to make four types of assumption:

1. *Assumption B.1.* No adjustment.
2. *Assumption B.2.* Lower bound to concentration where wealth is allocated as far as reasonable to lowest wealth groups.
3. *Assumption B.3.* A central estimate—based on best available information.
4. *Assumption B.4.* Upper bound to concentration where wealth is allocated as far as reasonable to upper wealth groups.

(The precise assumptions are described in greater detail in [B 3].)

* It should also be noted that the balance sheet totals quoted in Table 4.2 correspond to values at December 31, whereas the estate duty estimates are a weighted average for the year as a whole. If the value of assets is rising, then the discrepancy can be partly explained in this way. In view of this, the balance sheet totals used by Atkinson and Harrison are, wherever possible, based on a weighted average of the figures for different dates in the year.

4.1.3 *Other Adjustments*

The third aspect of these studies which should be noted is the paucity of other adjustments to the estate data. Settled property is the only one which has received much attention. Mallet and Strutt ([B 18], pp. 573–5) suggested totals for the extent of settled property but Daniels and Campion, whilst acknowledging this ([QRL 7], p. 38), argued that its exclusion does not vitiate comparisons between distributions for different years. Campion ([QRL 3], p. 108) was similarly disposed and it was left to Barna ([QRL 2], p. 260) to make some allowance adding 'settled' estates proportionately to other estates. Langley, like others before, made no attempt at distributing an estimated total for settled property ([QRL 9], p. 33) utilizing Campion's arguments on the insignificance of the effect of its exclusion. Lydall and Tipping [QRL 12] made some very approximate adjustments for this deficiency and added to their total of £40,000 million for personal wealth, a further £1,000 million for discretionary trusts, £3,000 million for property settled on a surviving spouse (both of which they assumed to belong entirely to the top 10% in the wealth distribution) and £3,000 million for pension funds (half of which they assumed to belong to the top 10%). Atkinson and Harrison [B 3] give a range of estimates based on a variety of sources.

4.2 Consistent Series Over Time

For many purposes it is interesting to know how the distribution of wealth has changed over time. The Inland Revenue series extends from 1960 to the present, but in order to make a longer-term comparison one has to go back to the studies just described. In this section we describe some of the main problems which arise in trying to produce a broadly comparable series of estimates. In order to help focus the discussion, it may be useful to have in mind the figures for the trend in wealth ownership usually quoted in public discussion, and those used by Polanyi and Wood [B 21] are shown in Table 4.3. It may be noted that these estimates cover only selected years. In large part the selection reflects the availability of the basic estate data in the required form, but there are certain years not included for which data are available. A listing of the published data, and its coverage, is given in Table 4.4.

There are a number of reasons why the figures in Table 4.3 do not give a consistent series over time, and amongst the most important are those outlined below. (For a fuller discussion of their quantitative significance and an attempt to construct a more satisfactory series, see Atkinson and Harrison [B 3].)

4.2.1 *Coverage of Estate Data*

The estate data originally only covered England and Wales, and all studies prior to that of Langley referred to this, whereas later estimates referred to Great Britain (for some intermediate years estimates were given on both bases). This causes a break in the comparability of the series presented by Polanyi and Wood, which they clearly recognize. On the basis of the later years for which data are available in both forms, it appears that in fact the estimates for Great Britain are not greatly different from those for England and Wales (see Atkinson and Harrison [B 3]).

A second break in comparability recognized by Polanyi and Wood is in the definition of adult, which was taken to be 25 and over in the earlier studies by Daniels and Campion. It could be argued that the difference between this and the age of 15 and over taken in the later years is appropri-

Table 4.3 Distribution of Wealth 1911–12 to 1970—Usually Quoted Figures

Proportion of adults	*England and Wales Adults aged 25 and over* 1911–13	1924–30	1936	1951–6	*Great Britain Adults aged 15 and over* 1960	1965	1970
Top 1%	66	60	56	42	39	34	31
Top 5%	86	83	81	68	64	62	56
Top 10%	90	90	88	79	76	75	70
Top 20%	—	96	94	89	91	89	87
Bottom 80%	—	4	6	11	9	11	13
Original source	Daniels and Campion		Campion	Lydall and Tipping	Polanyi and Wood		

Source: Polanyi and Wood [B 21], Tables 3 and 4. They in turn took the first four columns from Lydall and Tipping ([QRL 12], Table 5), rounding to the nearest percentage point.

ate in the light of the fall in the average age at which people achieve economic independence. On the other hand, the use of the same definition throughout the period would lead to a greater downward trend in the share of top wealth groups.

Table 4.4 Availability of Estate Data Classified by Range of Estate and Age

Financial Year	*Country*	*Classified by Sex*	*Published in*
1911–12	EW	No	AR 55
1912–13	EW	No	AR 56
1913–14	EW	No	AR 57
1914–15	EW	No	AR 58
1920–1	EW	No	AR 64
1923–4	EW	Yes	AR 67
1924–5	EW	Yes	AR 68
1925–6	EW	Yes	AR 69
1926–7	EW	Yes	AR 70
1927–8	EW	Yes	AR 71
1928–9	EW	Yes	AR 72
1929–30	EW	Yes	AR 73
1930–1	EW	Yes	AR 74
1936–7	EW	Yes	AR 80
1938–9	EW & S	Yes	AR 82
1950–1	EW & S	Yes	AR 94
1951–2	EW & S	Yes	AR 95
1952–3	EW & S	Yes	AR 96
1953–4	EW & S	Yes	AR 97
1954–5	EW & S	Yes	AR 98
1955–6	EW & S	Yes	AR 99
1956–7	EW & S	Yes	AR 100
1957–8	EW & S	Yes	AR 101
1958–9	EW & S	Yes	AR 102
1959–60	EW & S	Yes	AR 103
1960–1	EW & S	Yes	AR 104
1961–2	EW & S	Yes	AR 105
1962–3	EW & S	Yes	AR 106
1963–4	GB	Yes	AR 107
1964–5	GB	Yes	AR 108, IRS 1970
1965–6	GB	Yes	AR 109, IRS 1970, 1971
1966–7	GB	Yes	AR 110, IRS 1970, 1971
1967–8	GB	Yes	AR 111, IRS 1970, 1971
1968–9	GB	Yes	IRS 1970, 1971
1969–70	GB	Yes	IRS 1971
1970–71	GB	Yes	IRS 1972
1971–2	GB	Yes	IRS 1973
1972–3	GB	Yes	IRS 1974

4.2.2 *Mortality Multipliers*

Polanyi and Wood rightly stress the importance of using social-class adjusted multipliers, but they overlook the fact that the multipliers applied in the years before the Second World War are not fully consistent with those used by Lydall and Tipping in their estimates for 1951–6 or by the Inland Revenue. The first difference is that the earlier studies used the Registrar General's data on occupational mortality without the adjustment for errors in occupational statements (problem (b) described in subsection 3.2.3). As a result, the social class multipliers are probably too low in relation to those applied in the 1950s and 1960s. As shown in Atkinson and Harrison [B 3], this is likely to lead to a higher estimate of the degree of concentration, and hence cause the trend towards equality to be overstated. Secondly, the results quoted by Polanyi and Wood do not in fact appear to have been obtained using social class multipliers, and the use of Daniels and Campion's results based on social class multipliers would tend to reduce the shares of top wealth groups in 1924–30 and 1936.*

4.2.3 *Treatment of Small Wealth-Holdings*

The proportion of total deaths covered by the estate duty returns, and the treatment of the wealth of those excluded, has varied over the period. In the period up to the Second World War, the estate duty exemption level was £100; and a variety of estimtes were made of the wealth of those below this level. The approach of Clay

* For example, from Daniels and Campion ([QRL 7], Table 23) it may be seen that according to the social class estimates those with wealth of more than £100 represented the top 23·7% of the population in 1924–30. Taking the mid-point of their range of total wealth for those below £100 gives an estimate of total capital of £14,955m. The percentage share of the top 23·7% is then calculable as 95·3%—whereas the figures in Table 4.3 show a smaller group (the top 20%) owning a larger share (96·0%).

[QRL 5], based on the likely value of personal effects and 'working-class savings', suggested a figure in 1920–1 of £912 million, but Daniels and Campion [QRL 7] for 1924–30 took the lower range £500–£900 million.*

With the rise in the estate duty exemption level to £2,000 (1946), reaching £5,000 in 1963 and £15,000 in 1972, the problem of allowing for the excluded population has become more acute. (If the exemption level had increased since 1938 in line with prices, it would only have reached some £500 in 1972.) The method adopted by Lydall and Tipping [QRL 12] in the case of the estimates for 1954 has been outlined above. This has not, however, been followed in the Inland Revenue figures which make no allowance for the wealth of the excluded population. Adjustments for the wealth missing on this account would lead to a significant reduction in the share of top wealth groups (see [B 3]). To this extent, the trend towards equality from the beginning to the end of the period is understated in the figures shown in Table 4.3.

4.2.4 *Missing Wealth*

The estate data by their very nature exclude some important types of wealth, such as certain forms of settled property and the value of pension rights. In general, the studies considered here make no allowance for these (an exception is Lydall and Tipping [QRL 12]). The bias in the trend depends on how the extent of missing property has changed over the period and on the method of valuation. In the case of missing wealth arising from estate duty avoidance, there are likely to be two opposing forces. The scope of estate duty has been extended: for example, the inclusion of immoveable property situated outside the UK from 1962, and of discretionary trusts from 1969. A countervailing pressure has, however, been the rise in the rates of estate duty and the consequent increased incentive for avoidance. Not all methods of avoidance mean that wealth is missing from the estate duty returns, but in certain cases, notably trusts, this may happen. In the case of pension rights, there can be little doubt that they have increased in importance over the period. The significance of this depends in large part on the method of valuation. A realization basis would mean that the growth of pension rights was not relevant, but on a 'going concern' basis they would clearly have a value.

* If the upper end of this range is used, in line with Clay, then the figure for the share of the top 23·7% referred to in the previous footnote becomes 94·1% rather than 95·3%.

4.2.5 *Special Problems with Data for 1911–14*

There are a number of special problems surrounding the use of the data for 1911–14. The first is that the estate data were not then classified by sex, so that it is not possible to apply appropriate multipliers. Daniels and Campion [QRL 7] made a number of *ad hoc* assumptions about the proportion of estates possessed by women and their allocation by ranges. This means that there is a greater degree of uncertainty surrounding the estimates for the pre-First World War period (the same problem also applies with the estate data for 1920). A second set of problems consists of those arising from the establishment of Northern Ireland and the Irish Free State as separate taxing jurisdictions which affected the comparability of the estate statistics before and after the First World War (see [QRL 7], pp. 35–6). Thirdly, there are the changes in the estate duty law in 1913, especially the abolition of the exemption for the settled property on which duty had once been paid. These again make difficult any comparison of the estimates for 1911–13 with those for later years. Finally the occupational mortality data were presented in a different form in the Registrar General's 1911 Decennial Supplement.

4.3 Northern Ireland

As we noted in the introduction, no official estimates of the distribution of wealth in Northern Ireland have so far been published and in consequence our geographical coverage is largely confined to Great Britain. However there have been two unofficial studies, both adopting the estate duty approach. The first by Corley [QRL 6] covered various years between 1920 and 1960 and more recently Lyons [QRL 13] has presented estimates for 1966. We briefly consider these here as the final part of our discussion of the use of estate duty statistics by private researchers.

Many of the defects which we have earlier noted apply equally to these two studies, and in addition, to the extent that the basic data are less comprehensive, the estimates are probably less reliable than those reviewed so far. Both Corley and Lyons point out that the availability of the data dictates the precise form that use of the estate method takes, the former writer noting that the exercise 'is capable of infinite elaboration, depending on the amount of information available' ([QRL 6], p. 15). Table 4.5 presents details of the studies in the same form as Table 4.1 for studies of Great Britain and the discussion which follows elaborates some of the more important aspects of the techniques adopted, where necessary making comparisons with British estimates.

The first point to note is that relatively greater restrictions are imposed by the lack of suitable data. For example, neither author is able to use social class mortality multipliers since these are not available for Northern Ireland, and in fact Corley for some of the earlier years has to rely on a single multiplier for all people aged over 25. The problem of the exclusion of small wealth-holdings is acknowledged but the adjustments made are only crude.

Corley does make some attempt to identify those groups who might own some wealth, arbitrarily assuming this average amount to be £50 for estates of less than £100. In addition he also has to include some estimate for estates between £100 and the higher exemption limits of later years and follows Isles and Cuthbert [B 13] by using the results of sample surveys. Lyons however makes no such adjustment (by 1966 the exemption limit had risen to £5,000), in order that his estimates can be compared with similar results for the Irish Republic.

There are two other aspects of these studies which should be mentioned, both of which are again the consequence of the nature and availability of the data. The first concerns the basic estate duty statistics. Corley, in his appendix ([QRL 6], p. 27) reveals that the information on values and amounts of estates for earlier years is unpublished, but that in later years it can be found in the Government of Northern Ireland's half-yearly *Digest of Statistics* [QRL 23]. Lyons however only uses this source to estimate the number of persons in each wealth category, deriving the amounts of wealth by multiplying the number of people in each range by the mid-point of the range, with the final mid-point of the open-ended

Table 4.5 Studies of Northern Ireland Using Estate Method

Author	*Year(s)*	*Coverage: Age*	*Types of Multipliers*	*Treatment of Small Wealth*	*Other adjustments*
Corley [QRL 6]	Various years 1920–60	25 and over	GMR (only age- and sex-specific for some years covered)	Assigns to part of the excluded population an arbitrary average wealth size; zero wealth to the remainder	None
Lyons [QRL 13]	1965–6 (averaged)	20 and over	GMR	Assigns zero wealth to the whole of the excluded population	None

highest range being assumed. Since the data on values of estates are available for the years of Lyons' investigation it seems strange that they should be replaced by an assumption, the validity of which is not made clear.

The second point to note is that, as with some investigators in Great Britain, both writers use an average of two or more years' data, presenting the result as an estimate for the middle of the period. The reason for this is to diminish the chance that the dying are not representative of the living, especially where, as in Northern Ireland, the number of estates in a particular age-group in any year is small.

5 Alternative Approaches

5.1 The Investment Income (Giffen) Method

This method has been mainly employed to prepare estimates of the total of personal wealth, and only a few authors have used it to estimate the size distribution among persons. The study by Campion [QRL 3], for example, devotes an entire chapter to the Giffen method but is concerned only with total wealth and, for this reason, it is not considered here. Subsection 5.1.1 briefly reviews the use of this method by different investigators, including the present authors, and subsection 5.1.2 outlines the major deficiencies of this approach.

5.1.1 *Use of the Method*

The main statistical source for this method is the size distribution of investment income taken from the income tax data, which is then capitalized to obtain the distribution of wealth. The investment income data are discussed by Stark in his companion review and we shall not discuss the source in detail here.

The principal studies using this method are Barna [QRL 2], Cartter [QRL 4], a short article in the *Economist* for 15 January 1966 [B 38] and Atkinson and Harrison [B 3], an early version of which is presented in [B 1]. However, not all of these were predominantly interested in the distribution of wealth, the first two being primarily concerned with relating capital holdings to income ranges. In the course of Barna's study, he first estimated the distribution of assets left at death for different ranges of estates expressed as percentages of the gross capital for that range. He next derived the average yield of the different types of assets from a variety of sources and on the basis of a number of assumptions. The yield of capital in different estate ranges was estimated from a weighted average of the different asset yields, the weights being the proportion of the gross capital in that estate range which each particular asset represented. This yield curve was then used to calculate the capital corresponding to a given income. Barna did not take the final step of estimating the implied distribution of capital which would have yielded a distribution which could have been compared with that estimated from the estate method. The study by Cartter followed closely that of Barna and similarly did not make any comparison of the results obtained by the two methods.

The details of the estimate by the *Economist* for 1959–60 are unfortunately not discussed in the text of the article. All that is revealed is that the estimates were based on 'the recorded investment income of the living' and estimated yields from different assets were then applied to the breakdown of wealth by asset type. Beyond this, however, there is no indication of the method of estimating yields, and the editor was unable to supply further details.

The most recent estimates are those by the present authors which were based on the studies described above, where possible improving on the sophistication with which these earlier studies were made. First an analysis of the yield on different assets was made (using in all twenty-eight categories of asset based on the classification adopted by the Inland Revenue; see for example *Inland Revenue Statistics 1971* [QRL 31], Table 115). Since the income data relate to income as defined for tax purposes, non-taxable income should be excluded from the yield calculations (certain earlier studies were in error in including non-taxable income, for example on national savings certificates). For each range of wealth a weighted average yield was then calculated, reflecting the different composition of portfolios at different wealth levels. In contrast to earlier studies, the weights were based on evidence about wealth-holdings rather than estates.*

As Revell [B 23] has demonstrated, the use of data on the asset composition of estates causes a serious distortion because of the systematic variation of portfolios with age. The weighted average yields were then multiplied by mean wealth in each range and the points joined to form a yield curve, so that for each level of investment income, it is possible to read off the level of wealth to which this corresponds. The yield multipliers were then applied to the basic investment income returns, which were the returns for surtax purposes for the year 1968–9. Since liability to surtax in that year began at approximately £3,000 (£2,000 assessed income plus personal allowances) this was taken as the lower limit.

The distribution of wealth obtained using the investment income method differs from that derived from the estate returns in three respects. Firstly, the investment income returns cover the tax year whereas the estate data are assumed to correspond to the calendar year. With asset values rising over time this suggests that the estimates are not strictly comparable. Second, the estate data relate to individuals, whereas in the investment income estimates the wealth of husband and wife is aggregated since the data relate to tax units not individuals. Thus the possession of wealth by wives will once again cause the estimates to differ. Thirdly the investment income data relate to the United Kingdom while the estate duty estimates are based on data for Great Britain. Finally the fact that the investment income estimates are not adjusted for missing wealth or differences in the method of valuation in the way described in Section 4 means that they should be compared with 'unadjusted' estimates such as those produced by the Inland Revenue.

* The data used are referred to in the footnote on p. 30.

5.1.2 *Deficiencies of the Investment Income Approach*

There are a number of deficiencies associated with this approach and some of the most important are described briefly below.

(a) *Missing Wealth-holders*

As in the case of the estate duty method, the investment income returns do not cover the whole wealth-holding population. The surtax returns by definition only relate to the upper income ranges, so that the data for 1968–9, for example, cover only some 100,000 out of 20·7 million tax-paying units. The quinquennial income surveys provide comparable information covering the whole income range (most recently for 1969–70), but there are a number of ways in which the coverage is incomplete.* For this reason, the investment income method is probably more useful in throwing light on the upper wealth ranges than on the distribution as a whole.

(b) *Asset Composition*

Since the asset composition data are based on the estate duty method, they are subject to the same deficiencies as those outlined earlier. Errors in the multipliers, for example, may lead to a bias in the asset composition, as may the exclusion of certain types of property. It should be remembered, however, that these errors may be less important in the present case. This point may be illustrated with reference to the mortality multipliers. These are only used here as a means for weighting the asset composition of the estates of different age/sex groups; the overall level of the multipliers, which is the main possible source of error, is not relevant to the investment income method. To this extent, the investment income method is less subject to error. At the same time, the use of asset composition data unadjusted for property which is missing or incorrectly valued (e.g. life assurance policies)

* There is reason to believe that below the surtax range investment income is not necessarily reported where tax has already been paid. No adjustment was made for this in the 1969–70 survey, but in 1954–5 the Inland Revenue added a further 307,000 income units—see Stark [B 33], p. 12.

involves the same error as the estate method, and adjustments of the kind described in Section 4 may be necessary.

(c) *Yields*
The yield data play a critical role in the construction of the estimates; at the same time there are at least three sources of error. Firstly, there is the systematic bias introduced via random fluctuations in the return to different individuals. The yield multiplier is based on the mean yield and does not allow for a distribution of yields about the mean. This is likely to lead to concentration in wealth-holding being overstated (the argument is similar to that concerning permanent and transitory incomes). Second, the estimates of average yields may be incorrect. This is more likely to be the case for certain assets than others, and particular reference should be made to real property, where the methods of estimation were extremely crude. Recent published results [B 1] give some ideas of the sensitivity of the results to the return on this group of assets. Finally, the yields may vary systematically with the level of wealth, so that the average yield is not appropriate for the large holdings considered here. The direction of the bias introduced is not clear. There is likely in general to be a higher overall return to large holdings but the *taxable* return is not necessarily higher. In certain cases, more of the income will be taxable: for example, less of the residential property owned by those in the upper wealth is likely to be owner-occupied. On the other hand, tax reasons provide a strong incentive for this group to hold assets with a low taxable return: for example, the wealthy are more likely to hold 'growth stocks'. Some indication of the sensitivity of the results is given by Atkinson and Harrison [B 3].

(d) *Net Versus Gross Investment Income*
The only data available in 1968–9 were those for income net of interest paid, particularly mortgage interest. This would not by itself necessarily lead to error, since the weights used for different yields were based on net worth. However, the estate data almost certainly understate mortgage liabilities. Revell has pointed out that in 1960 the estate duty estimate of house mortgages was only 29 % of the total known from the issuing sources ([B 24], p. 173) and argued that the deficiency was mainly attributable to loans secured by life policies (which were netted out when the person died). Some guide to the approximate effect of such a possible understatement is obtained in [B 1] by increasing the mortgage liability by a factor of 3 and adding this amount to the asset side in the form of life policies.

5.1.3 *Investment Income Method—Summary*
In view of the deficiencies described above, we would conclude that the investment income method in its present form is unlikely to replace the estate duty method as the principal source of information about the overall wealth distribution. At the same time, given that the two techniques are largely independent, the investment income method may provide a valuable cross-check on the estate duty estimates for the group of top wealth-holders.

5.2 Sample Survey Method
The best-known sample surveys covering wealth-holding are those carried out by the Oxford Institute of Statistics in the early 1950s, the results of which were used by Lydall and Tipping [QRL 12] to estimate the lower tail of the distribution. While the Oxford surveys have not been repeated, a more recent survey of household income and wealth was carried out in 1968–9 by Abel-Smith and Townsend (the Essex Poverty Survey), and there have been a number of surveys by market research organizations (most recently the Economists Advisory Group study, *Personal Savings and Wealth in Britain* [QRL 14]). In subsections 5.2.1–3, we describe the main features of these surveys, and in subsection 5.2.4 we examine the problems inherent in this approach and their implications for the accuracy of the results which are obtained.

5.2.1 *Oxford Savings Surveys*★

The aims of the Oxford surveys were: 'to build up a complete picture of the financial position and behaviour of individual persons or families' (Hill [QRL 8], p. 129). Their main focus was on incomes and saving, but the 1953 and 1954 surveys also collected information about net worth. The unit of analysis was defined as the 'income unit' being the closest approximation to the ideal 'group of persons who could be expected to pool their income and their assets' (Lydall [QRL 11], p. 197). The surveys covered Great Britain, and were restricted to income units living in private households (i.e. excluding those living in institutions).

The 1953 survey was based on a two-stage sample design. At the first stage, the rating authorities of Great Britain were grouped into sixty-nine strata and within each one authority was selected at random. Within each rating area, a further stratification into two groups was made: an upper stratum with dwellings having a rateable value of at least £30 (£40 in London) and a lower stratum with a rateable value below this level. The sampling fractions for the two sub-strata were in the ratio 8:1. The final total of completed questionnaires was 2,104, representing a response rate of 66·1%. The response achieved in the lower sub-stratum (68·9%) was considerably higher than that in the upper sub-stratum (47·2%)—see ([QRL 8], p. 160). These differences were large enough to justify the use of weights not only for the differing sampling fractions but also for the differential non-response. This of course requires the assumption that, although there are differences in response rates between identifiable groups of the population, there are no important differences *within* these groups. As Hill, Klein and Straw point out, this 'may still leave serious biases' ([B 12], p. 90).

The 1954 survey was based on a rather different sample design. The first-stage units were electoral wards stratified by region, degree of urbanization, and proportion of jurors. At the second stage, liability for jury service was made the stratifying characteristic, and addresses containing jurors had a sampling fraction ten times that of others. The final total was 2,463 successful interviews with income units. The overall response rate (67·2%) was only slightly higher than in 1953, but there was much less difference between the upper and lower strata (in the case of 1954, jurors and non-jurors).

The main results of the 1953 and 1954 Oxford surveys are described in Hill [QRL 8] and Straw [QRL 16]. The former presents estimates of mean net worth per income unit, and the average holding of different types of asset, in 1953 and 1954. It also gives tables for the distribution by ranges of net worth, and of the following components: total liquid assets, total National Savings, real property, and mortgage debt outstanding. Straw's article [QRL 16] concentrates on the data for 1953, providing a more detailed analysis of the distribution of net worth by age and sex, occupation, housing status, and income, as well as of the distribution of individual assets.

Lydall and Tipping [QRL 12] made use of the results of the 1954 Oxford survey, which was regarded as the more reliable of the two (see Hill [QRL 8]), to establish the likely distribution of wealth below the exemption limit. They did this by first extrapolating the cumulative frequency distribution of those above the estate duty exemption level plotted on a double-logarithmic scale, to pass through the point corresponding to the total population and a minimum level of wealth. This yielded a frequency for a number of classes below exemption equivalent to the classes in the savings survey so that multiplication of the frequency by the mean value of net worth in each class yielded an estimate, when the class totals were added together, of total wealth owned by the excluded population. This total was checked by adopting a similar approach for each main class of asset, where the control amounts of total wealth held in each asset were also derived from the surveys. Some

★ See also Stark, Companion review, subsection 3.8.

adjustments were necessary, notably for house-ownership and to a lesser extent life insurance and the result was a further increase in estimated total net capital.

5.2.2 *Essex Poverty Survey*

The Poverty Survey was a much more ambitious attempt to obtain information about income and wealth (Townsend, [QRL 18]). The questionnaire was thirty-nine pages long, compared with seven pages in the case of the Oxford survey, and contained nine separate sections. The survey was conducted in order to provide details which were representative of the population and also specifically to illuminate the position of four communities in poor areas, hence the expressed aim that the report of the survey's findings would be a report of the extent of poverty in the United Kingdom.

The section of the questionnaire which concerns us here—Section V: Savings and Assets—attempted to establish estimates of the total value of savings and assets owned by the surveyed households in order to ascertain the extent to which poor families had 'reserves' of any kind. The respondents were asked seventeen questions relating to assets they owned or debts they owed and the interest received or paid. For each type of asset or debt they were asked to give an estimated value, although in the case of liquid savings (for example Post Office Savings Bank deposits, building society deposits, etc.) the total held was sometimes not disaggregated.

The unit of whom these questions were asked was in this case the household, that is one person living alone or a group of persons living together, but *not necessarily* pooling their resources. Unlike the Oxford surveys, the Poverty Survey also sampled institutions, and treated persons in them as separate households if they occupied separate quarters and, for the most part, cooked for themselves. The area covered by the sample was the United Kingdom, but in addition to this national sample, concentrated studies were made in four areas where the proportion of low-income households was expected to be high, in the hope of identifying members of minority groups.

The total number of households sampled was 2,495, which yielded 1,886 complete interviews and 166 incomplete interviews. This represents a response rate of 75·6% complete interviews and 82·3% overall. Of the remaining households, nearly nine-tenths were refusals. The 2,052 interviews covered a total of 6,098 individuals. The representative nature of this sample is discussed at some length in the published results of the survey, which notes, for example, that there was a noticeable variation in response rate between regions and also between other variables when these were identifiable in the limited information supplied on non-respondents by interviewers.

5.2.3 *Economists Advisory Group Survey*

This survey, carried out in 1974, is the most recent of a number of surveys undertaken by market research organizations (earlier studies include, for example, that by the British Market Research Bureau in 1965–6). The survey was particularly directed at the ownership of stock exchange securities and other financial assets, and the author recognized it to be very different from the Oxford surveys 'both in objectives and methods' ([QRL 14], p. 2). The fieldwork was carried out in 1974 by NOP Market Research, and involved the following three samples:

(i) Sample 1 with 3,705 actual respondents was asked questions covering ownership of financial assets, household composition, housing tenure, income and other personal characteristics,

(ii) Sample 2 with 9,388 actual respondents was interviewed using a shorter questionnaire with less detail of personal characteristics.

(iii) Sample 3 consisted of the subsample of 534 respondents from Sample 2 who stated that they owned any of the following assets:

> unit trusts, property bonds, other bonds, investment trusts, stocks and shares, government or local authority securities.

The response rates reported (excluding those who had died or moved away) were 70% for Sample 1 and 66% for Sample 2. The results are published in [QRL 14] and a limited number of copies of a volume of supplementary tables is available at a price of £200.00.

5.2.4 *Deficiencies of the Sample Survey Approach*
In this section we describe some of the principal difficulties associated with the use of sample survey data for estimating the distribution of wealth:

(a) non-response,
(b) incomplete information,
(c) incomplete coverage in survey design,
(d) sampling error.

In discussing these problems, we pay particular attention to the 1953 and 1954 Oxford surveys, but reference is also made to the more recent Economists Advisory Group Survey.

(a) *Non-Response*
The relatively low response rate was referred to in the previous section, and this is a problem inherent in any sample survey. As Lydall described the position in his analysis of the 1952 Oxford survey: 'In all surveys, there are some people who are unable or unwilling to be interviewed; and the question arises whether these "non-respondents", as a group, differ materially from the rest of the population in respect of the characteristics that are under observation' ([QRL 11], p. 228). The Oxford Institute made a number of external checks on representativeness using, for example, Population Census Figures. In their discussion of the 1953 Survey, Hill, Klein and Straw [B 12] devoted considerable attention to the problem of non-response. First, it is interesting to note that of all failures to achieve a satisfactory response, two-thirds were direct refusals, and only a third were caused by non-contact or rejection at the editing stage. Secondly, there appeared to be a marked association between the rateable value of the property and the response rate—see Table 5.1. The authors also concluded that 'response is lowest from the self-employed (businessmen, farmers, etc.). There is also a relatively low response from the professional, technical and executive classes, and from the retired and unoccupied—especially, it seems, the more wealthy retired people' (p. 100). There are, therefore, strong reasons to expect the upper wealth groups to be under-represented by the results of the survey. Although the information on rateable value was not available for 1954, Hill [QRL 8] argued that at least in the case of the self-employed the occupational distribution was more satisfactory in 1954. This is one reason why he regarded the 1954 survey as more reliable, although it seems unlikely that the bias was completely eliminated.

Table 5.1 Response Rate—1953 Oxford Survey

Rateable value (£ per annum)	*Success rate (as % of identified income units)*
0–4	86
5–9	79
10–14	76
15–19	69
20–29	65
30–39	62
40–49	52
50–59	51
60–79	51
80 and over	48

Source: Hill, Klein and Straw [B 12], p. 92

(b) *Incomplete Information*
Even where an interview is successfully completed there remains the possibility that the information provided may have been incomplete. Firstly, the respondent may have understated the value of his assets or omitted to tell the interviewer of certain possessions. This may reflect deliberate dishonesty, but probably more important are the problems of remembering all items of wealth and of making an

accurate valuation. As Hill [QRL 8] points out, 'the valuations given by informants can only be rough and ready in many cases . . . This problem is of course most acute in the case of shares in private companies, and several informants frankly admitted that the values they placed on such shares were hypothetical' (p. 151). Secondly, certain components of net worth may not be ascertained in the interview. The procedure followed at the editing stage in this case was to impute an amount for each type of asset based on the known characteristics of the income unit: e.g. the value of stocks, shares or property was calculated from the income data using a yield multiplier (20 for interest and dividends). Lydall [QRL 11] expresses the hope that 'in the aggregate, such errors of estimation would be randomly distributed' (p. 229), but it is difficult to be very confident about this.

In the Economists Advisory Group survey, the author similarly recognized that 'respondents may be either unable or unwilling to give answers that disclose "the truth, the whole truth and nothing but the truth"' ([QRL 14], p. 3). They may find it difficult to recall everything they own, and simply forget to mention holdings. They may fear that their answers would be divulged to the tax authorities and understate the value of their holdings. For these reasons 'there is little doubt that some underestimation does occur' (p. 3).

(c) *Incomplete Coverage in Survey Design*

The third problem is that savings surveys typically cover only certain types of asset, and the resulting definition is not comprehensive. The components of net worth in the 1953 Oxford survey are described below:

Assets	*Liabilities*
Liquid financial assets (see Table 5.2)	Hire purchase debt
Stocks shares and other securities	Overdrafts
Property	Mortgage debt
Cars	
Unincorporated businesses	

Among the items *not* taken into account were: life, industrial and endowment (except in conjunction with mortgages) insurance policies, pension rights, furniture, household goods, jewellery, holdings of notes and coin, and settled property. The Economists Advisory Group survey did cover life assurance, but on the other hand was exclusively concerned with financial assets and did not include the value of real property.

(d) *Sampling Error*

The sampling errors associated with the Oxford savings surveys are discussed by Lydall [QRL 11] and Klein and Vandome [B 14], the latter presenting estimates of the sampling error for the 1953 and 1954 surveys. The general conclusion reached by Lydall for the 1952 survey was that 'it is a fair guess that more serious errors are caused by reporting and processing errors than by sampling fluctuations' ([QRL 11], p. 240). At the same time, the Economists Advisory Group survey drew attention to the fact that 'a special case that is important in this context is the very rich . . . millionaires are so few that even a large sample is unlikely to include one at all' ([QRL 14], p. 2). (In relation to this, it is interesting to note that the Inland Revenue estate data included sixty-four millionaires in the three years 1970–1 to 1972–3.)

The quantitative importance of the first two of these problems may be illustrated by comparing the totals obtained by 'blowing up' the sample means with those known from external sources. This was discussed by Hill, Klein and Straw [B 12] in relation to the liquid asset holdings indicated by the 1953 Survey. Table 5.2 shows the survey estimates together with the external figures, from which the authors concluded that 'there seems little doubt that in all . . . types of assets the Survey estimates are too low' (p. 118). As they recognize, the external totals are not strictly comparable since they include holdings by other sectors (as well as persons not living in private households), but even allowing for this the survey estimates are in most cases still well short of the total. Hill, Klein and Straw concluded that 'the most probable explanation for the Survey's low liquid assets figures seems to be that those persons with the largest asset holdings were the least co-operative and more inclined to understate their wealth' (p. 118). This is supported by the fact that understatement was less for the assets which were more widely held: for example, the number of certain types of durable goods (cars, motor cycles, and television sets) appeared to be fairly accurately measured by the Survey (Hill, Klein and Straw, p. 121). (Evidence about understatement in American sample survey data is provided by Ferber *et al.* [B 8].)

5.2.5 *Sample Survey Method—Summary*

The experience to date suggests that sample surveys are unlikely to provide a fully satisfactory source of information about the size distribution of wealth as a whole. In particular they are likely to provide an inadequate picture of wealth-holding at the top: 'survey studies can tell nothing about the very rich, whose holdings loom so large in many studies of inequality' ([QRL 14], p. 60). They may however have considerable value in providing evidence about wealth-holding below the estate duty exemption limit (as demonstrated by Lydall and Tipping) and about the holding of certain types of asset.

Table 5.2 Comparison of Survey Results with External Sources—1953

Type of Asset	*Survey Estimate* *£m*	*External Total* *£m*
Post Office Savings Banks Deposits	920	1802
Trustee Savings Banks Deposits	440	949
National Savings Certificates	880	1749
Defence Bonds	480	820
Building Society Shares and Deposits	330	1401
Co-operative Society Shares and Deposits	110	230
Joint Stock Bank Personal Deposits	920	2100

Source: Hill, Klein and Straw [B 12], p. 117

6 Balance Sheet Data and Individual Assets

In this section we describe some of the sources of information about personal wealth-holding which do not provide evidence about the size distribution of total wealth, but may be valuable for other purposes. The first two parts deal with the national balance sheet data, already referred to in Section 4; the third part with information about the holding of individual assets derived from a range of special surveys.

6.1 Balance Sheet Data for the Personal Sector

6.1.1 Estimates of the total value of private and public property were presented by Campion in his pioneering pre-war study [QRL 3]. His results were cast in a balance sheet form by Hicks in early editions of *The Social Framework* [B 11], which remains one of the few introductory textbooks which deal adequately with this subject. Work on balance sheet data has been further developed by Morgan [B 19], and in the important study by Revell, subtitled *The National Balance Sheet of the United Kingdom, 1957–1961* [B 24]. The aspect of the balance sheet which concerns us here is that for the personal sector; the role played by the net worth of other sectors is discussed briefly in the next section.

6.1.2 Revell outlines three possible methods of deriving total holdings by the personal sector which he uses in addition to estimates obtained from the estate duty approach. The first of these, the use of sample survey data, has been dealt with in subsection 5.2 above. Since no data of this type were available for the period Revell was considering, their use will not be discussed further. The second method makes use of information from the issuing source. In some cases non-personal holdings are likely to form an insignificant proportion of the total, as with assets such as national savings certificates, building society deposits and the like. In consequence 'providing the extent of these non-personal holdings can be estimated, the remainder of the total amount in issue can safely be ascribed to persons' [B 24]. In other cases, estimates of personal holdings can be obtained from the information contained in the register of holders (e.g. of ordinary shares). As a third method Revell suggests that since the personal sector is the only one which lacks balance sheet information, it is possible to regard personal holdings as the residual of the known total after allowance for other sectors, although the margin of error is clearly likely to be substantial in this case.

6.1.3 Adopting a combination of these approaches Revell draws up a personal sector balance sheet for forty-three asset categories and fourteen categories of liabilities. In certain cases, the estate duty estimate is accepted as the final estimate for the asset in question. For other assets the estate duty figure was not regarded as satisfactory and Revell therefore either adjusted the figure or used independent estimates from alternative sources. Table 6.1 shows the main asset categories grouped according to whether the estate duty estimate in each case was adjusted, and if so the source of the alternative total used for the adjustment. In addition, alongside each asset type we reproduce Revell's 'subjective assessments' of the accuracy and reliability of his final estimates ([B 24], pp. 375–6).

In the first column are listed asset categories for which there was no reason to doubt the estate duty estimate. For example in the case of cash at the bank the estate duty affidavit requires that each bank account be detailed separately so that it is unlikely that overdrafts in one account will be netted against deposits in another. By way of contrast the second column contains items where the estate duty estimate was adopted with some adjustment. The adjustment entailed either treating the item as constant or smoothing the figures to follow an 'apparent trend' ([B 24], p. 376). Consequently miscellaneous rights and house mortgages were constant, the latter, it is important to note, being only those held as assets, not as liabilities which appear in column (4). Loans to and loans from persons were necessarily identical, following a smoothed trend. Finally the figure for trade debtors was an adjustment from the estate duty figure for 'book debts', smoothed and increased by 50% 'to allow for the trade debtors included under "unallocated share of partnership"' ([B 24], p. 156).

Table 6.1 Sources of National Balance Sheet Data for Personal Sector

(1) Unadjusted estate duty estimates used	*(2) Adjusted estate duty estimates used (see text)*	*(3) Register information used*	*(4) Estimated from known total in issue*	*(5) Others—see text for details*
Cash at bank (B)	Miscellaneous rights (C)	Quoted UK local authority (C)	Deposits of all kinds (A and B)	All loans (B)
Quoted UK government (B)	House mortgages as (assets) (C)	Unquoted UK local authority (B)	Unquoted UK government (A)	Unquoted company securities (D)
Quoted UK debentures (C)	Loans to persons (C)	Quoted UK preference (C)	Unit Trust units (A)	Notes and coin (D)
Other debtors (B)	Trade debtors (C)	Quoted UK ordinary (B)	Life policies of all kinds (A and B)	Mortgages overseas (A)
Bank advances (B)	Loans from persons (C)		Hire purchase (B)	Sinking fund policies (part of life policies in (4)) (B)
Creditors Overseas (B)			Other instalment credit (B)	
			House mortgages (liabilities) (B)	

Key: (A) A very reliable figure; (B) A fairly reliable figure; (C) Not very reliable; (D) A very unreliable figure.
Source: Revell, *The Wealth of the Nation* [B 24]

6.1.4 The items in column (3) were based on register surveys which were used to estimate the extent of personal holdings of these assets. In the case of quoted ordinary shares, this was derived from the surveys of company registers carried out by the Department of Applied Economics, Cambridge. The results of the first of these surveys (from 1957) were published in *The Times* by Feinstein and Revell [B 7]; this was followed by a second survey in 1963 by Revell and Moyle [B 27]. Since the balance sheet data were completed, there has been a further survey in 1970 by Moyle [B 20]. The method used may be illustrated by the 1970 survey which involved a two-stage sample, the first stage being the selection of 290 companies from the Stock Exchange list, the second being the drawing of a sample of shareholdings from the registers for these companies. The final sample contained 284,000 holdings. The holdings were valued at the quoted share price at 31 December 1969 to give the market value, and classified according to sector of *beneficial* ownership (i.e. nominee holdings were allocated to the appropriate categories of beneficial ownership). Similar enquiries for local authority securities in 1957 are reported in Revell and Hockley [B 25 and B 26] and in Revell [B 24]. The register surveys used by Revell in general only related to one or two years. Where only a register figure for the beginning of the period (1957) was available, Revell used a constant percentage of the total in issue to derive his estimate. When a later figure was available, the unknown percentages were interpolated linearly.

The fourth column is straightforward since the issuing bodies were able to supply reliable data on the extent of personal holdings and this was substituted for the estate duty estimate. The interesting item to be adjusted in this way was house mortgages, the estate duty estimate for which formed about 'one-quarter of the sums known to have been advanced' ([B 24], p. 157). According to Revell, this problem is caused by the practice of taking out life policies to cover outstanding mortgage repayments, so that when the person dies the estate only reveals the net amount remaining after the mortgage has been paid. Mention was also made of this in connection with the investment income method (see subsection 5.1.2).

Specific techniques were used to derive estimates of the items in the final column. Loans other than interpersonal items were taken from other sector balance sheets, while estimates of unquoted company securities were 'made from comparison of evidence in estate duty estimates, register surveys and estimates of total in issue' ([B 24], p. 376). Notes and coin was taken to be 15% of the average estimated amount in circulation so that the estate duty estimate (the transactions demand) was increased to take account of the hoarding demand. Mortgages overseas were interpreted to apply to Jersey and Guernsey and finally, for sinking fund policies, the estimate was taken to be 50% of the value of the funds.

6.1.5 The resulting estimates of the personal holding of each asset are given in Table BS.1.0 of Revell [B 24] and cover the years 1957–61. Since that time, a further study by Roe has appeared giving an integrated set of financial accounts for the UK relating to the years 1957–66, thereby extending the coverage of Revell's work. The balance sheet estimates up to 1961 are in fact a straight reproduction of Revell's figures, except for certain changes of definition and classification, and the remaining years, at least for the purposes of the personal sector, are treated entirely analogously with Revell. Roe pays particular attention to the financial flows, distinguishing between transactions in assets and their revaluation. The results for the personal sector are given in Table 2, subsection 1.1.1 of [B 29], pp. 72–3, and (in less detail) in the article by Revell and Roe [B 28]. More recently still, Rothman [B 30] has made estimates of the national balance sheet as at March 1974, including holdings by the personal sector classified by asset type, and the first report by the Royal Commission on the Distribution of Income and Wealth has published estimates for the personal sector balance sheet for the years 1971–3 [B 39].

6.2 Sector Balance Sheets

Revell, like the earlier investigators, was concerned not just with the personal sector but also with the balance sheets of other sectors, and with total national wealth. Full details are given in [B 24]. Here we are only concerned to draw attention to one issue which is relevant to the personal sector: the treatment of the positive net worth of the non-personal sectors.

The issue may be seen clearly from the following estimates given by Revell and Roe ([B 28], pp. xvi–xix) for 1966:

	net worth (£ million)
personal sector	104,900
financial institutions*	2,900
industrial and commercial companies*	25,800
public sector	6,300
all national sectors	139,900

(* where share capital is treated as a liability at its market value)

From this it is clear that the estimated net worth of the personal sector in 1966 was only 75% of the national total. Of the remainder, the public sector accounted for 5 %, and industrial and commercial companies for 20 %.

This raises the question as to whether the net worth of these sectors should be allocated in some way to the personal sector. In the case of the public sector, it has been suggested that this should be allocated on a *per capita* basis, or possibly with a greater allocation to groups such as local authority tenants, who, it is argued, benefit more than proportionately. In the case of the company sector, the net worth can be seen in part as the premium for control and may be allocated to shareholders as a body or, if the information is available, to those more likely to have a controlling interest. (In this allocation, allowance would have to be made for the possible capital gains tax liability.) It is suggested by Rothman [B 30] that part of the net worth of the company sector should be allocated to the management, the workers and to a lesser extent, the customers.

6.3 Data on Holdings of Individual Assets

In this section we describe briefly some of the main sources of information about the holdings of individual assets. The treatment is far from exhaustive and there are many surveys, published and unpublished, to which no reference is made. The groups of assets considered are houses, cars, consumer durables and financial assets.

6.3.1 *Owner-Occupation*

Housing statistics are discussed in detail in the review by Farthing [B 6] in this series. The reader is referred to this and to Chapter 5 in Edwards [B 5]. Here only brief reference is made to statistics on housing tenure and the characteristics of owner-occupiers.

The main source of information about home ownership is the Census of Population and the Sample Census which collect information about the distribution of housing by tenure. The results are published in the reports on respective censuses [QRL 21]. It should be noted that the post-enumeration surveys have demonstrated significant understatement of certain housing types: e.g. furnished accommodation in 1966 [B 10]. The Department of the Environment prepares estimates for intervening years and the resulting series is published in *Housing and Construction Statistics* [QRL 30] (formerly *Housing Statistics*). The figures are also summarized in *Social Trends* [QRL 35]. For discussion of earlier years, see, for example, Cullingworth [B 4]. Evidence about the distribution by tenure is given in the *Family Expenditure Survey* [QRL 26] and the *General Household Survey* [QRL 28]. The estimates for these two surveys for 1971 are compared with the Department of Environment figures in the General Household Survey [QRL 28] *Introductory Report*, Chapter 5. Information on the characteristics of owner-occupiers and those buying on mortgages is also given in the bulletins published by the Building Societies Association [QRL 25] and the Nationwide Building Society [QRL 33]. Evidence on the joint ownership of homes is given in Todd and Jones [QRL 17].

6.3.2 *Cars*

In the case of both cars and consumer durables, there are a wide range of sources, from the Census of Population to market research surveys. It is important to note, however, that some of this information relates to items of which households have use but do not necessarily own (e.g. rented television sets). From the point of view of wealth ownership, we should distinguish between (i) outright ownership, (ii) hire purchase, and (iii) rental, with only the first two being taken into account. (In the case of (ii) it is clearly the value net of the HP commitment which is relevant.)

In the case of cars, the 1966 Sample Census and the 1971 Census contained questions on their availability, and the results for 1971 showing the number of households with 1, 2, 3 or more cars were published in the report *Availability of Cars* [QRL 22]. Similar information has been provided by the Family Expenditure Survey since 1969 [QRL 26]. A series from 1961–71 is published in the Department of Environment publication *Passenger Transport in Great Britain 1971* [QRL 34]. The data in this series are based on a number of sources including the National Travel Survey, the Family Expenditure Survey, and the 1966 Sample Census of Population. Finally, the report of the General Household Survey [QRL 28] for 1972 shows the number of households having use of one car, or two or more cars. It should be emphasized that these figures in general relate to households 'owning or having use of' cars, so that they cover all three categories distinguished above. The General Household Survey questionnaire quite explicitly includes 'any provided by employers if normally available for use by informant'. It is therefore incorrect to regard these figures as corresponding to ownership, as in [B 21]. Some insight into the pattern of ownership is provided by the *Motor Transactions Survey 1971* [QRL 32].

6.3.3 *Consumer Durables*

Information about the availability of household consumer durables has been published in the *Family Expenditure Survey* [QRL 26] since 1969. This shows the percentage of households (by region) owning or having use of central heating (full or partial), washing machine, refrigerator and television. The same information (apart from that on central heating) is reprinted in *Social Trends* [QRL 35]. Again it should be emphasized that the data are not restricted to *ownership*. The Family Expenditure Survey question concerned with washing machines, refrigerators and central heating asks 'are any of these items owned or continuously available for use?' (It may be noted that the study by Todd and Jones on matrimonial property [QRL 17] collected data on the *ownership* of cars and durables.) The report of the General Household Survey [QRL 28] for 1972 contains information on items 'normally available for use' covering washing machines, refrigerators, vacuum cleaners and television sets. Similar information is collected in market research surveys, for example, the annual Target Group Index survey [QRL 36] carried out by the British Market Research Bureau with a national sample of some 24,000 adults. The results are not published but have been used by academic investigators: for example Pyatt [B 22]. The AGB Home Audit [QRL 29] is based on a sample of 35,000 households and provides data on major consumer durables, heating appliances, television sets, personal and kitchen appliances.

6.3.4 *Financial Assets*

The poor state of statistical information about financial asset holding was emphasized by the Radcliffe Committee in 1959, and their recommendations led to considerable improvement in the data on the totals of assets and liabilities (e.g. as published in *Financial Statistics* [QRL 27]). The data on the size distribution of holdings are, however, still relatively limited as may be illustrated by reference to the report of the Page Committee to Review National Savings [B 40] in June 1973. In order to examine the proportion of the population holding financial assets they made use of a sample survey (similar to that reported in Morgan [QRL 14]). The results published by the Page Committee showed the proportion of the sample holding deposits and the size distribution of holdings in the National Savings Bank, or Trustee Savings Banks, National Savings Certificates, Premium Bonds, bank deposit accounts, building society shares and deposits, unit trusts, stocks and shares, and local authority securities. The Committee did make some use of information from the issuing source. For example, the data on the distribution of holdings of Premium Bonds were derived from the internal records of the Department for National Savings. However, such information is not published on a regular basis. The main sources of information about the size of holdings of individual financial assets remain therefore sample surveys coupled with, in certain cases, the Inland Revenue estimates.

7 Desirable Improvements

In this section we describe briefly some of the developments, both in source statistics and in methods of estimation, which would in our view improve the currently available information about the distribution of wealth. The discussion is in large part based on evidence submitted to the Royal Commission on the Distribution of Income and Wealth in January 1975.* Recognizing that any selection of recommendations is likely to reflect our personal viewpoint, we have set out a fairly lengthy list. Given that the necessary resources may not be available to carry out the entire programme, it is open to the reader to attach his own priorities.

7.1 Source Statistics

We begin with the 'raw materials' for the estate method: the estate data and the mortality multipliers. In the former case, any recommendations must be seen in the light of the introduction of the Capital Transfer Tax, which may well affect the presentation of the statistics even if, as suggested earlier, their basic form remains essentially unchanged. For this reason, we confine ourselves to recommendations of a rather technical nature:

Recommendation 1. The procedure for the treatment of the delay between death and an estate appearing in the statistics be re-examined, and statistics be provided on a calendar year basis by date of death.

Recommendation 2. The Inland Revenue be asked to publish a guide to the most important changes in estate duty legislation and practice which have affected the comparability of the statistics over time, indicating where possible their likely quantitative importance.

Recommendation 3. The estate data be classified according to marital status (for the years for which this has been collected) as well as by estate size and the age/sex of the deceased.

The second key element in the estate method is the choice of mortality multipliers. In general we feel that the procedure followed by the Inland Revenue is very reasonable; at the same time in subsection 3.2.3 we made a number of detailed criticisms. As a result we should like to recommend that the basic method be continued but that:

Recommendation 4. Multipliers be developed taking account of marital status.

Recommendation 5. The occupational distribution of estates by size be examined and the multipliers more smoothly graduated with the size of estate than at present.

Recommendation 6. The present Inland Revenue practice of combining multipliers across age groups be re-examined.

Under the heading of source statistics we should also refer to the balance sheet data for the personal sector. As shown in Section 4, these data have played a major role in the adjustments made to the estate estimates by academic investigators, and their use was discussed in the first report of the Royal Commission on the Distribution of Income and Wealth. We regard the provision of these data on a regular basis as essential for the development of work on the distribution of wealth:

* This section was first written before the publication of the Royal Commission's first report, and it is gratifying to note that they have already acted on Recommendations 7, 9, 10 and 12.

Recommendation 7. The personal sector balance sheet data be compiled and published by the Central Statistical Office on a regular basis.

Finally, the proposed introduction of an annual wealth tax promises to provide valuable information on wealth-holding at the top of the scale, and we hope that:

Recommendation 8. The wealth tax, if enacted, be accompanied by provisions to collect and publish statistical information on wealth-holdings covered by the tax.

7.2 Official Estimates

The introduction by the Inland Revenue of official estimates was a major departure and the continuing series since 1960 has contributed greatly to knowledge about the size distribution of wealth. At the same time, we have suggested a number of ways in which these estimates could be developed, among the most important being those listed below:

Recommendation 9. The estimates be modified to allow for the average wealth of those not covered by the estate statistics, making use of balance sheet and other evidence, with the results being presented if necessary in the form of a range of estimates.

Recommendation 10. The extent of wealth missing from the estate returns be further investigated, and an attempt made to estimate the missing wealth by size of holding, again in the form of a range of estimates if necessary.

Recommendation 11. The estimates be adjusted as far as possible to a consistent basis of valuation, or to a range of possible bases (such as the realization and 'going concern' bases discussed above).

Recommendation 12. The Inland Revenue examine the extent to which upper and lower bounds on the concentration of wealth on a family basis can be calculated using extreme assumptions about the correlation between wealth-holdings and evidence about wealth, and investment income, by marital status.

7.3 Alternative Sources

For the reasons set out earlier, we agree with Lydall and Tipping's assessment that 'the estate returns remain our major source of information and the cornerstone of this analysis' [QRL 12, p. 85], and do not believe that the estate method can be totally replaced by the alternative sources described in Section 5. None the less, we feel that both the investment income method and the sample survey approach can provide valuable supplementary evidence. We should therefore like to see these sources further investigated:

Recommendation 13. The use of the investment income method be further explored by the Inland Revenue with particular reference to the refinement of the yield multipliers.

Recommendation 14. The role of sample surveys as a supplement to the estate data be investigated, with particular attention to the problem of securing a more satisfactory response rate and a wider coverage of assets than in the past.

7.4 Methodological Issues

At a number of junctures we have referred to questions which concern not so much the collection of data as the development of appropriate techniques of analysis. There are in fact a large number of methodological problems which have been neglected and warrant further study.

To illustrate this point, we may take some examples relating to the estate method and the investment income approach (the use of sample surveys has been much more thoroughly treated). The first example is the use of mortality multipliers and the consequences of different assumptions. Does the use of social class multipliers lead to higher or lower estimates of concentration? Are the estimates highly sensitive to the choice of multipliers? In [B 2] the authors have made a start on these problems, but otherwise they have been scarcely discussed, despite their obvious importance for the estate method. The second example concerns the appropriate method of valuing contingent rights: for example to income from a trust fund or to occupational or state pensions. What relation should such valuation bear to the capital fund, and what should be done where there is no such fund? This raises, particularly in the context of an imperfect capital market, a host of conceptual problems. Thirdly, in the analysis of the final data use is frequently made of methods of interpolation. A method of interpolation is necessary, for example, to estimate the wealth owned by the top 1 %, 5 %, etc. since these groups only coincide by chance with the wealth ranges employed in classifying the original data. How sensitive are the results to the choice of method of interpolation? Finally, turning to the investment income method, the theoretical considerations underlying its use have never been fully spelled out. In particular the way in which the estimates are likely to be affected by random variation in the return to a particular type of asset, and by differences in portfolio composition among people with the same wealth, need further analysis.

7.5 Relationship Between the Distributions of Income and Wealth

In this review we have concentrated on the distribution of wealth, but for a number of purposes we are interested in the relation between income and wealth. For example, Barna [QRL 2] made use of this relationship to allocate taxes on capital by income groups in his study of the redistribution of incomes. Stark [B 33] followed a rather similar procedure in estimating the capital gains accruing to different income groups. More recently, in considering the proposed wealth tax, it is necessary to know the joint distribution of income and wealth in order to assess the effect of suggestions to limit the combined burden of wealth tax and income tax.

The main method employed in the past to link the two distributions is similar to the investment income procedure. In broad terms, it involves the following steps (see Stark, [B 33]):

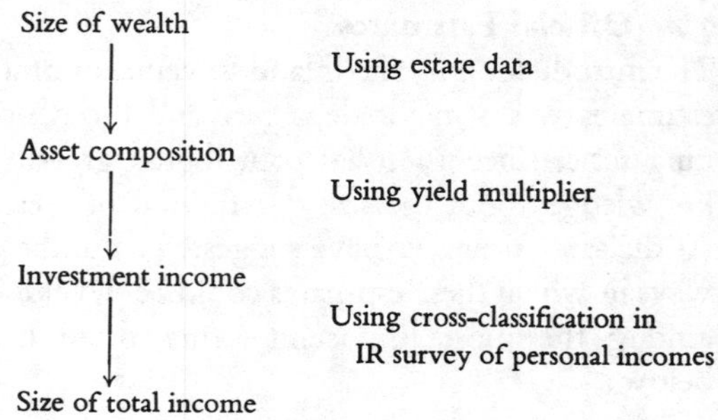

It is clear that this suffers from the same kind of shortcomings as the investment income method, and in particular that it can only provide adequate coverage at the top of the distribution. In view of this, a sample survey containing data on both incomes and wealth would have to be employed to give an overall picture.

In our view this aspect deserves more attention than it has received in the past, and the official statisticians should consider producing a joint distribution of income and wealth.

Quick Reference List—Table of Contents

N.B. In the case of I and II the period covered is from 1960 to the time of writing. Information on the estate data for earlier years is given in Table 4.4.

Quick Reference List

Title	*Breakdown*	*Area*	*Frequency*	*Publication*	*Text Reference and Remarks*
I Estates					
Estates: number by ranges and net value	—	GB, E & W and S	Annual up to 1967–8	[QRL 20]	2.1–2.3
	—	GB, E & W and S	1968–9 onwards	[QRL 31]	
Estates: analysis by type of property	Range of estate	GB, E & W and S	Annual up to 1962–3	[QRL 20]	2.1–2.3 (classification of property has varied slightly from year to year)
	Range of estate	GB, E & W and S	1963–4 to 1964–5	[QRL 20]	
	Range of estate	GB	1965–6 to 1967–8	[QRL 20]	
	Range of estate	GB	1968–9 onwards	[QRL 31]	
Estates: analysis by age and sex of deceased	By range	GB, E & W and S	Annual up to 1962–3	[QRL 20]	2.1–2.3
	By range	GB	1963–4 to 1967–8	[QRL 20]	
	By range	GB	1968–9 onwards	[QRL 31]	
Analysis of gifts *inter vivos*	By date of gift before death	GB, E & W and S	Annual up to 1967–8	[QRL 20]	2.1–2.3 (within five years of death)
	By date of gift before death	GB, E & W and S	1968–9 onwards	[QRL 31]	(within seven years of death)
Analyses of property by title and mode of disposition	—	GB, E & W and S	Annual up to 1967–8	[QRL 20]	2.1–2.3
	—	GB, E & W and S	1968–9 onwards	[QRL 31]	
II Wealth (official estimates)					
Distribution of wealth by ranges	M & F	GB	Annual, 1960–7	[QRL 20]	3.1–3.3 (see also [QRL 24] for 1973, ref. 3.1.4)
	M & F, G	GB	1968 onwards	[QRL 31]	

Total wealth by asset type (number of cases and amount)	M & F	GB	Annual, 1960–7	[QRL 20]	3.1–3.3
	M & F	GB	1968 onwards	[QRL 31]	(See also [QRL 24] for 1973, ref. 3.1.4)
	—	GB	Various years	[QRL 35]	In form of pie chart
Number of holdings of selected assets by range of wealth	—	GB	Annual, 1964–7	[QRL 20]	3.1–3.3
	—	GB	1968 onwards	[QRL 31]	(See also [QRL 24] for 1973, ref. 3.1.4)
Classification of property by range of wealth	—	GB	1971, 1972	[QRL 31]	3.1–3.3 (See also [QRL 24] for 1973, ref. 3.1.4)
Distribution of wealth by percentage of owners	G, M & F (1968)	GB	1961, 1966–8	[QRL 35]	In 1970 edition
	G, M & F (1969)	GB	1961, 1966–9	[QRL 35]	In 1971 edition
	G, M & F (1970)	GB	1961, 1965–6, 1969–70	[QRL 35]	In 1972 edition
	G, M & F (1971)	GB	1961, 1965–6, 1970–1	[QRL 35]	In 1973 edition
	G, M & F (1972)	GB	1961, 1965–6, 1971–2	[QRL 35]	In 1974 edition
Gini coefficients (Series A) covering only those with wealth	—	GB	Annual, 1960–	[QRL 31]	3.1.5
	—	GB	Annual, 1960–	[QRL 35]	First appeared in 1970 and from 1972 onwards in appendix
Gini coefficients (Series B) covering whole population	—	GB	Annual, 1960–	[QRL 31]	3.1.5
	—	GB	Annual, 1960–	[QRL 35]	First appeared in 1972 in appendix

III Wealth

(unofficial estimates using estate method)

Distribution of wealth by range	Number of persons and amount	E & W	1912, 1920–1	[QRL 5]	4.1–4.2 (see Table 4.1)
	(M & F for 1924)	E & W	1912, 1924	[QRL 19]	4.1–4.2 (see Table 4.1)
	Number of persons and amount (M & F for 1924–30)	E & W	1911–13, 1924–30	[QRL 7]	4.1–4.2 (see Table 4.1)
	Number of persons and amount (M & F for 1936)	E & W	1911–13, 1926–8, 1936	[QRL 3]	4.1–4.2 (see Table 4.1)
	Number of persons and amount, including and excluding 'settled' estates	UK	1937	[QRL 2]	4.1–4.2 (see Table 4.1)

Title	Breakdown	Area	Frequency	Publication	Text Reference and Remarks
	Number of persons and amount	E & W GB	1911–13, 1924–30, 1936–8, 1946–7	[QRL 9]	4.1–4.2 (see Table 4.1)
	Number of persons and amount	GB	1948–9	[QRL 4]	4.1–4.2 (see Table 4.1)
	Number of persons and amount	GB	1936, 1936–8, 1950, 1951	[QRL 10]	4.1–4.2 (see Table 4.1)
	Number of persons and amount	GB	1954	[QRL 12]	4.1–4.2 (see Table 4.1)
	Number of persons and amount	GB	1968	[QRL 1]	4.1–4.2 (see Table 4.1)
Distribution of wealth by richest percentage of people	—	E	1911–13	[QRL 19]	4.1–4.2 (see Table 4.1)
	—	GB	1911–13, 1924–30, 1936, 1951–6	[QRL 12]	4.1–4.2 (see Table 4.1)
	—	E & W	1911–13, 1924–30, 1936–8, 1954, 1960	[QRL 15]	4.1–4.2 (see Table 4.1)
Distribution of wealth by age group	Richest percentage of people	E	1911–14, 1923–5	[QRL 19]	4.1–4.2 (see Table 4.1)
	Range	E & W	1924–30	[QRL 7]	4.1–4.2 (see Table 4.1)
	Number of persons and amount	GB	1936–8, 1950–1	[QRL 10]	4.1–4.2 (see Table 4.1)
	—	GB	1954	[QRL 12]	4.1–4.2 (see Table 4.1)
	M & F	E & W	1927	[QRL 15]	4.1–4.2 (see Table 4.1)
	M & F	GB	1960	[QRL 15]	
Distribution of wealth by asset type	Range	GB	1930	[QRL 7]	4.1–4.2 (see Table 4.1)
	Range	GB	1936	[QRL 3]	4.1–4.2 (see Table 4.1)
	Range	GB, UK	1937	[QRL 2]	4.1–4.2 (see Table 4.1)
	—	GB	1954	[QRL 12]	4.1–4.2 (see Table 4.1)
IV Wealth—Northern Ireland					
Distribution of wealth by range	Number of persons and amount	GB, NI, Irish Republic	1920, 1924, 1938, 1949, 1954, 1960	[QRL 6]	4.3
	Number of persons and amount	NI, Irish Republic, All Ireland	1966	[QRL 13]	4.3
Distribution of wealth by age group	—	NI, Irish Republic	1966	[QRL 13]	4.3
Components of wealth	—	GB, NI, Irish Republic	1920, 1924, 1938, 1949, 1954, 1960	[QRL 6]	4.3
	—	NI, Irish Republic	1966	[QRL 13]	4.3

Estimate of total wealth	—	NI, Irish Republic, All Ireland	1920, 1924, 1938, 1949, 1954, 1960	[QRL 6]	4.3
V Wealth—Sample Survey Data					
Distribution of net worth by net worth group	% of income units	GB	1953, 1954	[QRL 8]	5.2.1 and 5.2.4
	Age, sex, occupation and housing status of head of income unit	GB	1953	[QRL 16]	5.2.1 and 5.2.4
Distribution of net worth by income	Age, sex, occupation and housing status of head of income unit. Region, town size and number of persons in income unit	GB	1953	[QRL 16]	5.2.1 and 5.2.4
Distribution of net worth	Income, household characteristics	UK	1968–9	[QRL 18]	5.2.2. and 5.2.4 (to be published)
Distribution of total liquid assets by range	% of income units	GB	1953, 1954	[QRL 8]	5.2.1 and 5.2.4
	Age, sex, occupation of head of income unit. Region, town size, number of persons in income unit	GB	1953	[QRL 16]	5.2.1 and 5.2.4
Distribution of property owned by range	% of income units	GB	1953, 1954	[QRL 8]	5.2.1 and 5.2.4
Distribution of mortgage debt outstanding by range	% of income units	GB	1952, 1953, 1954	[QRL 8]	5.2.1 and 5.2.4
VI Holdings of Particular Assets					
1. *Home ownership*					
Stock of dwellings by tenure	—	E, W, S, GB	Annual, 1966–	[QRL 30]	6.3.1 (see also [QRL 25, QRL 33])
Stock of dwellings by tenure	Household spaces, rooms, building type	E & W	1951, 1961	[QRL 21]	6.3.1
Private households by tenure	Rooms, building type, sharing of dwelling	E & W	1951, 1961	[QRL 21]	6.3.1

Title	*Breakdown*	*Area*	*Frequency*	*Publication*	*Text Reference and Remarks*
Households by tenure	Household type	GB	1971, 1972	[QRL 28]	6.3.1 (1971 data in Introductory Report)
	Age of head of household	GB	1971, 1972	[QRL 28]	6.3.1 (1971 data in Introductory Report)
	Age of building	GB	1971, 1972	[QRL 28]	6.3.1 (1971 data in Introductory Report)
	Type of accommodation	GB	1971, 1972	[QRL 28]	6.3.1 (1971 data in Introductory Report)
	Amenities	GB	1971, 1972	[QRL 28]	6.3.1 (1971 data in Introductory Report)
	Socio-economic group of head of household	GB	1971, 1972	[QRL 28]	6.3.1 (1971 data in Introductory Report)
	Gross weekly income of head of household	GB	1971, 1972	[QRL 28]	6.3.1 (1971 data in Introductory Report)
	Highest qualification level obtained	GB	1971, 1972	[QRL 28]	6.3.1 (1971 data in Introductory Report)
	Region	GB	1971, 1971/2	[QRL 28]	6.3.1 (1971 data in Introductory Report)
	Gross value	GB	1971, 1971/2	[QRL 28]	6.3.1 (1971 data in Introductory Report)
Owner occupation by region	Leasehold or freehold	GB	1971, 1971/2	[QRL 28]	6.3.1 (1971 data in Introductory Report)
2 *Cars*					
Households and persons by number of cars available	Area, age composition of household	E & W	1971	[QRL 22]	6.3.2
Households by number of cars available	Tenure of household's accommodation	E & W	1971	[QRL 22]	6.3.2
Households with 1 or 2 or more cars	Region, tenure, socio-economic group of head of household	GB	1972	[QRL 28]	6.3.2
Households with 1 or 2 or 3 or more cars	Region, household income, household composition	UK	Annual from 1969	[QRL 26]	6.3.2

Households with 1, 1 or more, or 2 or more cars	—	GB	Annual from 1961	[QRL 34]	6.3.2
Number of private vehicles and taxis licensed	—	GB	Annual from 1961	[QRL 34]	6.3.2
Business and private purchases of cars	New/used cars, engine capacity	GB	1971	[QRL 32]	6.3.2
Business and private purchases of new cars	Number of hire purchase transactions	GB	1971	[QRL 32]	6.3.2
Expenditure and average cost of cars purchased	New/used cars, method of finance	GB	1971	[QRL 32]	6.3.2
3 Consumer Durables					See also [QRL 29, QRL 36]
Households with telephone, central heating, washing machine, refrigerator, television	Region, income of household, composition of household	UK	Annual, from 1969	[QRL 26]	6.3.3
Households with telephone, washing machine, refrigerator, vacuum cleaner, television	Region, tenure, socio-economic group of head of household	GB	1972	[QRL 28]	See also [QRL 29, QRL 36] 6.3.3.
4 Financial Assets					
Holdings of selected liquid assets	—	UK	Quarterly from 1965	[QRL 27]	6.3.4
	Socio-economic group, size of holding, age	GB	1974	[QRL 14]	6.3.4

Quick Reference List Key to Publications

Reference Number	Author or Organization Responsible	Title	Publisher	Frequency or Date of Publication
[QRL 1]	Atkinson, A. B.	'The Distribution of Wealth in Britain in the 1960s—the Estate Duty method re-examined' in *Personal Distribution of Income and Wealth* (ed. Smith, J. D.)	National Bureau of Economic Research, New York	1975
[QRL 2]	Barna, T.	*Redistribution of Incomes*	Oxford University Press, Oxford	1945
[QRL 3]	Campion, H.	*Public and Private Property in Great Britain*	Oxford University Press, Oxford	1939
[QRL 4]	Cartter, A. M.	*The Redistribution of Income in Post-War Britain*	Yale University Press, New Haven	1955
[QRL 5]	Clay, H.	'The Distribution of capital in England and Wales' in *Transactions of the Manchester Statistical Society*	Manchester Statistical Society, Manchester	1925
[QRL 6]	Corley, T. A. B.	'The Personal Wealth of Northern Ireland 1920–1960' in *Journal of the Statistical and Social Inquiry Society of Ireland*, **21**, 1		1962–3
[QRL 7]	Daniels, G. W. and Campion, H.	*The Distribution of National Capital*	Manchester University Press, Manchester	1936
[QRL 8]	Hill, T. P.	'Income, Savings and Net Worth—the Savings Survey of 1952–54' in *Bulletin of the Oxford University Institute of Statistics*, **17**, 2		1955
[QRL 9]	Langley, K. M.	'The distribution of capital in private hands in 1936–38 and 1946–47' in *Bulletin of the Oxford University Institute of Statistics*, **12**, 12 and **13**, 2		1950 and 1951
[QRL 10]	Langley, K. M.	'The distribution of private capital, 1950–51' in *Bulletin of the Oxford University Institute of Statistics*, **16**, 1		1954
[QRL 11]	Lydall, H. F.	*British Incomes and Savings*	Basil Blackwell, Oxford	1955
[QRL 12]	Lydall, H. F. and Tipping, D. G.	'The distribution of personal wealth in Britain' in *Bulletin of the Oxford University Institute of Statistics*, **23**, 1		1961
[QRL 13]	Lyons, P. M.	'The distribution of personal wealth in Northern Ireland' in *Economic and Social Review*, **3**, 2		1972
[QRL 14]	Morgan, E. V.	*Personal Savings and Wealth in Britain*	Financial Times, London	1975
[QRL 15]	Revell, J. R. S.	'Changes in the social distribution of property in Britain during the twentieth century' in *Actes du Trosième Congrès International d'Histoire Economique*	Munich	1965

[QRL 16]	Straw, K. H.	'Consumers net worth—the 1953 savings survey' in *Bulletin of the Oxford University Institute of Statistics*, **18**, 1		1956
[QRL 17]	Todd, J. E. and Jones, L. M.	*Matrimonial Property*	HMSO, London	1972
[QRL 18]	Townsend, P.	*Poverty in the United Kingdom*	Allen Lane, The Penguin Press, London	Forthcoming
[QRL 19]	Wedgwood, J.	*The Economics of Inheritance*	Penguin Books, Harmondsworth	1939
[QRL 20]	Inland Revenue	*Annual Report of the Commissioners*	HMSO, London	Annual
[QRL 21]	General Register Office	*Census 1951, England and Wales, Housing Report. Census 1961, England and Wales, Housing Tables*	HMSO, London	1956 and 1964
[QRL 22]	Office of Population, Censuses and Surveys	*Census 1971, England and Wales; Availability of cars*	HMSO, London	1973
[QRL 23]	Department of Finance, Northern Ireland	*Digest of Statistics, Northern Ireland*	HMSO, Belfast	Biannual
[QRL 24]	Inland Revenue	*Estimated Wealth of Individuals in Great Britain 1973*	HMSO, London	1975
[QRL 25]	Building Societies Association	*Facts and Figures*	Building Societies Association, 14 Park St, Mayfair, W1Y 4AL	Occasional
[QRL 26]	Department of Employment	*Family Expenditure Survey*	HMSO, London	Annual
[QRL 27]	Central Statistical Office	*Financial Statistics*	HMSO, London	Monthly
[QRL 28]	Office of Population Censuses and Surveys	*General Household Survey*	HMSO, London	Annual
[QRL 29]	Audits Great Britain	*Home Audit*	Not published but contact AGB, Audit House, Ruislip, Middlesex HA4 9LT	
[QRL 30]	Department of the Environment	*Housing Statistics* (1966–72) *Housing and Housing Construction Statistics* (1972–)	HMSO, London	Quarterly
[QRL 31]	Inland Revenue	*Inland Revenue Statistics* (abbreviated to IRS)	HMSO, London	Annual since 1970
[QRL 32]	Central Statistical Office	'The Motor Transactions Survey 1971' in *Economic Trends*, 242	HMSO, London	December 1973
[QRL 33]	Nationwide Building Society	*Occasional Bulletins*	Nationwide Building Society, New Oxford House, High Holborn, London WC1V 6PW	Occasional
[QRL 34]	Department of the Environment	*Passenger Transport in Great Britain, 1971*	HMSO, London	1973
[QRL 35]	Central Statistical Office	*Social Trends*	HMSO, London	Annual since 1970
[QRL 36]	British Market Research Bureau	*Target Group Index*	Not published but contact British Market Research Bureau, 53 The Mall, Ealing, London W5 3E	—

Bibliography

[B 1] Atkinson, A. B. and Harrison, A. J., 'Wealth distribution and investment income in Britain', *Review of Income and Wealth*, **20**, 2, 1974.

[B 2] Atkinson, A. B. and Harrison, A. J., 'Mortality multipliers and the estate duty method', *Oxford Bulletin of Economics and Statistics*, **37**, 1, 1975.

[B 3] Atkinson, A. B. and Harrison, A. J., *The Distribution of Personal Wealth in Britain*, Cambridge University Press, Cambridge, forthcoming.

[B 4] Cullingworth, J. B., *English Housing Trends*, Bell and Sons, London, 1965.

[B 5] Edwards, B., *Sources of Social Statistics*, Heinemann, London, 1974.

[B 6] Farthing, S. M., 'Housing in Great Britain', in Maunder, W. F., (ed.) *Reviews of United Kingdom Statistical Sources*, Vol. III, Heinemann Educational Books, London, 1974.

[B 7] Feinstein, C. H. and Revell, J. R. S., 'Who owns ordinary share capital?', *The Times*, 23 June 1960.

[B 8] Ferber, R., Forsythe, J., Guthrie, H. W. and Maynes, E. S., 'Validation of a national survey of consumer financial characteristics: savings accounts', *Review of Economics and Statistics*, **51**, 4, 1969.

[B 9] Giffen, R., *Statistics*, Macmillan, London, 1913.

[B 10] Gray, P. and Gee, F. A., *A Quality Check on the 1966 Ten Per Cent Sample Census of England and Wales*, HMSO, London, 1972.

[B 11] Hicks, J. R., *The Social Framework*, Oxford University Press, Oxford, 3rd edition, 1960.

[B 12] Hill, T. P., Klein, L. R. and Straw, K. H., 'The savings survey 1953: response rates and reliability of data', *Bulletin of the Oxford University Institute of Statistics*, **17**, 1, 1957.

[B 13] Isles, K. S. and Cuthbert, N., *An Economic Survey of Northern Ireland*, HMSO, Belfast, 1957.

[B 14] Klein, L. R. and Vandome, P., 'Sampling errors in the savings surveys', *Bulletin of the Oxford University Institute of Statistics*, **19**, 1, 1957.

[B 15] Lampman, R. J., *The Share of Top Wealth-Holders in National Wealth, 1922–56*, Princeton University Press, Princeton, 1962.

[B 16] Lyons, P. M., 'The size distribution of personal wealth in the Republic of Ireland', *Review of Income and Wealth*, **20**, 2, 1974.

[B 17] Mallet, B., 'A method of estimating capital wealth from the estate duty statistics', *Journal of the Royal Statistical Society*, **71**, 1, 1908.

[B 18] Mallet, B. and Strutt, H. C. 'The multiplier and capital wealth', *Journal of the Royal Statistical Society*, **78**, 4, 1915.

[B 19] Morgan, E. V., *The Structure of Property Ownership in Great Britain*, Oxford University Press, Oxford, 1960.

[B 20] Moyle, J., *The Pattern of Ordinary Share Ownership 1957–1970*, Cambridge University Press, Cambridge, 1971.

[B 21] Polanyi, G. and Wood, J. B., *How Much Inequality?*, Institute of Economic Affairs, London, 1974.

[B 22] Pyatt, G., *Priority Patterns and the Demand for Household Durable Goods*, Cambridge University Press, Cambridge, 1964.

[B 23] Revell, J. R. S., 'Assets and age', *Bulletin of the Oxford University Institute of Statistics*, **24**, 3, 1962.

[B 24] Revell, J. R. S., *The Wealth of the Nation*, Cambridge University Press, Cambridge, 1967.

[B 25] Revell, J. R. S. and Hockley, G. C., 'A survey of the holders of local authority debt', *Local Government Finance*, **64**, 7, 1960.

[B 26] Revell, J. R. S. and Hockley, G. C., 'Holders of local authority stocks and bonds', *Local Government Finance*, **64**, 12, 1960.

[B 27] Revell, J. R. S. and Moyle, J., 'A survey of the owners of quoted ordinary shares', *A Programme for Growth*, Vol. 7, Chapman and Hall, London, 1966.

[B 28] Revell, J. R. S. and Roe, A., 'National balance sheets and national accounting—a progress report', *Economic Trends*, 211, May 1971.

[B 29] Roe, A., *The Financial Interdependence of the Economy 1957–66*, Chapman and Hall, London, 1971.

[B 30] Rothman, J., *The Wealth of the United Kingdom*, prepared for Sandelson and Co., Ltd., 1974.

[B 31] Simons, H. C., *Personal Income Taxation*, University of Chicago Press, 1938.

[B 32] Smith, J. D., 'The concentration of personal wealth in America 1969', *Review of Income and Wealth*, **20**, 2, 1974.

[B 33] Stark, T., *The Distribution of Personal Income in the*

United Kingdom 1949–1963, Cambridge University Press, Cambridge, 1972.

[B 34] Tristram, T. H. and Coote, H., *Probate Practice*, Butterworth, London, 1970.

[B 35] Registrar General, *Decennial Supplement, England and Wales, 1931, Occupational Mortality Tables*, HMSO, London, 1938.

[B 36] Registrar General, *Decennial Supplement, England and Wales, 1951, Occupational Mortality Tables*, HMSO, London, 1958.

[B 37] Registrar General, *Decennial Supplement, England and Wales 1961, Occupational Mortality Tables*, HMSO, London, 1971.

[B 38] ——, 'The indefensible status quo', *The Economist*, January 15, 1966.

[B 39] Royal Commission on the Distribution of Income and Wealth, *Initial Report on the Standing Reference*, Report No. 1, Cmnd. 6171, HMSO, London, 1975.

[B 40] Committee to Review National Savings, *Report*, HMSO, London, 1973.

[B 41] The Hudson Institute Europe, *The United Kingdom in 1980: The Hudson Report*, Associated Business Programmes, London, 1974.

[B 42] ——, *Wealth Tax*, Cmnd. 5704, HMSO, London, 1974.

Appendix

Reporting Document Completed by Estate Duty Offices

This appendix contains specimens of these forms, which are referred to as Stat. No. 4. The first is typical of the period before the introduction of capital transfer tax and relates to 1970–1. The second is the most recent available when the review was completed, and relates to 1975–6.

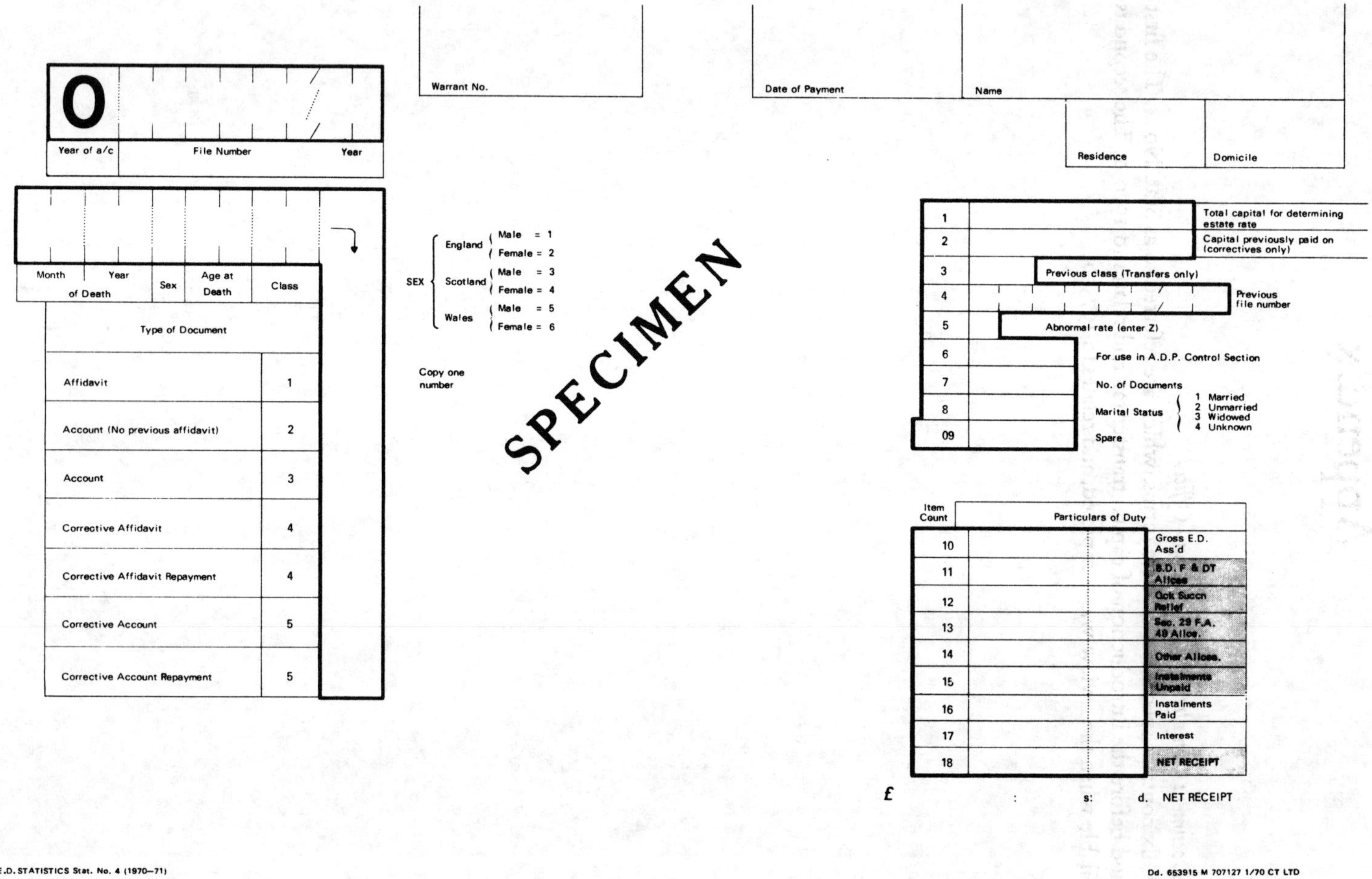

SPECIMEN

Year of a/c	File Number	Year
O		

Warrant No.

Date of Payment

Name

Residence	Domicile

Month	Year	Sex	Age at Death	Class
of Death				

Type of Document	
Affidavit	1
Account (No previous affidavit)	2
Account	3
Corrective Affidavit	4
Corrective Affidavit Repayment	4
Corrective Account	5
Corrective Account Repayment	5

SEX: England (Male = 1, Female = 2); Scotland (Male = 3, Female = 4); Wales (Male = 5, Female = 6)

Copy one number

1		Total capital for determining estate rate
2		Capital previously paid on (correctives only)
3		Previous class (Transfers only)
4		Previous file number
5		Abnormal rate (enter Z)
6		For use in A.D.P. Control Section
7		No. of Documents
8		Marital Status: 1 Married, 2 Unmarried, 3 Widowed, 4 Unknown
09		Spare

Item Count	Particulars of Duty	
10		Gross E.D. Ass'd
11		B.D. F & DT Allces
12		Qck Succn Relief
13		Sec. 29 F.A. 49 Allce.
14		Other Allces.
15		Instalments Unpaid
16		Instalments Paid
17		Interest
18		NET RECEIPT

£ : s: d. NET RECEIPT

E.D. STATISTICS Stat. No. 4 (1970–71)

Dd. 653915 M 707127 1/70 CT LTD

SPECIMEN

Item Count

Item	Description	Sub-group	Group
19	Nat. Sav. & Prem. Bds.		Govt. & Munpl. Securities
20	5 yrs	British Govt. Securities	Govt. & Munpl. Securities
21	5 – 14 yrs	British Govt. Securities	Govt. & Munpl. Securities
22	15 or over	British Govt. Securities	Govt. & Munpl. Securities
23	Undated	British Govt. Securities	Govt. & Munpl. Securities
24	Def. Bds. etc.		Govt. & Munpl. Securities
25	U K Munpl.		Govt. & Munpl. Securities
26	N. Ireland Govt.		Govt. & Munpl. Securities
27	Overseas Govt.& Munpl.		Govt. & Munpl. Securities
28	Ords.	NO	Shs. In. Br. Cos.
29	Pref. Debs. etc.	NO	Shs. In. Br. Cos.
30	Ords.	Q	Shs. In. Br. Cos.
31	Pref. Debs. etc.	Q	Shs. In. Br. Cos.
32	N. Ireland		Shs. In Other Cos.
33	Overseas		Shs. In Other Cos.
34	Quoted Inv. Trusts		
35	Unit Trusts		
36	Money on M'gage		
37	Building Socs.		Money on Bonds
38	Munpl. Mortgages, Debentures & Bonds		Money on Bonds
39	Co-op Societies		Money on Bonds
40	Loans to Ltd. Cos.		Money on Bonds
41	Loans to Persons		Money on Bonds
42	Other Money		
43	Other debts		
44	H'hold goods		
45	Policies		
46	Cash in house		
47	P.O. & T.S. Bk.		Cash at Bank
48	Deposit A/c		Cash at Bank
49	Drawing A/c		Cash at Bank
50	Agric.	P... etc.	Trading Assets
51	Other	P... etc.	Trading Assets
52	Book debts		Trading Assets
53	Farming Stock		Trading Assets
54	Other Stock		Trading Assets
55	Goodwill		Trading Assets
56	P'ship Unapp'd		
57	Cash Gifts		
58	Income due		
59	Int. in Expectancy	•	Also Box 130
60	Unadministered Estates		GROSS P.E.
61	Not classified		

Item	Description	Sub-group	Group
62	Non-Leasehold		Land
63	Leasehold		Land
64	Owner-Occp	Residential / Non-Leasehold	Buildings
65	Not own-occ	Residential / Non-Leasehold	Buildings
66	Not known	Residential / Non-Leasehold	Buildings
67	Other	Non-Leasehold	Buildings
68	Owner-Occp	Residential / Leasehold	Buildings
69	Not own-occ	Residential / Leasehold	Buildings
70	Not known	Residential / Leasehold	Buildings
71	Other	Leasehold	Buildings
72	Timber		
73	Rents		GROSS R.E.
74	Not classified		

Item	Description	Sub-group	Group
75	Bank Loan O'draft	To G.B. Residents	Debts
76	Loan from Ltd. Co., (Not Ins'ce Co.)	To G.B. Residents	Debts
77	Loans From Persons	To G.B. Residents	Debts
78	Other	To G.B. Residents	Debts — TOTAL DEDUCTIONS P.E.
79	F.E.		Debts
80	To Residents Abroad		NET P.E.
81	C.G.T. Dedn. (S.26, F.A.1965)		

Item Count

Item	Description	Group
82	To Local Auth'y	Mortgages
83	To Building So	Mortgages
84	To Insurance Co.	Mortgages
85	To Persons	Mortgages
86	Other	Mortgages
87	Other deductions	

TOTAL DEDUCTIONS R.E.

NET R.E.

88	Life Policies Annuities etc. NA *
89	Settled NA with free *
90	Not Free Aggregable with Free
91	Free

NET TOTAL ESTATE

92	*Total capital for determining estate rate on N/A ppty

GROSS

Item		Country	Group
93	P.E.	England	FREE
94	R.E.	England	FREE
95	P.E.	Scotland	FREE
96	R.E.	Scotland	FREE
97	P.E.	N. Ireland	FREE
98	R.E.	N. Ireland	FREE
99	P.E.	Overseas	FREE
100	R.E.	Overseas	FREE
101	P.E.	England	NOT FREE
102	R.E.	England	NOT FREE
103	P.E.	Scotland	NOT FREE
104	R.E.	Scotland	NOT FREE
105	P.E.	N. Ireland	NOT FREE
106	R.E.	N. Ireland	NOT FREE
107	P.E.	Overseas	NOT FREE
108	R.E.	Overseas	NOT FREE

NET

Item		Description	Group
109	P.E.	Settled by Decd.	DISPOSITION
110	R.E.	Settled by Decd.	DISPOSITION
111	P.E.	Settled by Others	DISPOSITION
112	R.E.	Settled by Others	DISPOSITION
113	P.E.	I.V. Gifts	DISPOSITION
114	R.E.	I.V. Gifts	DISPOSITION
115	P.E.	Joint	DISPOSITION
116	R.E.	Joint	DISPOSITION
117	P.E.	Other	DISPOSITION
118	R.E.	Other	DISPOSITION

Amount before relief

Item	Description	Sub-group	Group
119	Charities		IV GIFTS
120	Within 1 year	Other	IV GIFTS
121	Within 2 years	Other	IV GIFTS
122	Within 3 years	Other	IV GIFTS
123	Within 4 years	Other	IV GIFTS
124	Within 5 years	Other	IV GIFTS
125	Within 6 years	Other	IV GIFTS
126	Within 7 years	Other	IV GIFTS
127	Unclass'd	Other	IV GIFTS

Item	Description	Group
128	Before Relief	Release of life interest etc.
129	After Relief	Release of life interest etc.

Int. in Expectancy

• 130	Value at death

Item	Description	Group
131	Gross	AGRIC
132	Net	AGRIC
133	Duty	AGRIC

Item	Description	Sub-group	Group
134	Shares	P.E. Cap	S.28. F.A. 54
135	Others	P.E. Cap	S.28. F.A. 54
136	R.E. Cap		S.28. F.A. 54
137	Sec. 55	Duty	S.28. F.A. 54
138	Other	Duty	S.28. F.A. 54

Warrant No.	Date of Payment	Name

5

Year of a/c.	File Number	Year	Residence	Domicile

Month	Year	Sex	Age at Death/Gift	Class
of Death/Gift				

SEX
- England { Male = 1, Female = 2
- Scotland { Male = 3, Female = 4
- Wales { Male = 5, Female = 6
- N.Ireland { Male = 7, Female = 8

Affidavit	1
Account (No previous affidavit)	2
Account	3
Corrective Affidavit/corrective Affidavit Repayment	4
Corrective Account/corrective Account repayment	5
Transfer by a living donor	

Boxes 1 - 6
Type of Document

Copy one number only

SPECIMEN

122		Spouse	Capital Exemptions
123		Charities	
124		Heritage	

125		Total of gifts to date
126		Total reduction of capital under S45 FA 1973
127		**A** Reserved
128		**B** Boxes

1		Total capital for determining CLASS of estate
2		Capital previously paid on (correctives only)
3		Previous class (Transfers only)
4		Previous file number
5		Abnormal rate (enter 2)
6		For use in A.D.P. Control Section
7		No. of Documents
8		Marital Status
9		Spare

Marital Status: 1 Married, 2 Unmarried, 3 Widowed, 4 Unknown

'9' if No count

			Particulars of Duty/Tax
10			Gross E.D./CTT Ass'd.
11			B.D., F. & D.T. Allces.
12			Qck. Succn. Relief
13			Other Allces.
14			Instalments Unpaid
15			Instalments Paid (Land)
16			Instalments Paid (Others)
17			Interest
18			NET RECEIPT

£ : NET RECEIPT

E.D.STATISTICS Stat.No. 4 (1975-76)

G.4269 Dd 082792 150,000 HPB Ltd. 960

'9' if No Count

Code		Item	Group	
19		Nat.Sav. & Prem.Bds.	Br. Govt.	Govt. & Munpl. Secs.
20		Br.Sav.Bonds etc.	Br. Govt.	Govt. & Munpl. Secs.
21		Qtd. Securities	Br. Govt.	Govt. & Munpl. Secs.
22		UK Munpl.		Govt. & Munpl. Secs.
23		N.Ireland Govt.		Govt. & Munpl. Secs.
24		Overseas Govt. & Munpl.		Govt. & Munpl. Secs.
25		Ords.	NQ	Shs. In U.K. Cos.
26		Pref. Debs. etc.	NQ	Shs. In U.K. Cos.
27		Ords.	Q	Shs. In U.K. Cos.
28		Pref. Debs. etc.	Q	Shs. In U.K. Cos.
29		Shares in Overseas Co.'s.		
30		Quoted Inv.Trusts		
31		Unit Trusts		
32		Money on M'gage		
33		Building Socs.		
34		Munpl.Mortgages, Debentures & Bonds		
35		Co-op. Societies		
36		Loans to Ltd. Cos.		
37		Loans to Persons		
38		Other Money		
39		Other debts		
40		H'hold goods		
41		Policies		
42		Cash in house		
43		Nat. & T.S.Bk.	Cash at Bank	
44		Deposit A/c.	Cash at Bank	
45		Drawing A/c.	Cash at Bank	
46		Agric.	Plant etc.	Trading Assets
47		Other	Plant etc.	Trading Assets
48		Book debts		Trading Assets
49		Farming Stock		Trading Assets
50		Other St...		Trading Assets
51		Goodwill		Trading Assets
52		P'ship Unapp'd.		
53		Cash Gifts		
54		Income due		
55		Int. in Expectancy		
56		Unadministered Estates		
57		PE Not classified		
TOTAL GROSS P.E.				

SPECIMEN

Code		Item	Group		
58		Non-Leasehold	Land		
59		Leasehold	Land		
60		Owner-Occp.	Residential	Non-Leasehold	Buildings
61		Not own-occ.	Residential	Non-Leasehold	Buildings
62		Not known	Residential	Non-Leasehold	Buildings
63		Other		Non-Leasehold	Buildings
64		Own-Occp.	Residential	Leasehold	Buildings
65		Not own-occ.	Residential	Leasehold	Buildings
66		Not known	Residential	Leasehold	Buildings
67		Other		Leasehold	Buildings
68		Timber			
69		Ground Rents			
70		R.E.Not classified			
TOTAL GROSS R.E.					

Code		Item	Group	
71		Bank Loan/O.draft	To U.K.Res.debts	Debts
72		Loan from Ltd.Co., (Not Ins'ce Co.)	To U.K.Res.debts	Debts
73		Loans From Persons	To U.K.Res.debts	Debts
74		Other	To U.K.Res.debts	Debts
75		F.E.		Debts
76		To Residents Abroad		Debts
77		C.G.T.Dedn.(S26-FA 1965)		
TOTAL DEBTS P.E.				
NET P.E.				

'9' if No Count

Code		Item	Group
78		To Local Auth'y	Mortgages
79		To Building Scy	Mortgages
80		To Insurance Co.	Mortgages
81		To Persons	Mortgages
82		Other	Mortgages
83		Other deductions	
TOTAL DEBTS R.E.			
NET R.E.			
84		Life Policies Annuities etc. NA*	
85		Settled NA with free*	
86		Not Free Aggregable with Free	
87		Free	
NET TOTAL ESTATE			
88		*Total capital for determining estate rate on N/A ppty.	

GROSS

Code			
89		P.E.	FREE
90		R.E.	FREE
91		P.E.	NOT FREE
92		R.E.	NOT FREE

NET

Code				
93		P.E.	Settled by Decd.	DISPOSITION
94		R.E.	Settled by Decd.	DISPOSITION
95		P.E.	Settled by Others	DISPOSITION
96		R.E.	Settled by Others	DISPOSITION
97		P.E.	I.V. Gifts	DISPOSITION
98		R.E.	I.V. Gifts	DISPOSITION
99		P.E.	Joint	DISPOSITION
100		R.E.	Joint	DISPOSITION
101		P.E.	Other	DISPOSITION
102		R.E.	Other	DISPOSITION

AMOUNT BEFORE RELIEF

Code		Item		
103		Charities		IV GIFTS
104		Within 1 year	Other	IV GIFTS
105		Within 2 years	Other	IV GIFTS
106		Within 3 years	Other	IV GIFTS
107		Within 4 years	Other	IV GIFTS
108		Within 5 years	Other	IV GIFTS
109		Within 6 years	Other	IV GIFTS
110		Within 7 years	Other	IV GIFTS
111		Unclass'd	Other	IV GIFTS

Code		Item	
112		Before Relief	Release of life Interest etc.
113		After Relief	Release of life Interest etc.

CAPITAL & DUTY AT REDUCED RATE

Code		Item	
114		Gross	AGRIC
115		Net	AGRIC
116		Duty	AGRIC

Code		Item		
117		Shares	P.E. Cap	S.28 F.A. 54
118		Others	P.E. Cap	S.28 F.A. 54
119		R.E.Cap		S.28 F.A. 54
120		Sec.55	Duty	S.28 F.A. 54
121		Other	Duty	S.28 F.A. 54

Subject Index

11 Personal Incomes

by

T. STARK

Lecturer in Economics
The New University of Ulster

Acknowledgements

I have received much valuable help in the preparation of this paper from many people concerned with the collection and processing of income distribution data. Discussions which have been of great assistance took place with Messrs M. Boreham, J. Hibbert and D. Ramprakash and Mrs Muriel Nissel of the Central Statistical Office, and Messrs S. James and W. Gonzalez of the Inland Revenue. Valuable written comments were received from Mr N. Davis of the Office of Population Censuses and Surveys; Mr R. Turner and others of the Department of Employment; Mr A. Johnson of the Royal Commission on the Distribution of Income and Wealth: and Mr S. Hodkinson of the Northern Ireland Department of Finance. I would also wish to acknowledge the assistance of Professor C. H. Feinstein, who clarified for me some queries on the interpretation of his most excellent book.

I am most grateful to the editor of the series, Professor W. F. Maunder, for his patience and support during the long process of drafting the paper. My thanks are also due to my wife who has typed the many drafts, and to Miss Catherine McAleavey who had the onerous task of preparing the reference lists and bibliography.

Reference Date of Sources Reviewed

This review is believed to represent the position, broadly speaking, as it obtained at December 1975. Later revisions have been inserted up to the proof-reading stage [Jan 1977] taking account, as far as possible, of any major changes in the situation.

List of Abbreviations

BIR	Board of the Inland Revenue
CIF	1971 Census of Population Income Follow-Up
CSO	Central Statistical Office
DHSS	Department of Health and Social Security
FES	Family Expenditure Survey
GHS	General Household Survey
GNP	Gross National Product
IRS	Inland Revenue Statistics
NBPI	National Board of Prices and Incomes
NES	New Earnings Survey
NPB	Non-Profit-Making Bodies
PI	Personal Income
PSU	Primary Sampling Unit
RPI	Index of Retail Prices
SPI	Survey of Personal Incomes

Contents

I Introduction

1.1 Definitions

The concept of income in economics is complex and ambiguous. It has for us all a particular, almost seemingly obvious meaning, yet in everyday language we change from concepts of accounting income to notional or normal income or real income without much thought. Income can be to us either what we receive in cash, or are taxed on, or what we normally receive or expect to receive or it can be our command over resources. All these concepts of income are different, though they can be all identical given the correct definitions and assumptions. Since our tract is not a discussion on the concept of income we shall opt for an uncomplicated *base* concept as our guideline, namely that personal income is as defined in orthodox national income accounting which is the flow of receipts over a period of time to the personal sector of the economy. We emphasize that this is a *base* concept. When we consider its use for personal income data we shall see that it ought to be modified and redefined. Some of this modification stems from the constraint in national income accounting that all flows must be related to the flow of output, either directly via exchange for labour or capital services, or indirectly via transfers from other sectors. Other aspects of desirable modification arise from the definition of the personal sector.

The personal sector in the United Kingdom national income accounts comprises individuals, grouped in either families or households, unincorporated businesses, charities, some educational institutes and life assurance and superannuation funds. It is in many respects a definition unsuitable for any particular purpose other than permitting the other major sectors of the accounts—the Public, Company and International—to be well defined. For instance if we wished to analyse the determinants of personal consumption or saving, or of the size distribution of income amongst persons, both of which would require data on personal incomes, then it is clear that the definition of the personal sector is far from ideal.

These peculiarities of definition would be unimportant were it not for the considerable significance personal income has as an economic entity. We have mentioned already two major roles, to which we can add the politically arresting analyses of living standards, tax changes, equity and social justice. These are areas of study which attract much attention in the media, parliament and in the academic world of the social scientist. For this reason we shall devote some discussion in each section to the relationship between definition and use of personal income statistics.

1.2 Coverage of the Study

Practically all uses for the variable personal income have a bias towards the macro or nationally representative factor. It is therefore not surprising that almost all data currently available on personal incomes are produced by the government authorities. This has been more or less so since the Second World War. Prior to that government statistics were very poor indeed and there were a number of isolated private or academic data sources. These have now dwindled. They are largely no longer required and even in those areas where the official data are unsatisfactory the cost of non-official collection of statistics is frequently prohibitive. It therefore follows that much of the analysis to follow shall focus on official data sources. Since most of these publish detailed accounts of the collection sources and processing methods, we shall limit ourselves to a brief analysis on these matters, except in the rare cases of major non-official data or where official information is not in one readily accessible source. The reader will be referred throughout to official publications containing further details.

The main emphasis of the survey will be on post-war data. Pre-war data, which we shall refer to as historical data, will be considered, though there will be less extensive coverage of this material. This was necessary, since many historical data are non-official and by virtue of that highly heterogeneous with regard to collection, source and definition, so that a comparable depth of analysis would have doubled the length of this work.

There are two final points with regard to coverage. First it is assumed throughout that the United Kingdom includes Northern Ireland and secondly that the emphasis is on personal income as an entity, so that the sources on particular types of personal income are not our concern unless they can be adapted to the study of total personal income. This means that the comprehensive earnings and labour cost surveys undertaken by the government will be considered in less detail than other income data sources. These are intended to form the core material of a later volume in this series.

1.3 Plan

The survey will be divided into three parts. In Section 2 we will deal with aggregate personal income. This variable is most important. It forms the basic control total to which all studies using personal incomes must ultimately relate. The third section concentrates on the distribution of income to persons and the relationship to aggregate personal income. As in this area the sources are more varied and the techniques of estimation more open to scrutiny, a greater emphasis will be placed on the technical aspects compared to Section 2. The final part, Section 4, will be a hotch-potch of miscellaneous minor sources of data on personal incomes. For the same reason as with the historical data, this section will be largely a summary of sources.

2 Aggregate Personal Income

2.1 Definition and Primary Sources

The Central Statistical Office (CSO) defines aggregate personal income as that income from either employment, property or transfers from other sectors which accrues in aggregate to the personal sector of the economy. The personal sector of the economy, in turn, is defined as being '... made up mainly of households and individuals resident in the United Kingdom as distinct from corporate businesses or organs of government. It includes individuals living in hostels and other institutions as well as those living in private households. The sector extends beyond households and individuals to include unincorporated private businesses of sole traders and partnerships, such as farms, retail shops and independent professional men. It also includes private non-profit-making bodies serving persons and private trusts' ([B 85], *Sources and Methods*, pp. 99–101). This last group includes charities, universities, trades unions, life assurance and superannuation funds, independent schools, voluntary hospitals and churches. However, contrary to expectation building societies and co-operative societies are not included.

Highly detailed definitions of the personal sector, its income and the means of collecting the data are published in the CSO's *National Income and Expenditure: Sources and Methods* [B 85, B 88]. The latest such publication was in 1968 and subsequent developments and changes since then are recorded in a section entitled 'Notes', that is usually the fourteenth and last section of the CSO's annual publication on National Income and Expenditure [QRL 37], hereafter referred to by its commonly accepted title, the *Blue Book*. In addition in each January edition of the CSO's *Monthly Digest of Statistics* [QRL 35] there is included 'A Supplement of Definitions and Explanatory Notes', which records new developments with respect to monthly and quarterly data.

The annual *Blue Books* are the primary published source of data on annual aggregate personal income. The data are presented both in summary form as a part of the national income accounting system and in detail as the statistics on the personal sector. In addition to these annual estimates, there are quarterly estimates published in the *Monthly Digest of Statistics* [QRL 35] and the *Financial Statistics* [QRL 29]. There is also in each October issue of *Economic Trends* [QRL 20] a much longer run of quarterly estimates than would normally appear in the other sources, which is specifically presented to tie in with the annual estimates from the *Blue Books*.

2.2 Itemization of Aggregate Personal Income

2.2.1 *Annual Data*

As mentioned in subsection 2.1 the personal sector is very broadly defined in the UK national accounting system. This can be illustrated by listing the items that form part of 'officially' estimated personal income. These are set out in Table 2.1, which reproduces the revenue side of the income and expenditure account of the personal sector. This form of presentation has always been standard for the summary tables in the *Blue Book* [QRL 37] (i.e. Section 1) and since 1965 a detailed version of the account has been published in the section on the personal sector. It is the latter detailed version which is presented in Table 2.1.

Details of the items in Table 2.1 are given in each *Blue Book*. All items are computed prior to direct income taxation. The estimates on wages and salaries include employee contributions to the

National Insurance system and contributions to private pension and superannuation schemes. They are however net of expenses incurred during employment which are deductible for taxation purposes. Up to and including the 1970 *Blue Book* [QRL 37] estimates have been presented separately for wages and salaries. Since the distinction is somewhat arbitrary the CSO ceased to do this in 1971. However, estimates consistent with those prior to 1971 can be obtained on request from the National Accounts section of the CSO.

Income from self-employment is a hotch-potch. It includes those personal incomes which are assessed for income tax purposes under Schedule D as profits of a trade, profession or vocation but before the provision of depreciation. This type of income is in effect a combination of labour and capital return and as such presents conceptual difficulties (see subsection 2.8.1). Similarly property income is also a mixture. It comprises the investment and rent income of life assurance and superannuation funds as well as that received by households. Furthermore the rent element includes an estimate of imputed owner-occupied rent. The investment income element includes not only dividends and yields on shares and securities but also bank interest, interest on building society shares and deposits and dividends from co-operative societies, but not interest on personal loans between persons. Again all these estimates are computed before taxation and are net of allowable expenses, such as maintenance and insurance expenditure against rent. It should also be mentioned at this stage that the estimates of property income are computed as a residual. The CSO computes property income for the whole economy, mainly from the expenditure and appropriation accounts, and then allocates the income to all the other sectors of the economy, thereby leaving a residual estimate for the personal sector. Data imperfections make it impossible to make reliable estimates for rent and investment income components of property income. However a rough estimate of personal sector rent is made for the distribution of GNP by sector [B 85, p. 67].

Table 2.1 Items of Personal Income as in the 'Blue Book' Income – Expenditure Account of the Personal Sector

(i)	Wages and salaries in cash and kind	Income from employment
(ii)	Pay in cash and kind of HM Forces	
(iii)	Employers' contributions:	
	(a) National Insurance, etc.	
	(b) Other	
(iv)	Professional persons	Income from self-employment
(v)	Farmers	
(vi)	Other sole traders and partnerships	
(vii)	Rent, Net Interest and Dividends:	Property income
	(a) Receipts by life assurance and superannuation funds	
	(b) Others	
(viii)	Current transfer to charities from Companies	Transfer incomes
(ix)	National Insurance benefits and other current grants from public authorities	
	TOTAL PERSONAL INCOME	

Finally the last items in Table 2.1, transfer incomes, not only comprise the standard categories of social security payments, pensions, and student scholarships, but also include post-war credits, death benefits, injury benefits to persons and up to 1969 the net cost of subsidized school meals, milk and welfare foods, plus recurrent grants to universities and other current grants to charities. It is argued that there is confusion in this area between capital and current payments. Post-war credits, death and injury benefits could be claimed to be capital transfers. However they amount to a negligible part of the total. The authorities are far stricter when it comes to large items of capital transfers such as the capital grants to universities which are excluded.

A more detailed description of the various items above, including an example of how personal property income is residually computed, can be obtained in the CSO's *Sources and Methods* ([B 85], pp. 103–4).

Since 1956 the *Blue Books* have always given an alternative presentation of aggregate personal income. This is again presented in the section on the personal sector and is generally captioned as 'Categories of Personal Income'. The items comprising this alternative approach are set out in Table 2.2.

The difference between the two presentations is that the latter is classified according to the manner in which income is received, i.e. cash, in kind, etc. whilst the former classifies according to factor or payment source. A very noticeable distinction thus arises with respect to transfer incomes. In Table 2.2 transfer incomes include pensions, benefits and policy monies from life insurances from private schemes, but exclude employers' contributions to such schemes. The reverse is the case in Table 2.1.

Table 2.2 Categories of Personal Income as given in the 'Blue Books'

(1) Wages and salaries	Direct income in cash from work and property
(2) Pay in cash of HM Forces	
(3) Income from self-employment	
(4) Rent, dividends and interest (gross receipts less interest paid)	
(5) Employers' national insurance, etc. contributions	Imputed income and income in kind
(6) Income in kind	
(7) Rent of owner-occupied dwellings	
(8) Accrued interest on National Savings certificates	
(9) Current transfers to charities from companies	Transfer incomes
(10) Current grants from public authorities:	
(a) Retirement pensions, widows' benefits, etc. non-contributory pensions	
(b) Grants to private non-profit-making bodies	
(c) Other current grants	
(11) Pensions and benefits from life assurance and superannuation schemes	
(12) Adjustment for life assurance and superannuation funds, namely contributions of employers plus rent, dividends and interest less pensions and other benefits paid	

The adjustment item (12) in Table 2.2 ensures that the totals from the two tables balance.

These complications concerning transfer payments arise simply from the fact that when grouping together individuals and life assurance and superannuation schemes in the personal sector, the double counting of certain incomes must be avoided. In national income accounting transfers within a sector on consolidation can only be counted as income of the donor or recipient, not both. For example, say in a two-person personal sector, person A has an 'initial' income of £1,000 and person B £500, giving an aggregate of £1,500. Now if A transfers £250 to B, each will have a 'final' income of £750, i.e. still £1,500 in aggregate. However, if we counted A's 'initial' income and B's 'final' then an aggregate of £1,750 would arise. This is clearly incorrect since the aggregate resources of the personal sector have not been increased, at this given period in time, by the transfers between A and B. The relevance of this example is that employee or self-employed contributions to life assurance superannuation and pension schemes organized within the personal sector, must be considered as part of 'initial' income and the pension and benefit payments out of these contributions as part of 'final' income. Thus since in Table 2.2 item (11) includes the pension and benefit payments as income there should be a corresponding deduction for the appropriate contributions in items (1), (2) and (3). However, these deductions are not made and the correct aggregate is preserved by the adjustment factor (item 12). If a consistent procedure were followed and these appropriate deductions made, then the adjustment item (12) would have to be increased by an equivalent sum. The adjustment factor would become simply the gross increase in life assurance and superannuation funds before the payment of taxes and other administrative charges. It is probably less misleading, however, to adopt the method of presentation given in Table 2.2.

These transfers within the personal sector are not to be confused with transfers via the public or company sectors, such as state pensions, employer contributions to life assurance and superannuation funds, etc. where both contribution and payment of benefits are recorded in personal income. Since the flows involve another sector, transactions are not self-cancelling on consolidation. We shall argue in a later section (see 3.10.4) that in some instances it would also be meaningful to include both the contributions and payments of the private personal sector schemes as well. Ideally this means splitting the personal sector into two sectors—a household sector and a life assurance fund and charities sector—a development that the Central Statistical Office introduced in 1976 (see subsection 2.8.1 for further details and discussion).

As a useful piece of information, not presented in official sources, the correspondence between Tables 2.1 and 2.2 can be represented by seven identities. The seven identities are given below (Table 2.1 items in Roman numerals):

(a) i + ii = 1 + 2 + 6, n.b. (i − 1) + (ii − 2) = 6
(b) iv + v + vi = 3
(c) viii = 9
(d) ix = 10a + 10b + 10c
(e) iiia = 5
(f) viib = 4 + 7 + 8
(g) iiib + viia = 11 + 12, i.e. 12 = iiib + viia − 11 as defined in Table 2.2

It is clear from these identities that a reader if he so wished could construct himself an alternatively itemized version of aggregate personal income. A maximum of sixteen items is the limit. Furthermore by consulting the 'Gross Domestic Product by sector and type of income and by type of employment' table in the *Blue Book* [QRL 37] (T. 13 in 1971) the total amount of rent income for the personal sector can be obtained. This comprises item (7) above plus part of the rent part of item (4).

2.2.2 *Quarterly Data*

The National Income and Expenditure section of each *Monthly Digest of Statistics* [QRL 35] and each *Financial Statistics* [QRL 29] give quarterly estimates of total personal income as defined in the *Blue Book* [QRL 37]. The tables published are a limited version of Table 2.1 (see subsection 2.2.1) from the *Blue Book* [QRL 37]. They comprise items (i), (ii), (iii) and (ix) from our Table 2.1 plus the conglomerate of all the other items under the title of 'other personal income'. The data are presented both unadjusted and adjusted for seasonal variations. An outline of the manipulations for seasonal adjustment is given in the CSO's *Sources and Methods* [B 85] pp. 53–7.

The *Monthly Digest* [QRL 35] generally provides quarterly data only for a three-year period and *Financial Statistics* [QRL 29] for a four-year period. The October issue of *Economic Trends* [QRL 20] reproduces much longer runs for quarterly data.

2.3 Methods of Estimation

As mentioned in Section 1, the methods of estimation are very adequately described in the CSO's

Sources and Methods [B 85]. However, for the sake of completeness a very brief outline is presented below.

2.3.1 *Annual Data—Wages and Salaries in Cash*
The system for estimating wages and salaries is currently under review. However, the present system is based on the PAYE Deducation Cards (see Appendix A for an example). The cards are made out in respect of every employee whose earnings in any week are in excess of an exemption limit, which is a limit related to the income tax personal allowance for a single person. There are, however, a number of adjustments and difficulties to be overcome before presentation in the *Blue Books*. The first is the conversion of the financial year returns to a calendar year estimate. This adjustment is made by interpolating the financial year data using the results of a sample survey of employers covering about a quarter of total wages and salaries, undertaken by the Inland Revenue each quarter and it forms the basis of the quarterly estimates (see subsection 2.3.11).

The second difficulty is the wage and salary earnings of those whose total in any one week does not reach the exemption limit. In these cases it is not required that the employer either records or makes out a card, though quite a number of employers do both. The Inland Revenue consider that the incomes of retiring persons and part-time incomes are likely to be covered by the cards even though they may be below the effective tax exemption limit on an annual basis. However persons with very low incomes, the unemployed and some school leavers entering the labour market may not have cards made out. The Central Statistical Office attempts to estimate the number of wage and salary earners involved by comparing the number of persons employed in the UK with the number of deduction cards received. The former is obtained from the Department of Employment for Great Britain and the Department of Manpower Services for Northern Ireland. As far as possible, the difference is classified into wholly unemployed, school leavers, part-time workers, etc. and average wages and salaries assigned by way of 'informed' guesswork.

Another important difficulty arises with respect to those receiving pension incomes while still employed. It is not always possible in these cases to distinguish pension income from wages and salaries on the deduction cards. An adjustment is made by reference to the Inland Revenue Surveys of Personal Incomes (see subsection 3.2). There are also other minor problems, particularly for farm workers. Details are given in the *Sources and Methods* ([B 85], p. 123).

2.3.2 *Annual Data—Wages and Salaries in Kind*
The *Sources and Methods* ([B 85], p. 125) gives a list of items that are included under this heading. The sources are varied, such as the Coal Board for miners' free coal, the Agricultural and Fisheries Departments for the board and lodging of agricultural workers. The *Family Expenditure Survey* [QRL 28] is used to estimate the total value of employer-provided accommodation and the former Ministry of Labour's enquiries into total labour costs [QRL 24, 33, 34] are the basis of estimates of subsidized factory meals. The *Sources and Methods* handbook [B 85] also mentions a number of items which ought to be included, but are not due to data inavailability. Notably, these include most transport services that might be subsidized by employers and those cases where uniforms or work clothes are provided free as personal equipment. Some information on these items is available from the *Labour Cost Surveys* [QRL 24, 33, 34].

2.3.3 *Pay in Cash and Kind of HM Forces*
The sources here are the figures provided by each of the service departments. They refer specifically to currently employed servicemen and women. Those receiving disability or death awards or educational, etc. grants are treated as current transfers by the public authorities to the personal sector.

2.3.4 *Annual Data—Employers' Contributions*

The National Insurance contributions are quite obviously obtained from the current income and expenditure account of the National Insurance and Industrial Injuries Fund, which is reproduced in the public sector section of each *Blue Book* [QRL 37]. The contributions by employers to the private sector superannuation, pension and lump sum schemes however present a very much more difficult task.

There are several sources of data for this latter group of contributions, for example certain public authorities and larger private schemes publish annual accounts and the Government Actuary conducts periodic surveys of occupational pension schemes. There have been three such surveys, for 1958 [B 90], 1966 [QRL 44] and 1968 [QRL 45], and a fourth began in July 1973. They provide detailed estimates of the structure of private pensions and superannuation schemes in the United Kingdom. In addition to the surveys an article appeared in the August 1971 issue of the *Department of Employment Gazette* ([QRL 21], pp. 690–711) which reproduced estimates for 1970 by the Department of Employment of the number of employees covered by occupational pension schemes derived from the results of the *New Earnings Surveys* [QRL 42].

Although there are a number of sources, it has proved in practice difficult to use them in making estimates required for the national accounts. The main basis of the estimates used to be the regular information received by tax inspectors on schemes approved for tax purposes. The Inland Revenue receive statistical reports from district tax officers in respect of private uninsured schemes while similar information on nationalized industry schemes is provided to the Inland Revenue by the Government Actuary. However, this system for various reasons has never worked very satisfactorily, the information for recent years is particularly poor and the CSO is currently reviewing alternative methods of estimation. In particular it is hoped that much greater use can be made of the current (1973) survey being undertaken by the Government Actuary. Contributions to insured schemes are derived partly from an analysis of insurance company accounts and partly from information published annually by the Life Offices Association [B 81].

The estimates of employers' contributions to superannuation funds also include a number of actual lump sum payments and pensions made to employees as opposed to those made on behalf of them. These comprise mainly payments by central government to HM Forces and civilians and payments to police and firemen. In most cases they are pensions paid less employee contributions. This treatment is not consistent with regard to other transfer incomes. For example with respect to Table 2.1 the employee contributions should be included in item (i)—wages and salaries, and the pensions net of these contributions should form an additional item for transfer incomes from the company sector. In Table 2.2 a consistent procedure would be to include the pensions in item (11)—pensions and benefits from superannuation schemes—the employee contributions in wages and salaries in item (1), with the adjustment factor, item (12), accordingly changed to counterbalance the double-counting. The estimates also include a very small amount covering employers' compensation payments not subject to tax and thus not included in the wages, salaries and pension bills; see *Sources and Methods* ([B 85], p. 128) for further details. Those subject to tax are included. The items not subject to tax include payments under industrial injuries schemes and the 1968 Redundancy Payments Act.

2.3.5 *Annual Data—Income from Self-Employment —Professional Persons*

The data source for this group of incomes is the tax assessments under Cases I and II of Schedule D. These categories comprise the profits of profession or vocation, subject to income tax and not dealt with under any other income tax schedule. They relate solely to single-person or partnership businesses which depend on personal qualifications. A detailed account of the method of collecting the data and subsequent adjusting is given in *Sources and Methods* ([B 85], pp. 146–7). The main points to note are first that overall the CSO attaches less than usual reliability to these estimates, predicting a probable margin of error between 3 to 10%, with the errors for the two most recent years being the largest for the reasons outlined in the following paragraph. For further details on the concept of probable margins of error, see *Sources and Methods* ([B 85], pp. 39–41) and subsection 2.7.

The second point to note is that there is a long time lag in assessing Schedule D income, which means that for any given *Blue Book* the estimates for the last two years are only very provisional; based on special returns from Tax Inspectors to the Inland Revenue; and subject to revision in later years. A final note of importance is that all forms of income from self-employment are estimated before depreciation and stock appreciation.

2.3.6 *Annual Data—Income from Self-Employment —Farmers*

The income of farmers includes the profits and labour income of those working and/or owning farms. It also includes the profits of companies engaged in farming, which in turn are excluded from the profits of the company sector. However, very small farms and smallholdings are not included, their income forming part of that of item (vi), other sole traders and partnerships. Furthermore farm income does not include any rent income with respect to the ownership of buildings and property. This is included under rent income in the personal sector.

The figures in the *Blue Book* are derived from the estimates of farm income as given in the *Annual Review and Determination of Guarantees* [QRL 14], a White Paper published each year by the government and issued each spring in connection with farm prices and subsidies. The figures in the White Paper are in turn obtained from the Ministry of Agriculture, Fisheries and Food, the Northern Ireland Ministry of Agriculture and the Scottish Department for Agriculture and Fisheries. The data is on a financial year basis. Furthermore it excludes depreciation but includes interest payments on borrowed capital as a part of income. The CSO makes adjustments for these items, in order to maintain consistency with the definition of other self-employed incomes, before presentation in the *Blue Book* [QRL 37]. Again a detailed analysis is available in the *Sources and Methods* ([B 85], pp. 142–4).

2.3.7 *Annual Data—Income from Self-Employment —Other Sole Traders and Partnerships*

This group includes the income of all sole traders and partnerships which are assessed under Schedule D of the income tax laws other than professional persons and farmers. It includes in addition an estimate by the CSO for the income of small-holders, i.e. those working holdings of one acre and less. The main data source is the Schedule D returns of the Inland Revenue. For further details see *Sources and Methods* ([B 85], pp. 146–7).

2.3.8 *Annual Data—Rent, Net Interest and Dividends*

This item is initially estimated as a collective residual. The CSO firstly estimates the total rent, interest and actual dividend payments by all sectors of the economy. These include the rent payments imputed on to owner-occupiers and estimated actual rent payments by household tenants. Both of these since 1964 have been estimated by utilizing data from the *Family Expenditure Surveys* [QRL 28]. Prior to 1963 the Ministry of Labour *Household Expenditure Inquiry* for 1953–4 [QRL 46] and a Savings Survey enquiry for 1955 [QRL 1] were used and their figures projected forwards. For the period 1946 to 1955 the same figures were projected backwards. Estimates of the stock of dwellings were used as index for these backward projections.

The payments of interest and dividends are based on estimates made for the company, public and international sectors. They include payments by public corporations, and payments by companies of profits due abroad gross of UK tax. The international sector also provides data on property income from abroad, i.e. payments by the international sector.

Summing together all these payments the CSO then subtracts receipts by all the sectors other than the personal sector. The personal sector receipts are then assumed to be the residual. The reason for this procedure is that data exist for the receipts of the other sectors but not the personal sector. The personal sector receipts are finally usually subdivided into that accruing to life assurance and superannuation funds and to other receipts, the latter group being effectively the residual of a residual.

2.3.9 *Annual Data—Transfer Incomes (i) From the Public and Company Sector*

The transfer incomes in Table 2.1 are items (viii) and (ix). The former, charitable donations to charities from companies, are figures obtained from the Inland Revenue. They cover covenanted and uncovenanted contributions which are not allowed as business expenses. There are data that come to light from the company returns to Inland Revenue with respect to the assessment of companies to income tax and profits tax (prior to 1965/6) and corporation tax (since 1965/6).

The second group, item (ix), is National Insurance benefits and other current grants from the public authorities. It is a summation of the current grants to the personal sector as given in the current accounts of the central government and local authorities. These accounts are published in the *Blue Books* [QRL 37], separately in the accounts for the central and local authorities. A combined total also appears in the combined public sector accounts as grants to the personal sector. The items included in the separate accounts are:

(a) *Central Government*
- (1) Post-War Credits
- (2) Education
  - (a) Scholarships and maintenance allowances for students
  - (b) Grants to universities and colleges
  - (c) Grants to other private non-profit-making institutions
- (3) Social Security
  - (a) Child care
  - (b) Milk and welfare food schemes
  - (c) National Insurance pensions and benefits
  - (d) War pensions and service grants
  - (e) Family allowances and Family Income Supplements
  - (f) Supplementary Benefits (formerly National Assistance)
  - (g) Other non-contributory benefits
- (4) Employment and other services

(b) *Local Authorities*
- (1) Scholarships and grants to universities, colleges, etc.
- (2) School meals and milk
- (3) Other

Since and including the 1969 *Blue Book* [QRL 37] milk and welfare food schemes and school meals and milk have been excluded as income of the personal sector and attributed as direct expenditure of the public authorities. These and similar other expenditures were estimated at the net cost to the public authorities.

The basic source for all the above estimates are the actual annual payments made by each of the departments, ministries, etc. concerned. These are published in the various annual accounts of the departments. Because of the coding procedures adopted by the government accounting system and interdepartmental transactions the separate accounts bear little resemblance to the figures that appear in the national accounts. Hence there has to be a long process of re-coding into economic categories as above and consolidation. The complexities of the process are set out in *Sources and Methods* ([B 85], Ch. IX, pp. 288–95). Further details of the departments, etc. who provide the basic data are also listed in Chs IX, X and XI of *Sources and Methods* [B 85]. Nevertheless the final outcome is highly reliable figures largely based on actual payments.

There are however two possible sources of error. First, in all cases the accounting data refer always to the financial year. The conversion to the calendar year is made by reference to the quarterly returns of the departments, etc. It is naturally only an approximation. The second possible error relates to the figures for the latest year of each *Blue Book* [QRL 37]. These are published before the final actual payments are wholly known, hence an element of forecasting is included. This explains why this figure is usually revised the following year.

2.3.10 *Annual Data—Transfer Income (ii) Within the Personal Sector*

The relevant item appears in the figures for the 'categories' of personal income, Table 2.2 (op. cit.) item (11), namely pensions and benefits from life assurance and superannuation schemes. The basic sources for this information are the revenue accounts of the above schemes which are presented in each *Blue Book* [QRL 37]. These accounts are estimated from the same sources as employers' contributions to such schemes (see subsection 2.3.4) and as interest, dividends and rent receipts of the schemes (see subsection 2.3.8). Finally, the balancing adjustment of Table 2.2 also is clearly derived from these sources.

2.3.11 *Quarterly Data*

The *Monthly Digest of Statistics* [QRL 35] publishes figures of five categories of personal income. They are: wages and salaries; Forces' pay; employers' contributions; current grants from public authorities; and lastly other personal income (see subsection 2.2.2). A greater breakdown cannot be given, because as we shall see in many instances the estimates are interpolations of annual data.

The wages and salaries figures comprise two elements, cash payments and payments in kind. The quarterly estimates of the former have been available since 1954/5. Up to 1959/60 the estimates were based on a sample survey of deduction cards. Since, however, a considerable number of employers only provide pay figures on annual deduction cards this sample has been from the second quarter of 1960 replaced by a panel of employers who provide quarterly reports. Further since January 1963 considerable use has been made of the Department of Employment's monthly index of average earnings in manufacturing and some other industries, combined with estimates of total employment. The quarterly figures are naturally revised when the annual figures become available. (See *Sources and Methods* [B 85], pp. 119, 125–7, 144, 146–7 for further details.)

For wages and salaries paid in kind, there exist no quarterly data at all. The quarterly figures are interpolations and projections of the annual data. The same is done for other items of personal income. These are, employer contributions to superannuation schemes (which forms part of employers' contributions), farm income, income of professional persons and some, but only a small proportion, of the forms of income of 'other sole traders and partnerships'. These three latter groups form part of the 'other income' category. The quarterly estimates of sole traders and partnerships in manufacturing, construction, transport and communication and distributive trades assume that income moves in accordance with the index of manufacturing production, the value of building work completed, the index of output at constant prices for transport and communication, and the index of retail sales for the distributive trades. The basic source, Inland Revenue data, for these groups of income permits such a fine division of the annual totals.

Also included in the 'other personal income'

group, in addition to the above, are the current transfers to charities from companies and all rent, interest and dividend receipts including those of life assurance and superannuation funds. All of these items are also smooth interpolations and projections of annual estimates. In 1971 approximately 17% of the quarterly estimates of total personal incomes are by way of smooth interpolations and projections.

The remaining items are Forces' pay and employers' contributions to the National Insurance scheme. The data for the former are provided quarterly by the service departments. The quarterly figures for employer National Insurance contributions are provided by the Government Actuary's department. Finally the estimates of employers' contributions also include a small item relating to employers' compensation payments which are not subject to tax. Some of these payments are again interpolated for quarterly figures, other than those paid under the Redundancy Payments Act where quarterly figures are provided by the Department of Employment.

In conclusion it would not be unfair to state that the quarterly estimates are much less reliable *in toto* than the annual figures.

2.4 Personal Disposable and Real Disposable Income

2.4.1 *Personal Disposable Income*

Annual figures on disposable personal income are published in each *Blue Book* as a footnote to the income and expenditure account. Seasonally adjusted quarterly figures appear in the *Monthly Digest of Statistics* [QRL 35] and *Economic Trends* [QRL 20] as part of the table on personal income, expenditure and saving. The *Monthly Digest of Statistics* [QRL 35] also publishes the unadjusted figures. Similar data, covering a greater span of years, appear in each October issue of *Economic Trends* [QRL 20] (see subsection 2.2.2).

Disposable income in these tables is defined as aggregate personal income less actual payments by the personal sector of United Kingdom taxes on income, all National Insurance contributions by employees, employers, self-employed and non-employed persons and finally net transfers of personal income overseas and taxes paid abroad. Additions to tax reserves are not deducted.

Taxes on income paid by the personal sector almost entirely comprise income tax and surtax which since 1973/4 have been replaced by the new Unified Tax System. This includes income tax deducted at source from income paid by the company, public corporation and government to individuals and the tax on the investment income of life assurance and superannuation schemes. Since the introduction of corporation tax in 1966 the personal sector is now the main source for income tax and virtually all surtax receipts. Though largely income and surtax, occasionally other categories of direct taxation creep in as a result of the UK's highly complex tax system. For instance, the estimates for the years immediately after the Second World War include small amounts of profits tax and excess profit tax paid by sole traders and partnerships, and right up to 1966 some profits tax payments paid by farmers and Lloyd's underwriters (which are part of the personal sector). The figures, however, do not include the payments of income tax on short-term capital gains, introduced in 1964 and charged under Schedule D of the Income Tax Code. The CSO considers this to be a capital transaction, arising from the basic concept adopted in the UK national accounting system that capital gains are not a part of income since they have no corresponding output flow. As we shall argue later (see subsection 2.8), this approach may not always be desirable with regard to the 'use' of personal income statistics.

The estimates of the income tax paid by the personal sector are provided by the Inland Revenue. Since the introduction of corporation tax in 1966 they are predominantly based on the financial and calendar year net receipts by the Inland Revenue for income tax and surtax. The financial year figures were formerly published in the annual reports of HM Commissioners of the Inland Revenue [QRL 48] and since 1972 in the annual *Inland Revenue Statistics* [QRL 31]. Aggregate calendar year figures appear in *Financial Statistics* [QRL 29] and the *Monthly Digest of Statistics* [QRL 35]. The figures refer to actual payments of income tax and surtax and do not include an estimate made of the tax due on the annual income of the personal sector. This can differ from actual payments because of assessment, etc. delays. However an estimate is published in the *Blue Books* [QRL 37] of the difference between tax accruals and payments and referred to as an addition to tax reserves. It is not however deducted in the estimates of disposable income.

In those years before 1966 the procedure for estimating the income tax paid by individuals was more complicated, by virtue of the fact that income tax at standard rate was also payable on profits in addition to profits tax. This required the Inland Revenue to estimate the income tax payments by companies and public corporations. The former were made by reference to Schedule D and profits tax returns and the latter by reference to annual published accounts. For further details see the first *Sources and Methods* ([B 88], pp. 63, 166 and 174). The recent *Sources and Methods* [B 85] contains also a detailed account of the procedure used in allocating income tax receipts to companies (see [B 85], pp. 211–14). The quarterly estimates of income tax payments are also made by the Inland Revenue. The Inland Revenue has figures on the weekly receipts of PAYE tax and monthly figures for all the other main schedules of tax.

The other major deductions to arrive at disposable income are the National Insurance contributions by employees, employers, self-employed and non-employed persons. The annual figures are obtained from the annual current account of the National Insurance Funds. The quarterly returns are estimated by the Government Actuary.

The two remaining small items are net transfer payments abroad and taxes paid abroad. The former are taken directly from the balance of payments accounts and the latter estimated by the Inland Revenue with reference to information on relief given against UK income tax under the double taxation agreements. The balance of payments accounts use Exchange Control records for transfers with the non-sterling area and proxy indicators, such as the number of migrants and other countries' balance of payments data for estimates within the sterling area. The non-sterling area transfers are reckoned to be substantially complete but those for the sterling area only very approximate. A detailed definition of the items involved is given in *Sources and Methods* ([B 85], p. 447).

Quarterly data are available for net transfer payments, based on Exchange Control records. However, the quarterly information is not available for taxes paid abroad. These are therefore grouped with the net transfers for the quarterly estimates after simple interpolation.

2.4.2 *Real Disposable Income*

Annual and quarterly data are published in the *Monthly Digest of Statistics* [QRL 35] and *Economic Trends* [QRL 20]. They are simply the current price estimates of disposable income revalued by the implied consumers' expenditure deflator. There are no published statistics on real aggregate personal income or the real values of the various items of personal income.

An important conceptual issue, with equally important practical implications, arises with respect to the meaning and definition of real personal disposable income. If it is accepted that changes in the real value of a flow of disposable income between any two given periods of time are simply the changes in the quantity of a standard bundle of consumer goods that potentially could be purchased, assuming zero saving, then the current method of measuring real income is quite acceptable. Supporters of this definition could further argue that the price of saving is no more than the real value of consumption forgone or postponed so that the zero saving assumption is essentially irrelevant to the justification of the procedure.

On the other hand if it were argued that the price of saving was not current consumption forgone or postponed, but something else, then the zero saving assumption could be conceptually crucial. For instance it might be argued that in the context of the present time period savings are used to purchase assets and it is the price of assets which is relevant rather than that of consumer goods in deriving the overall price of saving. Hence on this basis the appropriate deflator to obtain real disposable income should include, appropriately weighted, the price of assets. This approach attaches to saving a greater significance than simply income which could have been spent. Moreover if this approach is accepted, then it must be concluded that current procedure adopted to estimate real disposable income is biased towards consumption *vis-à-vis* saving.

The important practical issue in this approach is the measurement of a general price level for assets. Economic theory simplifies the problem a little by allowing the price of assets to be interpreted as the reciprocal of their rate of interest or yield. Thus a solution may be to construct a general index of interest rates on a similar basis to the Retail Price Index. The two indices could then be combined, weighting them by the current savings and consumption ratios respectively, to produce a 'Purchasing Power' Index which could be used as the deflator to derive real disposable income. The major obstacle in this procedure would be the choice of weights for the different types of assets purchased by the personal sector. This is a problem that cannot be considered in detail in this work. Nevertheless the above reasoning emphasizes that the current procedure for measuring real disposable income could be open to a fundamental criticism, over and above the familiar criticisms levied at any indexing process such as changes in the structure of purchases, new commodities, changes in quality and so forth (see Abraham [B 3] for details).

2.5 Northern Irish Data

Northern Ireland is at the moment the only region of the United Kingdom which produces estimates of aggregate personal income. They are presented in the *Northern Ireland Digest of Statistics* [QRL 18] which is published at six-month intervals. The estimates differ in presentation from those for the United Kingdom. First they are for financial as opposed to calendar years, extending back to 1951–2. Secondly the various components of personal income are grouped into four categories, namely income from employment, income from self-employment, current grants from public authorities and finally rent, interest and dividends.

The *Northern Ireland Digest of Statistics* [QRL 18] does not publish details of how the statistics contained therein are compiled. However the Department of Finance of the Government of Northern Ireland, which undertakes the estimation of the province's total personal income, kindly supplied a detailed description of the estimation. We quote liberally from this description.

The method of estimation can be summarized as follows:

1. Schedule E PAYE Incomes
2. − Agricultural Schedule E Income
3. Schedule E (excluding Agriculture) adjusted
4. + Agricultural Income (Department of Agriculture)
5. + Schedule E Tax Evasion
6. + Imperial Civil Servants' Income
7. + HM Armed Forces' Income
8. + Employers' National Insurance Contributions
9. + Employers' Contributions to Private Schemes
10. + Under Tax Limit Income

A = TOTAL CASH INCOME FROM EMPLOYMENT

11. Agricultural Workers' Perquisites
12. + Imputed Rent of Rent-Free Households
13. + Housekeepers' Income
14. + Net cost to Employers of Meal Vouchers, etc.
15. + Imputed Income of Owner-Occupation

B = TOTAL IMPUTED INCOME AND INCOME IN KIND

A + B = C TOTAL INCOME FROM EMPLOYMENT

16. Schedule D Income—Individuals
17. + Schedule D Income—Firms
18. − Schedule D Agricultural Income
19. + Agricultural Income (Department of Agriculture)
20. + Tax Evasion
21. − Excess Rent

D = TOTAL INCOME FROM SELF-EMPLOYMENT

22. Public Sector Current Grants to Persons and Private Bodies
23. + United Kingdom War Pensions
24. + Post-War Credits

E = NATIONAL INSURANCE AND OTHER CURRENT GRANTS FROM PUBLIC AUTHORITIES

F = RENT, DIVIDENDS AND NET INTEREST

C + D + E + F = G = PERSONAL INCOME

Item 1. Schedule E PAYE incomes are obtained from the Inland Revenue. They are adjusted to include Northern Irish employees paid at pay points in Great Britain and to include Schedule E tax evasion (item 5). A separate estimate is made for Schedule E agricultural income (item 4), and it is supplied by the Northern Ireland Department of Agriculture and is to be found in the agricultural statistics published in the *Digest of Statistics* [QRL 18]. Items 6 and 7 represent the incomes of government employees in Northern Ireland but paid by the United Kingdom Treasury. The calculations are based on employment and earnings supplied by the Civil Service Department in London and the Registrar General's Office in London.

Employers' National Insurance contributions, item 8, are obtained from the Northern Ireland Department of Health and Social Security, whilst contributions to private schemes, item 9, are based on projections from the 1968 *Northern Ireland Labour Cost Survey* [QRL 23] and the national income *Blue Books* [QRL 37]. Item 10 is based on the number of tax deduction cards returned by employers for employees whose earnings are below the exemption limit. Employers are not required to do this, but many of the larger firms in fact do.

The main item in section B is the imputed income of owner-occupation, item 15. This is calculated from the *Northern Ireland Family Expenditure Survey* [QRL 43] as is item 12, the imputed rent of rent-free households. The other items in this sub-group are separately estimated. The Northern Ireland Department of Agriculture provides the figures for item 11. Item 13, housekeepers' income, is based on the number of tax allowances granted to persons who have resident housekeepers multiplied by a guessed imputed income paid to housekeepers. The 1968 *Northern Ireland Labour Cost Survey* [QRL 23] in conjunction with the Retail Price Index is used to give an estimate of the net cost to employers of meal vouchers, etc. item 14.

Apart from agricultural income, the income in section D, self-employed income, is based on Schedule D returns for individuals and firms, from the Inland Revenue. The agricultural figures are provided by the Department of Agriculture. The tax evasion factor, item 20, is calculated adopting the evasion ratios used by the Central Statistical Office in London for the United Kingdom data. The total is reduced by the payment for excess rent, item 21, based on data from the Inland Revenue.

Figures for Public Sector Current Grants to Persons and Private Bodies in section E are derived from the various central and local government accounts. The main proportion, social security benefits, is provided by the Northern Ireland Department of Health and Social Security. Finally, since there is no possible means of directly estimating rents, dividends and interest for Northern Ireland, these factor incomes are thus based on a percentage of the United Kingdom estimate.

There is no doubt that the Northern Ireland Department of Finance is to be congratulated for its courage and ingenuity in making these estimates. The estimates are probably quite reliable. The data in section E are very reliable, whilst much of that in sections A and D is derived from Inland Revenue material. In 1968–9, £615m out of a total personal income of £748m was calculated from the standard data of the Inland Revenue and other government departments. The major sources of error clearly arise with regard to rent, interest and dividend income, incomes below the tax limit and the calculations of under-reporting due to tax evasion. Tax evasion in Northern Ireland is likely to be higher than in the rest of the UK due to the increased opportunities afforded by economic transactions with the Republic of Ireland.

Nevertheless, in spite of these difficulties, it is a pity that the other countries of the United Kingdom have not attempted similar estimates. The *Scottish Abstract of Statistics* [QRL 64] and its forerunner, the *Digest of Scottish Statistics* [QRL 17], and the *Digest of Welsh Statistics* [QRL 19] do provide extensive data on social security incomes (see subsection 4.2.7). They also produce regional data on earnings from the various national earnings surveys (see subsection 3.6), as also does the *Northern Ireland Digest of Statistics* [QRL 18]. There is, however, no clear reason why the Scottish and Welsh Offices could not produce data similar to those for Northern Ireland. Practically all government departments treat Scotland as a separate accounting entity and the Inland Revenue and the Department of Health and Social Security do provide separate estimates for Wales, though the Departments of Agriculture and Fisheries and Education do not.

2.6 Historical Data

2.6.1 *Official Data—1938–45*

The intense interest generated in the 1930s by Keynes with respect to National Income Theory, coupled with the pioneering studies of Bowley and Stamp [B 14] and Clarke [B 21], culminated in the first official estimates of National Income for 1938 and 1940, published in a 1941 White Paper entitled *An Analysis of the Sources of War Finance and An Estimate of the National Income and Expenditure in 1938 and 1940* [QRL 12].

This publication broadly adopted the concepts and definitions used today and briefly summarized in the previous sections of this chapter. It contained data on the personal sector, which included charities, life insurance companies, etc. as at present, though the title of the data confusingly varied between private income and personal expenditure and savings. Estimates were published for wages, salaries, pay and allowances of the Armed Forces, rents, profits and interest and social security and other transfer incomes. There were also figures for disposable private income. Wages and salaries included income in kind, employee contributions to National Insurance and superannuation, etc. funds, plus employer contributions to the latter but not to the former. Employers' National Insurance contributions were in those days considered an indirect tax. However this figure can be readily obtained from the Revenue Account of the National Insurance Funds, reproduced in the White Paper.

The rent incomes were based on the Inland Revenue Schedule A tax returns, plus an allowance for rent incomes below the effective exemption limit and after deduction for maintenance and repair. They inevitably included rent incomes, both imputed and real, of the company sector. Similarly the estimates of profits and interest, assumed that all profit income belonged to the (private) personal sector, whether distributed or not, hence this item included not only professional incomes, farm incomes and national debt interest but also all company profits. Both of these groups of income are computed after an allowance for depreciation, which is of course contrary to the current practice. The transfer incomes comprised old age pensions, contributory pensions, supplementary pensions, family allowances and gifts and donations from the Ministry of Food and the National Milk Scheme, etc. Unemployment insurance relief, and allowances were also included but not grants to universities. Furthermore, there were no data on net transfers of income abroad from the personal sector, and the UK tax payments also included payments of capital taxes. This latter item, however, was usually shown separately and can readily be deducted to conform with current practice.

It is generally stated that the estimates for 1938 were reasonably sound, but still crudely done in comparison to the data and sources available today. The Central Statistical Office, which made the estimates, quite specifically announced that the estimates were drawn up from information collected by various government departments and private organizations for purposes other than the preparation of estimates of national income. For 1938 they also had the benefit of the first *Inland Revenue Survey of Personal Incomes for 1937/38* [QRL 51]. The 1940 figures are usually assumed less reliable, resulting from an unavoidable break in figures between 1938 and those for 1940 due to the war, especially with respect to figures for public authorities.

Similar White Papers were published in April of each year up to and including 1945. They formed part of the Budget information. Estimates were also subsequently produced for 1939. Though the figures for the war years were consistent with each other, they were never really comparable with those for 1938 and in themselves were always subject to much variation. In April 1946 the name of the White Paper was changed to *National Income and Expenditure of the United Kingdom 1938–1945* [QRL 39]. The format and procedures however were not changed. The first significant development appeared in the 1948 National Income White Paper [B 86] when the private sector was subdivided into the private corporate sector and the personal sector. The profit, interest and rent income of the personal sector was accordingly revised for all previous years and the tables for aggregate personal income resembled those used today. By 1950 [B 87], after further revisions and changes of definitions, the National Income White Papers were almost identical to the present *Blue Books*, mainly differing in that employers' contributions to National Insurance were still treated as an indirect tax and adjustments for the addition of depreciation and stock appreciation to self-employment income were not made. In 1951 the CSO published a *Statistical Digest of the War* ([QRL 67], T181) which reproduced estimates of national income, including the Revenue Account of the Persons (Personal Income), using the definition of the 1950 White Paper, for the years 1938 through to 1945.

2.6.2 *Official Data—1946 to date*

The ever-growing complexity of estimation and the changing concepts of National Income accounting led the authorities to conclude that to encompass the estimates as part of the budget literature was no longer feasible. Therefore in 1952 the White Papers were supplemented by the now familiar *Blue Books*.

This first *Blue Book* contained a summary table of personal income and expenditure for the years 1946 to 1951. The definitions were almost identical with those currently adopted. The main difference was the exclusion of depreciation and stock appreciation from self-employment income. However these items were incorporated in the 1953 *Blue Book* with adjustments back-dated to 1946. The only other item missing was current transfers to charities from companies. This did not appear until the 1957 *Blue Book* at which point estimates were made back to 1954. The pattern of presentation in the 1952 edition has remained largely intact. The personal sector income and expenditure account always appears in the summary tables in Section 1. In addition there is a section on the Personal Sector providing data on distribution (see subsection 3.3), the capital account, expenditure and since 1954 we have had the Categories of Personal Income table (see Table 2.2, subsection 2.2.1).

Each annual *Blue Book* provides data up to and including the previous year. The extent of the backrun of years provided in each *Blue Book* however has varied considerably, much to the annoyance of users. Recent practice, since the 1969 *Blue Book*, has been to provide a twenty-two-year backrun with respect to the personal income and expenditure account in the summary tables and a ten-year series for the tables in the personal sector section. The extent of the backrun appears to be solely determined by the number of columns that can be fitted into a double page for the former and a single page for the latter category. Prior to 1969 the practice was for eight to eleven-year backruns for the tables in the Personal Sector section other than for Income Distributions (see subsection 3.3) and eleven-year runs in the summary tables except in the very first two *Blue Books*. The first four *Blue Books* only provided data for 1946 onwards though from 1955 to 1967 revised and redefined data were also published for 1938. Finally each year the estimates of previous years are subject to revision as new and better information, techniques, etc. become available. Purely from a user's point of view it would be of great value if the Central Statistical Office every five or ten years were to publish complete revised backruns of National Income statistics in the *Blue Book*, incorporating quarterly data where feasible and wartime data.

The present series of quarterly figures first appeared as a regular series in the 1960 editions of the *Monthly Digest of Statistics* [QRL 35] and the series both adjusted and unadjusted extended back to 1955. The January 1958 edition of *Economic Trends* [QRL 20] also has published unadjusted figures for 1954. These estimates again are subject to constant revision.

2.6.3 *C. H. Feinstein's Data*

The definitive work on National Income and Expenditure is surely that published in 1972 as the sixth and last in a series of volumes on *Studies in the National Income and Expenditure of the United Kingdom* under the general editorship of Richard Stone. Volume 6, entitled *National Income, Expenditure and Output of the United Kingdom, 1855–1965* by C. H. Feinstein [QRL 2] marks the end of thirty years' work and must be regarded as one of the most monumental pieces of research ever undertaken on the United Kingdom economy. The extensiveness of the research is aptly summed by Professor Prest in his review [B 47]: 'It would be rash to predict that no improvements will be made to any of the figures in, say, the next twenty years but at least one can say that strongly diminishing returns are likely to characterise further efforts in this, by now, very well-tilled area.'

Feinstein presents annual data in his Table 10 on aggregate personal income, as currently defined, for the period 1920 to 1965, excepting 1939–45. The data are subdivided into the following categories:

(1) Income from employment, including National Insurance and Health contributions
(2) Income from self-employment, including National Insurance and Health contributions
(3) Rent, dividends and net interest
(4) Current grants from public authorities
(5) Transfers abroad (net) and taxes paid abroad
(6) Current transfers to charities from companies (from 1954 only)

There are also data on direct taxes on income, additions to tax reserves, National Insurance and Health contributions so that a continuous estimate for personal disposable income from 1920 is also available. In addition data are available on income from employment from 1855 ([QRL 2], Table 21, p. T54), and farm incomes from 1855 ([QRL 2], Table 23, p. T60). In the following sections we give a very brief outline of Feinstein's sources and methods, with respect to his data on personal income. We omit however any discussion on the 1946–65 data which is simply drawn from the *Blue Books*.

2.6.4 *Unofficial Data—1939–45*

Feinstein's summary table on personal income does not contain any estimates for this period. However his detailed tables on income from employment (T21), farmers' income (T23) and the summary table on factor incomes in GNP (T1) do contain figures. Both series are largely based on, but not wholly derived from, the CSO *Statistical Digest of the War* [QRL 67]. For instance, the employment income series from this source is adjusted, by the addition of employers' National Insurance contributions. These data were obtained from the 1947 White Paper [QRL 40].

The adjustments to income from self-employment are somewhat more complex. For non-farm self-employment income the *Statistical Digest* [QRL 67] figures are used after minor adjustments to include depreciation and the rent of owner-occupied property. The depreciation estimates were interpolations of the 1939 and 1945 figures ([QRL 2], p. 42). For farm income, Feinstein adopts an entirely different method. He interpolates the official 1939 figure given in the *Annual Abstract of Statistics* ([QRL 13], 1961, No. 98) and the 1948 CSO estimate. The basis of his interpolation is J. R. Bellerby's article [B 10] on agricultural income. Again minor modifications are made to include depreciation in the official estimates. Feinstein's wartime series for self-employment incomes varies between 7 to 12% higher than those in the *Statistical Digest*. Most of this variation can be attributed to the adjustments for depreciation.

With regard to the other items of personal income Feinstein provides little data. There are data on transfer incomes from the public sector. These comprise central government and National Insurance benefits and the education and poor relief given by the local authorities. The data are shown in Feinstein's Tables 12 and 13 respectively. His sources for the above figures were: first for the central government transfers, the *Statistical Digest of the War* [QRL 67] with adjustment for grants to universities which were omitted from the official data, and, secondly, for the local authorities, estimates by Peacock and Wiseman ([B 46], p. 205) were adopted.

Feinstein does not, however, accept the *Statistical Digest of the War* estimates ([QRL 67], T181) for rent, dividend and interest income for the personal sector. With this vital link missing he is thus unable to compute a series for aggregate personal income for the war years. His reasons for not accepting the *Statistical Digest* estimates were twofold. First there were only data on constituent components for 1938 and 1946 and the substantial changes in the proportions of these components negated the possibility of extrapolating for the intervening years. Secondly the different definitions used in the above estimates and those subsequently published in the *Blue Books* for 1938 and 1946 onwards indicated a marginal effect on the overall aggregate total. Further to this there was no satisfactory means of adjusting for comparability.

Feinstein does not provide any figures of disposable income for the war years. Assuming for the moment that we had estimated total personal income then to estimate disposable personal income we would have to subtract actual UK income tax paid, all National Insurance contributions and net transfers of income abroad including taxes paid abroad. The first two items are readily available, the former from the Revenue Account of Persons in the *Statistical Digest of the War* ([QRL 67], T181) and the latter from Feinstein's Table 12. The other items are also estimated by Feinstein for his Table 15 on International Transactions but are not published as separate series (see pp. 112–13 of Feinstein [QRL 2] for details of the method of estimating).

It follows from our discussion that the bulk of figures necessary for a wartime series do exist, albeit in some instances unreliable, and it is a pity that such a series was not attempted by Feinstein or the CSO.

2.6.5 *Unofficial Data—1920–38*

Feinstein's Table 10 publishes estimates on total personal and personal disposable income for this period. The estimates of income from employment in this period are essentially improvements of the early pioneering estimates of A. L. Chapman [B 18] for wages and salaries and A. L. Bowley's and Sir Josiah Stamp's National Income figures for 1924 [B 14]. A considerable use is made of the censuses of production for 1924, 1930, 1935, the population censuses of 1921 and 1931 and the unemployment statistics which then were published regularly in the Ministry of Labour *Gazette* [QRL 21]. Feinstein also utilizes the eleven Ministry of Labour enquiries into earnings which were made during this period. The income from employment figures are thus reasonably reliable (see [QRL 2], Ch. 2:1 for further details).

The same can also be said for income from self-employment and the figures for rent, interest and dividends. The latter were estimated as at present, by the residual technique, allocating to the personal sector that of all income of this nature which cannot be allocated to other sectors. Given that the reliability of unofficial GNP figures for aggregate rent, interest and dividend figures was not much less than today and that the allocation to all other sectors was likewise, then this technique is quite acceptable. With respect to income from self-employment, that of farm incomes was for the period 1923–38 an extrapolation of the 1938 figure, using Bellerby's series [B 10] and the 1920–22 estimates were based on data from Ojala [B 44] (see Feinstein [QRL 2], Ch. 2:2, p. 40 for further details). Non-farm self-employment incomes were built up in a very complex manner. Broadly, much unpublished material from the Inland Revenue was made available to Feinstein who used it extensively. In addition he made allowances for evasion, fraud and incomes below the exemption limit. The procedure followed closely that which he adopted for estimating all company profits for the period ([QRL 2], pp. 129–47 for further details).

National Insurance and Health contributions for the period were readily obtained from the *National Health and Insurance Accounts* [B 67, B 68, B 69]. Similarly grants to persons from the public sector were largely obtained from government accounts, including the accounts of the National Insurance Funds, the *Local Government Financial Statistics* [B 83, B 70], the *Annual Reports of the Scottish Department of Health* [B 72] and the *Local Taxation Returns for Northern Ireland* [B 84]. The only unofficial source utilized was the scholarship figures in Peacock and Wiseman ([B 46], p. 205).

The two remaining series in Table 10 of Feinstein's work are taxes on income and net transfers of income abroad. The former are calculated from Inland Revenue data ([QRL 2], subsection 2:5, for further details) whilst the latter was essentially an extrapolation of the 1938 estimates using Board of Trade figures on investment income from abroad and some Inland Revenue figures as proxies (see [QRL 2], Chs 6:3 and 6:5 for further details).

2.6.6 *Unofficial Data—pre 1920*

There are no complete data for aggregate personal income prior to 1920. However Feinstein does give estimates for some of the items comprising personal income for these earlier periods. The series that are available are: from 1855, wages and salaries (Table 21) and farmers' income (Table 23); from 1900 Forces' pay in kind and cash; from 1912 Employers' National Insurance and Health contributions. These series all include figures for the First World War years. Details of the estimation procedures and sources, which are complex and ingenious, are given in Chapter 2 of Feinstein's book. It hardly needs emphasizing that the degree of reliability is nowhere near modern standards.

2.7 Reliability

It is natural that the users of personal income statistics would wish some indication as to the 'soundness' and reliability of the data they wish to use. One method of evaluation might be to compare estimates of the same item produced from independent sources. This technique is quite feasible for the pre-1938 period when there existed no official figures but a number of unofficial estimates. The first two chapters of Feinstein [QRL 2] contain such detailed comparisons relevant to personal income statistics.

However since 1938 there has, in the main, only been official data. As a result the Central Statistical Office has developed a system of grading statistical series in order to give some indication of reliability. These grades are subjective guesses by the estimator; to quote from the *Sources and Methods* ([B 85], p. 40): 'They may be taken to mean that, in the opinion of the estimators and in their present state of knowledge, there is, say, a 90 per cent chance that the true value of the figures referred to lies within the limits set by the gradings.' The present state of knowledge is the key factor. Ever-increasing knowledge may well mean that figures previously considered highly reliable could be subject to revision. This is not to say however that all revisions result from increasing knowledge. Changes in definition are frequently the cause of revision. There is also the possibility of arithmetic errors, allocating errors, etc. in compiling. These only come to light after checking. It must also be emphasized that the lags caused by data compilation, etc. mean that the most recent year figures in the *Blue Book* are less reliable and always subject to subsequent revision.

At present the CSO adopts three reliability gradings, namely:

grade A = less than 3% margin of error
grade B = 3 to 10% margin of error
grade C = more than 10%

There is no doubt that in the absence of perfect knowledge this is the only method of evaluating macro statistical series. Those who have collected, compiled and manipulated statistics, often searching tediously for sources, proxies and the like will readily testify that an 'intuition' for reliability is developed. Such 'intuitions' cannot usually be explained or described. They are not dissimilar to the 'intuitions' that engineers, chemists or other pure scientists experience. In any field of study or analysis there will always be room for intuition and experience.

The reliability grading system used by the CSO was also adopted by Feinstein to evaluate his historical series. In fact he extended the grades and changed the limits slightly. The grades used by Feinstein were:

grade A = 5% margin of error
grade B = 5 to 15% margin of error
grade C = 15 to 25% margin of error
grade D = more than 25% margin of error

In Table 2.3 below we have attempted as far as possible to attach reliability gradings to the items of aggregate personal income. The two sources for our gradings have been the CSO's *Sources and Methods* [B 85] and C. H. Feinstein's *National Income and Expenditure* [QRL 2]. The only assumption that has been made is that with the exception of the First World War periods, figures derived from the accounts of government bodies will rate a grade A reliability. This in keeping with the reliability gradings of our two sources with respect to government current expenditure and National Insurance and Health contributions. The gradings adopted are:

	Margin of error:
Grade A*	= less than 3%
A	= less than 5%
B*	= 3 to 10%
B	= 5 to 15%
C	= 15 to 25%
D	= more than 25%

Table 2.3 Reliability Grades

Years	*Income from Employment* Forces Pay and Wages	Salaries	Employer National Insurance Contributions	Other Contri-butions	*Income from Self-Employment* Farm	Non-farm	Rent, Dividends and Interest	Transfers from the Public Sector	Taxes on Income
1855–66[1]	C	D	–	–	D	–	–	–	
1867–79[1]	C	D	–	–	C	–	–	–	
1880–9[1]	B	C	–	–	C	–	–	–	
1890–1914[1]	B	C	–	–	C	C	–	–	
1915–19[1]	C	C	B	–	D	–	–	B	
1920–3[1]	B	B	A	–	C	C	B	A	A
1924–6[1]	A	A	A	–	C	C	B	A	A
1927–38[1]	A	A	A	–	B	B	B	A	A
1939–45[2]	B	B	A	–	B	C	B	A	A
1946–[3]	A*	A*	A*	B*	B*	B*	B*	A*	A*

Notes: 1. Feinstein's data [QRL 2]; 2. Digest of War Statistics [QRL 67]; 3. 'Blue Book' data [QRL 37].

2.8 Critical Evaluations

The ideal definitions of a variable and the value of the consequent measurement approximation vary according to the particular aspect of economic or other analysis which is being served. Though there may be many minor uses for National Income statistics incorporating personal incomes, there are only two broad major uses relevant to aggregate personal income statistics. These are, first, the requirements of macro-economic analysis, particularly with respect to consumption function studies and sector income flows and, secondly, the requirements of the applied welfare analysts who want data relevant to living standards and the like. We shall consider each of these requirements in turn.

2.8.1 *Macro-economic Analysis—Aggregate Household Income*

In macro-economic theory the personal sector refers specifically to households. It is the economic activity of households that is relevant to National Income determination, multiplier and consumption function theory. Furthermore the income flow into the household sector is usually defined to comprise factor incomes from employment, transfer incomes from other sectors and income from the ownership of capital, all received by households or persons living in institutions. In these respects the UK definition of personal income to date has not been perfect. First it includes the income of charities, churches, trades unions and other non-profit-making bodies serving persons, universities and colleges, and the property income of life insurance companies and superannuation funds. However, it does not include the companies which administer these funds. Secondly it also includes all the income of unincorporated businesses which in turn will include depreciation, stock appreciation and an undistributed net profit element, which rightfully should be placed in the production or company sector, especially that of income of agricultural companies which is still placed in the personal sector accounts.

This unsatisfactory definition of the personal sector has received some considered attention by the Central Statistical Office, and a recent article by John Moyle and David J. Reid in *Economic Trends* [QRL 9] has produced the first semi-official estimates of aggregate household income as opposed to personal income. The estimates are for the years 1966 to 1972 inclusive. There is no indication given in the article whether these estimates are to be produced regularly or not, though they have been reproduced in the 1964–74 *Blue Book* [QRL 38]. The authors emphasize that the estimates are tentative. Nevertheless they give an insight into the difference between the official definition of personal income and that required by macro-economists.

The items of personal income which are not household income and which Moyle and Reid extract from the personal sector and put in an all-embracing residual sector are:

(i) the income of life assurance and superannuation funds;
(ii) the income of charities, universities and other non-profit-making bodies;
(iii) the undistributed income of unincorporated businesses and agricultural companies, including stock appreciation and depreciation.

Let us consider each of these categories in turn. The procedure with respect to netting out life assurance, etc. funds is to subtract employers' (but not employees') contributions and the property income of such schemes. The pensions and benefits of the schemes on the other hand are included and the employee contributions enter the expenditure side of the current account of the new household sector. These changes effectively take care of the criticisms of the presentation of personal sector accounts which we referred to in subsection 2.2.1. In the 1970 estimates by Moyle and Reid this procedure led to £607m being subtracted from total personal income, i.e. 1·4% of the original total. It could be argued that the property income of the life assurance companies and superannuation funds theoretically ought to be part of household income, inasmuch as it represents future bonuses on life policies, pensions, annuities, etc. Similar logic however could be applied and has been applied in the past to some income distribution studies (see Section 3) with respect to the relationship between undistributed company profits and dividends. Apart from the necessity for consistency, it could be argued that most macro-economic theory refers entirely to income actually received by households or over which they can exercise a high degree of command. This is certainly not so in this case.

The second group of non-household incomes presented Moyle and Reid with numerous estimation problems. The present practice in the National Accounts is to approximate the income of non-profit-making bodies (NPBs) as transfers received currently from the public and company sectors plus wages and salaries paid by the NPBs to households. The property income of the NPBs is brought in by the 'residual' method of computing this item for the personal sector as a whole (see subsection 2.3.8). Thus to separate the NPBs from households required the compilation of a balance sheet for the NPBs where current income comprises transfers from companies, households and the public sector; rent, interest and dividends; and the trading surplus. The expenditure side of the account in turn would comprise wages and salaries paid to households, transfers to households, transfers to other sectors and expenditure on goods and services. The present personal sector accounts are adjusted first by subtracting all the income items of the NPBs, other than transfers from households, which in fact accounted for approximately 40% of total income. These naturally remain as household income, and are entered in the accounts as part of household expenditure. The second step then adds in the transfers from the NPBs to households, but not the wages and salaries paid out as these are already included. There is also a minor change made to the data on consumer expenditure by households to allow for expenditure on these items by NPBs. The overall outcome for 1970 was a reduction in aggregate 'personal' income by £581m, i.e. by 1·3%.

To compile the above balance sheet the authors divided the NPBs into five categories, universities and colleges, trades unions, friendly societies, housing associations and finally charities and other NPBs. Over 70% of their collective income was accounted for by the last group. The data sources for the first four groups were good and presented few problems. The final group did present problems and necessitated a survey for 1970 of 568 major charities. The results of the survey and that for the whole NPB area fared well in a number of consistency checks against independently estimated control totals already used in estimating the *Blue Book* data. However the survey meant that 1970 became a benchmark for this group and the figures for the other years in the series are extrapolations.

The final group—the undistributed profit factor (including depreciation, etc.) of unincorporated business and so on—was estimated by 'deducting from income from self-employment those costs that might be regarded as necessarily incurred in order to maintain the business in its pre-existing state' ([QRL 9], p. 86). These items were defined as capital consumption, stock appreciation and untaxed interest charges. They amounted to £653m in 1970, that is 1·5% of aggregate personal income. The 1964–74 *Blue Book* [QRL 38] gave a total of £2518 m, i.e. 3·4% of aggregate personal income.

Bringing together all the deductions the overall effect of the authors' calculations in 1970 was that the income of households, persons living in institutions and private trusts amounted to approximately 96% of aggregate personal income as officially defined.

The above estimates can be viewed as overestimates of household aggregate incomes. There are still two further elements that should be taken out and put in the residual sector. These are the undistributed income of private trusts and the undistributed net profits of unincorporated companies after depreciation and stock appreciation. Unfortunately there are very little data on both these items. An estimate of the undistributed net profit element was made by L. R. Klein [B 38] from the 1953/4 Oxford Savings Survey. A very approximate assumption to make might be that it averages at the same rate as the company sector, namely 36% of all company income in 1970 using *Blue Book* data, though Klein's estimates would indicate a figure at least double this size. On this basis we would conclude that a further £1,318m (i.e. 3·6%) of total personal income was not household income, giving an overall total in the order of 7 to 8%. It is impossible to hazard even a guess at the undistrubuted income of private trusts in 1970.

Two important points arise from these estimates. First they imply that the propensity to save magnitudes, currently published in the *Blue Book*, are not an accurate reflection of household behaviour and hence may be quite unsuitable for consumption function studies. This point can be illustrated by the figures presented in Table 2.4. In this table we compare five savings ratios. The first is that for the personal sector as officially defined; the second for the household sector as estimated by Moyle and Reid [QRL 9]; and third, the Moyle and Reid estimates extended to exclude the undistributed net profits of unincorporated companies. The two final ratios are a rough approximation to discretionary savings, in that they exclude employee contributions to superannuation and life assurance funds and current transfers to non-profit-making bodies. They do not exclude mortgage capital payments or Save-As-You-Earn savings which are also contractual savings or the undistributed profits of private trusts. If they did then it is clear that there is a strong possibility that part of household consumption expenditure is financed by borrowing. This is certainly not a regular feature of time series consumption functions estimated by economists, generally using 'official' definitions. It is quite evident from the foregoing analysis that the savings ratio is sensitive to changes in the definitions adopted in estimating disposable income and savings.

The final important point concerns the restructuring of the personal sector accounts. There can be no doubt that the personal sector ought to be redefined to exclude the non-household sector. Whether the non-household element becomes a new residual sector or is placed in the company sector is open to debate. However none of these developments can really take place until there is a regular supply of satisfactory data on charities and the undistributed profits of unincorporated businesses.

However further criticisms of official data depend largely on the object of a particular study and the definition required. For example any study that adopts the well-known and widely accepted Simons' definition of income immediately runs into problems. This definition of income is briefly that personal income is the algebraic sum of (1) the market value of rights exercised in consumption and (2) the change in the value of the store of property rights between the beginning and the end of the period (see H. Simons for further details [B 54]). It was a concept of income strongly adhered to by the *Minority Report of the Royal Commission on Taxation* [B 97]. The major implication of this definition is that the second part comprises savings and capital appreciation. We use the term capital appreciation to distinguish from capital gains as defined for taxation purposes. The latter are only realized forms of capital appreciation and frequently refer to realization of appreciated values over more than one period. It is normal practice in national income accounting to exclude capital appreciation, on the

Table 2.4 Savings Ratios, 1970

Disposable Income Definition (1)	*Source* (2)	*Amount £m* (3)	*Savings Definition* (4)	*Amount £m* (5)	*Savings Ratio* (5)/(3)
1. Aggregate Personal Disposable Income	*Blue Book*	34,367	Disposable Income *less* consumption	2,963	8·6
2. Aggregate Household Disposable Income	Moyle and Reid	32,772	Disposable Income *less* consumption	2,743	6·5
3. Aggregate Household Disposable Income excluding undistributed net profits of unincorporated companies	op. cit.	31,454	Disposable Income *less* consumption	1,425	4·5
4. Aggregate Household Disposable Income	Moyle and Reid	32,772	Disposable Income *less* consumption and some contractual savings	511	1·5
5. Aggregate Household Disposable Income excluding undistributed net profits of unincorporated companies	op. cit.	31,454	Disposable Income *less* consumption and some contractual savings	−807	−2·6

Sources: Moyle and Reid [QRL 9]; *Blue Book* [QRL 37] 1973

2.8.2 *Welfare Studies*

A second major purpose for total personal income statistics is for applied welfare studies such as living standard analysis, international comparisons of income *per capita*, income tax equity problems, redistribution studies and so on. Contrary to the dictates of the macro-economists this group of analysts prefer to have available data on a broad range of items of personal income. On the other hand in conjunction with macro-economists there is universal acceptance that personal income ought only to refer to households and persons. In this respect the criticisms in subsection 2.8.1 are relevant.

grounds that it has no real counterpart in the output of goods and services, though for computational reasons stock appreciation is included in the estimates of the component parts of GNP, being deducted in the summary tables only. Nevertheless this is clearly a deficiency in data. We shall return to this problem in Section 3.

Simons' definition also highlights the problem of transfers within the personal sector, namely private pensions received and contributions to the superannuation funds that finance them. In subsection 2.2.1 it was pointed out that to avoid double-counting only one of the above items should be included. However if we were to define contributions to private pension schemes as increases in property rights and pensions received on the other hand as rights exercised in consumption, etc. then there is a case for including both items. The problem arises because one part of income is serving and benefiting two groups of people at two different periods of time. Put another way if two economies had identical populations and aggregate personal income, conventionally defined, but one had no transfers within the personal sector of this nature, then it would be spurious to claim, *ceteris paribus*, that the benefit to the personal sectors of the two economies would be identical. Whether on the other hand we can weight income committed to future as highly as currently received income is of course another conceptual problem. (For further discussion on this issue see subsection 3.10.4.)

The above two paragraphs have focused attention on conceptual issues and their measurement implications that arise from the second part of Simons' algebraic sum. There is in addition a conceptual problem that arises with the first part, namely what constitutes an income in kind and how should it be valued? Subsection 2.3.2 itemizes the incomes in kind that the CSO consider part of an individual's income. There is also mention of incomes in kind that are not evaluated due to data inavailability. We could add to this list such factors as recreational benefits provided by firms, free or cheap products made available to employees, luncheon vouchers, plus some of the personal benefit that is derived from employer-provided cars, even though this item is 'technically' taxed. We could add to the latter part of the expenses claimed by self-employed persons with respect to business travel by car, again assuming a high degree of tax evasion. All these enable an individual to benefit from savings in consumption expenditure. Whilst it is difficult to compute the items regularly each year, tentative estimates could be obtained from the *Family Expenditure Survey* [QRL 28], the Ministry of Labour (now the Department of Employment), *Cost Surveys* [QRL 24, QRL 33, QRL 34] and private surveys on labour costs such as that by Reid and Robertson [B 49]. Estimates of these additional incomes in kind are available for 1954, 1959 and 1963 in Stark [B 59].

Given that data is difficult for many incomes in kind, there arises the conceptual problem of evaluation. First such incomes ought perhaps to be measured at their market value. This is rarely so. According to *Sources and Methods* ([B 85], p. 120) many of the items are measured at the net cost to the employer. Secondly, with respect to pre-tax (or pre-disposable) personal income estimates an income tax element ought to be included. This is, of course, the case with those items of income in kind that do get caught in the tax net such as in the agricultural sector. However, much income in kind does not get reported for tax purposes. This is indicated by the fact that many incomes in kind must be imputed. From the 'welfare' aspect the omitted tax factor in imputation is clearly a deficiency.

2.8.3 *Tax Evasion*

We have seen that a considerable proportion of the data on personal incomes is derived from income tax sources. This means that an obvious source of error is tax evasion, as opposed to avoidance. The latter is the legal reduction of a tax burden by arrangement of income, but not by the under-reporting of income received, which is tax evasion and is illegal. Naturally there is very little information available on tax evasion. The Inland Revenue does add on charges and penalties imposed as an estimate for detected evasion and the CSO makes a further adjustment for expected evasion. However there must be many cases that go undetected. Most of the cases that are detected refer to self-employed or similar incomes. Feinstein estimated [QRL 2] for example that the *Blue Book* estimates for 1938 had made an adjustment amounting to 37% of the income from sole traders and partnerships (other than farmers and professional persons) for tax evasion. This figure he then demonstrates is in excess of the 18% estimated by Stamp [B 58] for 1913. Feinstein concluded that tax evasion is on the increase and used the two figures as benchmarks for interpolating the intervening years.

There are no available figures for the post-war adjustments that have been officially made for Schedule D evasion, but to suggest that the pre-war rate of increase was maintained would be absurd. Given that evasion might range between 10 to 50%, this would produce totals for 1972 of £291m to £1,456m or roughly 0·4 to 2% of total personal income. However these estimates could be quite paltry in comparison to the tax evasion by other income recipients, even those who it is invariably assumed are trapped by the PAYE network and for whom no allowances are made. The types of evasion that might come under this heading comprise the private after-hours work by craftsmen (electricians, painters, etc.); casual labour work, especially by students; by those who squeeze into the labour market without National Insurance cards, especially in the contracting industry; and by those who are remunerated unofficially for their pastimes and leisure, such as many sportsmen. If £100 p.a. for every employed adult is accepted as an example of this type of evasion, then it would total approximately £2,000m or 4% of total personal income.

In a national accounting framework the above type of evasion implies that the personal sector also incorporates an unrecorded production sector, particularly with regard to the service and servicing industries. Furthermore if we were to assume that some of this evasion appeared on the expenditure side of the personal sector balance sheet, then doubt is cast on the estimates of personal saving and the savings ratios published in the *Blue Book*.

3 The Distribution of Personal Income

3.1 Introduction

It could be claimed that a nation without a substantial collection of evidence on the size distribution of incomes, which nevertheless uses its tax rates as economic policy parameters or introduces new taxes, subsidies and social security provisions to alleviate economic injustice, must be, by virtue of the data deficiency, basing many of its decisions on intuition and hope. The value of income distribution data to the policy-maker and the social commentator is immense. There are a few key statistics that are essential to any economic analysis such as balance of payments figures, money supply, prices, national income and expenditure. The closer an equitable distribution of income ranks with growth, price stability and international solvency as an ultimate or final economic target, then the closer income distribution (and wealth) data become to joining the list of key statistics. The recent formation of a permanent Royal Commission on the Distribution of Personal Income and Wealth (cf. subsection 3.7) suggests that this point may have been reached.

There are three major types of policy analysis which require income distribution data. These are: Inequality, comprising dispersion, low income and poverty studies; Income Tax management; and Redistribution. They could also be used in conjunction with consumer expenditure data, to improve and expand the National Income Accounts, such as the construction of a household as opposed to a personal sector (cf. subsection 2.8.1 and Boreham and Semple [B 11]). Finally social scientists require these data to analyse the causes and trends in the distribution of income.

There are currently five official sources of income distribution statistics in the United Kingdom. All of them attempt to quantify the size of income (or types of income) over a specified period of time accruing to individuals, be they grouped either in households, income tax paying units or on a *per capita* basis. The choice of the time period and the recipient unit are important conceptual as well as practical issues. They will clearly vary according to the predominant use required of the data source and the nature of the data collection. The definition of income is also a crucial issue. As pointed out in subsection 2.8.1 a proportion of personal income as officially defined cannot be considered as the income of households or persons living in institutions. As it happens none of the UK sources include the income of charities, universities, etc. life assurance and superannuation funds or even that part of self-employed persons' income covered by depreciation allowances. However the definition of income required by analysts in the field of inequality or welfare studies often extends to capital gains, fringe benefit from employment and the like. These items are rarely available. Throughout Section 3 we shall make brief reference to these conceptual issues raised by the definition of income and recipient and the time period involved. For a fuller discussion on these matters and the theory of income distribution in general the reader is referred to A. B. Atkinson's *The Economics of Inequality* [B 5].

Though official UK income distribution statistics omit most elements of non-household income, it does not follow from this that each source covers the whole area of household income. Two of the sources, the *New Earnings Surveys* [QRL 42] and the Department of Health and Social Security's statistics on annual earnings in [QRL 11] are restricted to income of employees and for this reason we shall examine them briefly in subsection 3.7. The other sources, however, do attempt to cover as wide a range of the income of persons as is feasible according to the nature and structure of the source. In no case is the coverage of the remaining items of aggregate personal income complete. In fact the coverage and the definition of income and the income recipients sometimes differs substantially between the sources. It is for this reason among others that much care must be taken in interpreting and comparing the statistics that are produced by these sources.

The sources are the *Family Expenditure Survey* [QRL 28], the new *General Household Survey* [QRL 30] and the Inland Revenue publications [QRL 32, QRL 53, QRL 68, QRL 69, QRL 70]. These last are the longest-standing source and for many years were the only source of income distribution statistics in the United Kingdom. We can also add to the above list the forthcoming 1971 Census Income Follow-Up [B 75]. In this section we shall consider each of these sources in detail. In addition we shall also examine the recently reinstated CSO *Blue Book* income distributions [QRL 37], which were an extension of the Inland Revenue data; the redistribution studies pioneered by Mr J. L. Nicholson and continued by the CSO, based on the *Family Expenditure Survey* and Professor Lydall's data from the Oxford Savings Surveys of the mid-1950s. There will also be some analysis of pre-war and historical data.

3.2 Inland Revenue Data—Post-War

3.2.1 *Sources*

Since the Second World War the Inland Revenue has periodically undertaken investigations which it originally called an 'Income Census' and now calls an 'Income Survey' and which up to 1970 were published in detail in the annual reports of the Commissioners of the Board of the Inland Revenue, hereafter known as the BIR reports [QRL 53]. Since and including 1970 the results of the Income Surveys have appeared in the new annual publication entitled *Inland Revenue Statistics* (IRS) [QRL 32]. In addition, highly detailed accounts of the 1969–70 and 1970–1 surveys have appeared in two separate publications entitled *The Survey of Personal Incomes* [QRL 68, QRL 69]. This practice was not repeated for the 1971–2 survey, but the summary tables of the 1972–3 survey were published in a separate booklet early in 1975 and for the 1973–4 survey in 1976. The detailed tables for 1972–3 appear in the *Inland Revenue Statistics* for 1975 and for 1973–4 in that for 1976.

The surveys are for the tax year 6 April to 5 April the following year. Originally they were undertaken every five years, with the first one being for 1949–50. The details and results of this 'census' appeared in the BIR reports numbers 94 (pp. 95–127, 1952) and 95 (pp. 91, 93–145, 1953). The next survey was for 1954–5 and was published in the 99th report (pp. 45–95, 1957). The 100th report (1959) and the 101st report (pp. 69–77, 84–7) contained some corrections relating to the 1954–5 survey. The 1959–60 survey was largely reproduced in the 105th report (1963) with some additional material appearing the following year in the 106th report.

After the 1959–60 survey the Inland Revenue decided to adopt a policy of having smaller annual surveys covering the years between the major quinquennial ones. The first of these was for 1962–3 in the 107th report (1965), followed by that for 1963–4 in the 108th report (1966). The fourth major quinquennial survey for 1964–5 was then published in the 109th (1967) and 110th (1968) reports. The 110th report (1968) also contained the 1965–6 annual survey. The 111th report contained the 1966–7 survey. Since then there have been further annual surveys for 1967–8 and 1968–9 which were published in the *Inland Revenue Statistics* for 1970 and 1971 respectively, culminating in the fifth quinquennial survey for 1969–70 referred to above.

We will consider the differences between the quinquennial and annual surveys in subsection 3.2.4. However a word of warning to the user of these statistics is necessary at this stage. Prior to

1962–3 personal income distributions using identical definitions, etc. can be found for the years not covered by the Inland Revenue quinquennial surveys, especially in the CSO *Blue Books* [QRL 37] and the *Annual Abstract of Statistics* [QRL 13]. These distributions, prepared by the Inland Revenue, are no more than simple extrapolations of the previous quinquennial survey and should be treated with caution.

3.2.2 *Definition of Income*

Income in the surveys covers all income received by persons which is subject to income tax. Specifically, it is that income computed for income tax purposes after making statutory deductions with respect to expenses, Schedule A and capital allowances, mortgage interest payments (see sub-section 3.10.3), contributions to approved superannuation schemes and other similar annual payments. For data referring to years before 1961 employee National Insurance contributions were included in these deductions, but not since as this item is no longer deductible for tax purposes. Income before these deductions is termed 'gross income' in the surveys. After deductions it is called 'net income' and it is this concept to which we refer as taxable income, and which forms the basis for allocating income by size in the surveys. It should be noted however that personal allowances and life insurance relief are not deducted in arriving at total net income. The only major change in the definition of taxable income since the war is abolition of Schedule A, owner-occupied rent income, in 1963, though there have been many changes in the statutes regarding deductible interest charges. Prior to 1969–70 most interest charges were deductible. The budget of 1970 restricted allowable deductions to interest relating to purchase or the improvement of property and business. In 1972 the budget allowed all interest relating to property and businesses plus all other interest exceeding £35 p.a. However by 1974 there was a return to the pre-1972 situation plus a restriction on the tax relief of house mortgages to the value of £25,000. In spite of these statutory changes the definition is nevertheless highly comparable in each survey.

Therefore not all personal income is covered by the Inland Revenue surveys. Incomes below the deduction card (or effective exemption) limit are excluded as are all types of non-taxable income such as most types of state benefits, student grants, the first £40 of savings bank interest and employer National Insurance and superannuation contributions. Approximately 75% of total personal income, as defined in Section 2, is covered. Of the remaining 25% about 6% referred to income below the effective exemption limit in 1949–50 and 3% in 1962–3. The proportion relating to this item has decreased substantially, in spite of the fact that the effective exemption limits, £135 in 1949–50 and £330 in 1969–70, have risen faster than the rate of increase of the retail price index. The rest refers to non-taxable income above the effective exemption limit which has risen noticeably since 1949–50, and the income of the non-household part of the personal sector including the undistributed profits of private trusts.

The income referred to in the surveys means the amount received or earned in the particular financial year under analysis. The only exception is for Schedule D income (broadly self-employment income together with some investment income). Here the assessments are normally based on the amount of income arising in a previous year. It is for this reason that it is difficult to link the surveys to other statistics published by the Inland Revenue.

3.2.3 *Definition of the Income Recipient*

The numbers of incomes in the Inland Revenue surveys refer to income tax units, that is adult single persons, each as one unit, plus married couples, each couple also as one unit, where the income received is taxable and above the effective exemption limit. Contrary to criticisms made by some academics, notably Titmuss [B 63], the Inland Revenue has not deviated at all from this definition in any of its surveys, even where wives' incomes are separately assessed from those of their husbands (see BIR 105 [QRL 53] for a clear denial by the Inland Revenue of any deviations in this respect). However the *Surveys of Personal Incomes* do publish separate tables on the distribution of employment income of wives.

It has long been the standard practice in British fiscal law to treat the income of husbands and wives together for taxation purposes. For a number of years it has been possible for wives to be taxed jointly with their husbands but separately assessed. Since 1972–3 it has also been possible for wives to be taxed separately. Nevertheless these provisions have not influenced the presentation of the data, where the incomes of husbands and wives are still combined. The income of minors, however, is much more confusing and has been subject to a number of recent statutory changes. Broadly the state of affairs from 1972–3 to date is that all income of minors is taxed separately unless it is the investment income from a deed of covenant provided by the parent, in which case the income is aggregated with that of the parents, providing the minor is unmarried and under 18 years old. However it has been announced that the present position will be entirely reversed in the near future so that all income of minors will be aggregated. In 1969–70 and 1971–2 all the unearned, but not the earned, income of minors was aggregated. Prior to 1969 arrangements similar to those in force from 1972 to 1975 were in hand.

The income of adult dependent relatives and permanent housekeepers is not and has never been aggregated. Income units can claim allowances for the above, provided the income of the claimees is below a certain limit. The extent of the allowances and limits has naturally varied over the period and a sliding scale offset principle has operated to determine the size of the allowance. The parameters of the system are such that it is not usually possible for an income unit, such as a dependent relative, to be included in the distributions both as a dependent and a separate income unit. There are a few exceptions to this generalization. In 1967–8 and 1968–9 the parameters did permit an overlap at the margin and it is possible also in the surveys for 1959–60 and 1965–6 that some dependent relatives were included as separate tax units but probably not paying tax. In all these instances we refer only to overlaps at the margins and the numbers involved were extremely small indeed.

The non-aggregated income of minors is treated in a similar manner to that of dependent relatives, etc. though a sliding scale principle did not come into operation until 1963–4. As with dependent relatives it is generally not possible for minors to appear as both a dependent child and an independent tax unit except for a very few cases at the margin in the 1959–60 survey and in each survey between 1963–4 to 1968–9.

3.2.4 *The Scope of Inland Revenue Data*

The 1949–50 and 1954–5 quinquennial surveys were almost identical in presentation and coverage. Both presented a summary distribution of personal taxable income before and after tax including adjustments for deficiencies in the survey (see subsections 3.2.6 to 9 inclusive). These were accompanied by a number of more detailed tables which were not so adjusted. The detailed tables came under three broad headings. First, the distribution of personal taxable income before tax by type of income, e.g. by employment, pension, investment profits, deductions, etc. These were further disaggregated into three categories, namely married couples, single males and widowers and single females and widows.

The second broad heading covers the distribution of taxable incomes by income size cross-classified by family circumstances. Family circumstances relate to the number of dependents and children for whom allowances are claimed. These tables are further disaggregated into the three marital status categories mentioned in the first heading.

The final heading covers regional data. Both surveys provided data on the income distribution of the four home countries, further disaggregated into marital status plus a summary family circumstance cross-classification for each country. The 1949–50 survey also provided detailed income distribution tables for each country in the United Kingdom. This data was not available for the 1954–5 survey. This latter survey however did contain data on the distribution of life insurance premiums by size of net income, a table that has reappeared for the second time in the 1967–8 survey and in every survey since.

It should be noted that in many tables the income recipient columns refer to the number of cases as opposed to the number of income units. This arises when the table is analysing incomes from different sources of income. A single income unit may be counted as a case under more than one heading of income.

The 1959–60 quinquennial survey followed a similar pattern to the two previous ones but provided much more detail and included many new tables. The degree of disaggregation in the first two headings was very extensive. For instance there was extensive cross-classification by type of main source income and marital status. Married income units were further grouped into those with wives earning and those with wives not earning. There was also detailed information on wives' earnings, trading profits and professional earnings which had not previously appeared. Furthermore all the tables in this survey were presented after adjustment for deficiencies in investment income and wives' earnings (see subsections 3.2.6 to 9 inclusive), though the Board did publish one table on the income distribution of married couples before the adjustment for unreported wives' earnings, thereby enabling the user to gauge the extent of the adjustment.

With respect to regional data, the summary data on the four home countries remained, but not the further disaggregation by family circumstance or marital status. Instead there were moderately detailed tables on the distribution of income by the regions of Great Britain, such as north-eastern England, the central Clydeside conurbation, etc. plus separate tables for the Armed Forces, Seamen and Public Departments. There were also summary size distributions for each county.

Three particularly interesting additions in 1959–60 were the cross-classification of, first, net earned income with total net income, secondly, net investment income with total net income and finally the proportionate change in wages and salaries from 1958–9 to 1959–60, with wages and salaries in 1958–9.

The 1964–5 and 1969–70 quinquennial surveys contained more or less the same format and structure of tables as the 1959–60 survey. The only notable addition was the cross-classification of income by size after tax with that before tax, subdivided into married and single person units. A notable omission in 1964–5 was the cross-classification of change in wages and salaries over two years, though this table was in the 1969–70 survey. One small difference between the 1969–70 survey and the others is that a change to the coding practices meant that, for all incomes except that of the self-employed (i.e. main source income charged under Schedule D), the basis of the regional data was now the place of residence of the taxpayer as opposed to the location of the local district tax office through which his claims were dealt with. The result is a small loss of units in England in favour of the Celtic countries.

The annual surveys since 1962–3 naturally contain much less information than the major quinquennial surveys. They contain approximately fifteen tables compared to the seventy or more of the major surveys. The most notable omissions are the county tables and the special tables. The information under the other two headings is quite extensive. An exception to this general rule is the 1970–1 survey, which was presented on the same scale as the major quinquennial surveys. It was also the first survey since 1949–50 to present family circumstance data for the four home countries. Unfortunately the data were grouped under only three family circumstance headings, though it was extended to the standard regions and conurbations in addition to the home countries.

3.2.5 *Method of Estimation*

A detailed account of the organization of the 1959–60 survey is given in the Central Statistical Office's *New Contributions to Economic Statistics* ([B 89], Third Series, pp. 149–55), *The Survey of Personal Incomes 1969–70* [QRL 68] and in 'The Survey of Personal Incomes' by F. R. L'Aiguille, *Statistical News* ([B 101], No. 17, May 1972). This was the first survey to make extensive use of computer facilities and broadly the same organization has been adopted for the two subsequent quinquennial surveys. The annual surveys also follow a similar pattern.

The basis of the survey is a questionnaire completed by each local tax office with respect to a selected number of taxpayers in its district. A copy of the questionnaire is given in Appendix B. The taxpayers are randomly selected from the main source of income classifications made by each local tax office. There are in addition further selections to cover areas where experience has shown that deficiencies and errors are likely to appear, such as the earnings of wives. Though the sample of taxpayers in each category of taxpayer is randomly chosen, a stratified sample design is used. The actual sampling fractions for 1959–60 and 1969–70 are given in Table 3.1. It can be clearly seen that the procedure involves filling in questionnaires or income reports for approximately 1 million taxpayers.

The actual selection of the sample is made over a two-day period in each local office in April soon after the end of the financial year. It then takes up to nine months for the local offices to complete and send in the questionnaires. This time lag results from the complexity and numbers of tax records involved. The response rate to the sample is excellent. In the 1969–70 sample over 95% of the forms were returned, though in certain categories, especially those covering the earnings of wives, there were larger deficiencies. These deficiencies arise from the difficulties sometimes encountered in tracing the earnings of husbands of the sampled earning wives, particularly those dealt with in a different district from their husbands.

The sample returns are then checked for consistency with respect to the tax laws and statutes. They are then processed by the computer. The process includes the 'grossing-up' of each of the sampled strata. A check is then made against independently estimated control totals for the various types of income, the amount of tax collected and the numbers of taxpayers. Adjustments

Table 3.1 *Sampling Fractions in the Inland Revenue Income Survey 1959–60 and 1969–70*

Main Source Income Classification	*Sampling Proportion (%)* 1959–60	1969–70	*Numbers in Sample ('000s)* 1959–60	1969–70
PAYE (simple one-source cases)	2·5	2·5	406	443
PAYE (complicated assessed cases)	10	10	316	96
Schedule D (self-employed)	5	5	73	88
Schedule A and repayment claims	5	5	33	28
Surtax cases up to £10,000 p.a.	25	25	97	123
Surtax cases over £10,000 p.a.	100	100	13	5
Simplified reports on wives and subsidiary earnings	2·5	2·5	111	139
PAYE earners ceasing employment in survey year	2·5	10	34	53
Total number in sample			1,083	975

Sources: *New Contributions to Economic Statistics*, Third Series, [B 89] CSO, 1964; and *The Survey of Personal Incomes 1969–70*, Inland Revenue, 1972 [QRL 68]

are made with respect to some of the deficiencies that emerge from the data.

The computer produces a preliminary set of tables which are then subjected to a number of further adjustments. Deficiencies with respect to some control totals still emerge, especially for investment income and the earnings of wives where these are above the PAYE limit (see sub-sections 3.2.6 and 7). The adjustments in these instances are somewhat arbitrary, and in the 1969–70 survey no adjustment was made for the investment income deficiency. Furthermore in 1959–60 an adjustment in the one major summary table has also been made for wives' earnings below the PAYE limit. The Inland Revenue can ascertain the numbers involved here by reference to National Insurance records. It has however to guess at the amounts of income involved and to which husbands they are 'linked'. This adjustment has not been made in any subsequent surveys.

Though the Inland Revenue can adjust for most detectable errors it cannot for undetectable or sampling errors. Sampling errors arise due to the natural chance of any sample. The computer programme for the survey therefore estimates the standard or sampling error of estimates. Examples of the percentage standard errors are reproduced in Appendix D of the 1969–70 survey and Table 76 of the 105th report for 1959–60, Tables 94 and 95 in IR 1970 for 1967–8, Tables 103 and 104 in IR 1971 for 1968–9.

The annual surveys from 1962–3 adopted a similar pattern to that outlined above. The major difference is that the sampling fractions are reduced. They vary from 0·083% (1–1,200) for the smaller PAYE cases to 100% for the surtax incomes in excess of £100,000 p.a., producing in total a sample of approximately 125,000 tax reports (see Appendix C for an example of the 1972–3 sampling fractions).

The quinquennial surveys of 1949–50 and 1954–5 differed quite substantially from that of 1959–60. The former adopted a uniform 10% sampling fraction, involving approximately 2 million cases and the latter a uniform 5% producing the now standard 1 million sample size. However in neither case was an electronic computer used. This severely curtailed opportunities for cross-checking and the adjustments for deficiencies and consistency. This is why only the summary tables and a very small number of the detailed tables of these surveys have been adjusted for known deficiencies (see sub-section 3.2.6).

3.2.6 *Deficiencies in Investment Income*

The Inland Revenue checks its sample survey estimates against data from independent sources where possible. This has led to the discovery of three important deficiencies in the sample data. These are in investment income, earnings of wives and the number of children reported in the family classification tables.

The deficiency in investment income for all the surveys up to 1964–5 is given in Table 3.2.

Table 3.2 Investment Income Deficiency

Year	*£m*	*As a percentage of taxable income (a)*
1949–50	150(290)[b]	1·8(3·5)[b]
1954–5	72	0·60
1959–60	60	0·40
1962–3	20	0·11
1963–4	30	0·15
1964–5	60	0·28
1965–6	80	

Notes: (a) i.e. after all adjustments for deficiencies; (b) £290m including the basic adjustment on surtax incomes (i.e. £150m + £140m)

Source: Information from the Inland Revenue and various Inland Revenue reports

Since 1965–6 the Inland Revenue has not computed the deficiency nor has it made adjustments to the summary tables on its account. Till recently the Inland Revenue argued that there was no satisfactory means of estimating an independent control total of investment income accruing to income tax units, mainly due to the problem of the unincorporated and charity element in the aggregate personal income control totals (see subsection 2.8.1). However recent developments in National Income Accounting (see subsection 2.8.1) have remedied some of these difficulties. Statisticians at the Board and the CSO now suspect a probable 12% deficiency in investment income, mainly in the middle income ranges. Nevertheless the Board still argues that the adjustments made in the earlier surveys were rather arbitrary and a satisfactory procedure has not yet been discovered.

In the earlier surveys the Inland Revenue did attempt to estimate a minimum level of deficiencies in investment income reported. The deficiency was also subdivided into various categories so that the shortfalls could be broadly located. In the 1949–50 survey a basic adjustment of £140m was also made on the basis of the surtax data. This was in addition to the £150m deficiency detected for incomes below the surtax limits. The Inland Revenue observed that investment income as a percentage of total income fell sharply below the surtax limits. Therefore on the hypothesis that the deficiency is mainly due to income receivers not reporting investment income where the standard rate tax had already been paid, the deficiency was allocated to those middle income range units paying standard rate tax which had reported no investment income. It is now believed that reports in some cases related to the previous year's income as the current year's was not yet known, or simply the investment income net of tax already paid. Both of these could cause under-reporting, though in an unusual year such as 1966–7 the opposite effect would have occurred since in the previous year very high dividends had been paid out in anticipation of the corporation tax, followed by a sharp cut-back in actual payments the following year. These additional factors were taken specifically into account on the adjustments made between 1962–3 to 1965–6 surveys (for further details see BIR reports [QRL 53]).

The number of income units affected by the adjustments made in the six surveys has not been available, except for 1954–5 where it caused an increase of 307,000 units receiving investment income. In no year, however, did they cause any significant increase in the total number of units receiving all types of taxable income. Only in the 1959–60, 1964–5 and 1965–6 surveys was the adjustment incorporated in all tables. In the other surveys they are only included in the 'after adjustment' summary tables, except in 1949–50 when the £140m 'surtax' adjustment was included in all tables. Finally by its own admission the nature of the adjustment by the Inland Revenue is somewhat arbitrary. It would appear that the Board's present statisticians are less prepared, rightly or wrongly, to be 'arbitrary' than their predecessors. Table 3.4 in subsection 3.2.9 gives a guide to the comparability of tables before and after adjustment.

3.2.7 *Deficiency in the Earnings of Wives*

The deficiencies attributable to wives' earnings were particularly substantial in the 1949–50 survey. The survey only indicated 1,416,000 working wives, which implied a deficiency of 1,584,000 wives when compared with the entirely independent National Insurance statistics. This deficiency also implied a deficiency of £171m worth of income, though it did not imply any tax loss due to the operation of the PAYE system. The main effect of the deficiency would be the placing of many income units in a wrong income range.

The Inland Revenue adjusted for the deficiency in 1949–50 by plotting graphically the number of wives per range and estimating the number of wives to be added by reference to the number of married units. Originally an independent sample had been taken of cases where wives' income had been reported, but this proved to be a fruitless exercise.

In the 1954–5 survey the deficiency was equally as large as in 1949–50 (see Table 3.3). The same adjustments were undertaken as in the 1949–50 survey. In both surveys these adjustments were incorporated only in the 'after adjustment' summary tables.

Table 3.3 The Deficiencies resulting from the 'Earnings of Wives' Deficiency

Year	Deficiency £m (1)	000's of units (2)	(1) as a percentage of taxable income	(2) as a percentage of taxable income units
1949–50	171	1,584	2·1	7·9
1954–5	264·6	1,940	2·3	9·6
1959–60	315·1*	111	2·0	0·5

Source: Information from the Inland Revenue and various Inland Revenue Reports

*£315·1m = £257·2m + £57·9m, i.e. the deficiency in the earnings of wives above the PAYE limit plus that of wives with earnings below the limit (see text).

In the 1959–60 and subsequent surveys an important change was made in the treatment of this deficiency. The survey structure now included a separate sample return of wives' earnings (see subsection 3.2.5) drawn from PAYE returns. In 1959–60 this sample indicated that the extent of the deficiency in the main sample was about one-third of wives' earnings, concentrated mainly in the lower income ranges. The estimated deficiency was £257·2m and 101,000 units (see *Inland Revenue Report*, No. 105, para. 12). In addition there was an estimated deficiency of £57·9m and 10,000 units with respect to the earnings of wives below the PAYE exemption limit. The 105th report stated that for those earning wives above the exemption limit 'The correction was made by adding wives' earnings to selected groups of husbands who had returned no such earnings, the selection being made by reference to the distribution of similar earnings of wives which had been duly returned by the husbands.'

In all subsequent surveys the correction has been made a little differently. The returns in the lower income ranges from the separate sample have simply been substituted for wives' earnings in the main sample. In the higher ranges the correction has been made by adjusting the grossing factor applied to the main sample.

In the 1959–60 survey and in all subsequent surveys the above adjustments were incorporated in all tables. Only for 1959–60 did the Inland Revenue publish any indication of the size of the deficiency. Also for 1959–60 the Inland Revenue included a correction in the 'after adjustment' summary tables for the deficiency in wives' earnings below the PAYE deduction card limit (i.e. effective exemption limit). This correction has not been reported in subsequent surveys. It is however implicitly included in the two earlier surveys.

3.2.8 *Deficiency in the Numbers of Children Reported*

The final major deficiency in the surveys relates to the numbers of children reported in the family classification tables. An independent control total of the number of children can be estimated, albeit imprecisely, from the Registrar General's statistics. The lack of precision arises from the existence of children in respect of whom children's allowances cannot be claimed. The eligibility for children's allowances depends upon whether the children in question are receivers of income and, if so, whether that income in its taxable form exceeds the limit above which the allowance is taken away. Children aged 16 and over must also be in full-time education.

Such independent checking suggested a deficiency of about 500,000 children in 1949–50 and 250,000 in 1954–5. In each case this was shown by a similar deficiency in the number of children's allowances. The Inland Revenue state that this deficiency occurs in the lower income groups, where in some families the income may already be protected from tax liability by allowances, etc. so that it is not worth claiming for any additional allowance. For example, they point to a large drop in the percentage of married couples claiming two children in the income ranges £300–350 and £250–300. A similar phenomenon is also cited for families with three or four children.

The Inland Revenue could not make any correction for this deficiency in the 1949–50 survey due to the lack of alternative information. However in the 1954–5 survey an arbitrary adjustment was made but only in a summary family classification table, not in the marital status and regional family classification tables.

By 1959–60 the problem of missing children had almost disappeared. The 105th report stated that there was a small deficiency for that survey which the author has estimated as a possible maximum of 42,000 children, i.e. 0·3 % of all children (see [B 59]). Since 1959–60 none of the surveys have reported any deficiency.

3.2.9 *Other Minor Deficiencies*

In the 1962–3 annual survey the Inland Revenue reported that a minor deficiency results out of the administrative problems with Code Cards and Deduction Cards (BIR 107 [QRL 53], p. 81, para. 6). Code Cards were formerly issued where income was above the effective exemption limit but not subject to tax because of child allowances, etc. Though these cards were being gradually withdrawn in 1962–3, there were still some in existence and unlike the 1959–60 survey they had not been included in the sample. This deficiency also existed in the 1963–4 annual survey but by the 1964–5 quinquennial survey Code Cards had been completely withdrawn.

Another problem arises with certain classes of employees such as farm workers, domestic servants and members of the Forces for whom there are no Deduction Cards. Estimates of the numbers involved were included in all the tables of the surveys up to and including 1959–60. However since then there have been no adjustments for the detailed tables and only in the quinquennial surveys for the 'after adjustment' summary tables. The annual surveys include no adjusted tables for this deficiency. The 1963–4 annual survey reports that the combined effect of the Code and Deduction Cards deficiencies involved 170,000 cases and approximately £75m of income (BIR 108 [QRL 53], p. 80, para. 6). This was slightly smaller than for 1962–3 where the respective figures were 220,000 and £95m. The 1969–70 survey reported that the Deduction Card deficiency amounted to 52,000 cases only and for 1970–1 the Inland Revenue stated that the raising of the Deduction Card limit left only such a negligible number of cases in this category that the adjustment was not attempted.

3.2.10 *Comparability*

The previous four sections outline the deficiencies and adjustments made to the surveys. They have unfortunately led to difficulties and frustration in comparing the tables of each of the surveys. Because of this we have drafted a tabular guide to comparability (see Table 3.4). Since the terms 'before' and 'after adjustment' do not appear in every survey we have also included in our guide the table numbers of each report under the different categories of tables in our guide. The guide is not comprehensive and is meant to be used in conjunction with the previous three sections.

The other main factor influencing comparability has been the changes in the estimation of regional data. From 1949–50 up to the 1968–9 survey the data was based on the place of main assessment of each unit which in most cases is the place of business as opposed to residence. The only exceptions to this rule were the Forces, merchant seamen and most civil servants who are assessed centrally and published in the regional tables as separate groups but included in England for the country distributions.

In the 1965–6 survey, however, the civil servant grouping was abandoned and civil servants allocated to the various regions according to residence. This mixture of place of assessment and residence was repeated in the next two annual surveys. In the 1969–70 and subsequent surveys most data have been changed to residential basis (see subsection 3.2.4). This major change in theory might have seriously affected the comparability of the country distributions. In practice it does not appear to have done so. The main effect has been a diminution in the number of units allocated to cities and conurbations. Details of this effect are given in the *Survey of Personal Incomes 1970–71* ([QRL 69], p. vii).

3.2.11 *Disadvantages of Inland Revenue Data*

There are two main uses for the Inland Revenue income distributions. The first is to provide a model for estimating the yield and specific effects of changes in the income tax parameters. The second is to analyse the welfare and social aspects of the distribution of income.

There is naturally little criticism, other than the technical deficiencies outlined in subsections 3.2.8–9, that is relevant to the first use. Broadly these deficiencies have been reduced with the changes in the organization of the tax system. The problem of the 'missing' children has disappeared and though some of the effects of the under-reporting of the earnings of wives remain, they are no longer such a serious deficiency as in the past. It is however unfortunate that the deficiency in investment income still remains though this is probably nowhere nearly as large as in the two early surveys. These are, however, technical rather than interpretative criticisms.

The main disadvantages relate to the second use of the statistics. They are quite simply that the definition of income as we saw in subsection 3.2.2 does not cover all personal income and furthermore it means that many low incomes below the tax limits are omitted. There are also disadvantages with the definition of the income unit recipient. This concept is only of value if accompanied by the family classification tables. Without these then there is no indication of how many persons may be attached, either as active income recipients or dependents, to each unit. Therefore equality conclusions based solely on the summary tables such as the Inland Revenue frequently makes could be quite misleading.

Even the use of the family classification tables

Table 3.4 Adjustments Included in Inland Revenue Surveys

		Summary Tables				*Detailed Tables*		
		Before Adjustment		*After Adjustment*				
Year of Survey	*Source*	*Table Nos.*	*Adjustments Made*	*Table Nos.*	*Adjustments*	*Table Nos.*	*Adjustments Made*	*Notes*
1949–50	BIR 94	90	5	110–11	1,2,3,5	90–109	5	Summary tables in BIR 95 revised
						112–15		
	BIR 95			86–7	1,2,3,5	89–185	5	
1954–5	BIR 99	55	5	80–1	1,2,3,5	55–99	5	
1959–60	BIR 105	75	1,2,5	75	1,2,3,5	76–137	1,2,5	
	BIR 106					74–8	1,2,5	
1962–3	BIR 107	71–2	2	71–2	1,2,4	73–83	2	
1963–4	BIR 108	59–60	2	59–60	1,2,4	61–71	2	
1964–5	BIR 109	69–70	1,2	69–70	1,2,5	71,127	1,2	
	BIR 110					71–100	1,2	
1965–6	BIR 110	101	1,2	101	1,2,5	102–44	1,2	
1966–7	BIR 111	64	2	64	2,5	66–106	2	
1967–8	IRS 1970	50	2	50	2,5	51–96	2	
1968–9	IRS 1971	58	2	57	2,5	59–105	2	
1969–70	IR Survey	1	2,5	1	2,5	2–75	2	
1970–1	IR Survey	1	2	1	2	2–72	2	
1971–2	IRS 1974	37	2	37	2	39–52	2	

Notation of adjustments made: 1. Investment income deficiency; 2. Wives' earnings above exemption limit deficiency; 3. Wives' earnings below exemption limit deficiency; 4. Code cards; 5. Deduction cards deficiency presents interpretative problems. When using them, there emerges an implicit definition of the income recipient commonly termed as the 'inner' family. That is husband, wife and dependent children. This definition has the advantage of being uncompromisingly basic and fundamental. On the other hand if we were to use it to estimate actual living standards, as in low-income or poverty studies, it has the disadvantage that it tends to exaggerate the number of low incomes. This arises because the 'inner' family is often a smaller unit than the household and does not allow for the 'income sharing' factors within a household. The most common examples of this are either young persons' earnings or old persons with low but taxable incomes living with either parents or relatives as the case may be. In the family classification tables of the Inland Revenue surveys this could amount to two 'inner' families, e.g. the parents as one unit and the young person as the other. The 'smallness' of the young person's income may grossly understate his or her actual standard of living even allowing for contributions to the household budget. The parents' income on the other hand will overstate their living standards. Therefore we have a misleading picture. The above example has assumed that the young person earns sufficient to be taxed. If he or she does not, then the problem is even more misleading since he or she will not enter the distributions as either an income recipient or dependent.

Though these criticisms are important, they must be considered in perspective. For instance, the alternative to an 'inner' family concept, namely the 'household' concept as we have it in the *Family Expenditure Survey* [QRL 28], suffers because it underestimates the number of low incomes (see subsection 3.4.3). The conversion of either source to a per adult equivalent basis as might be imagined, would not solve the problem. The different treatment in each source regarding income sharing would still produce correspondingly different distributions. The Inland Revenue data however have two major advantages, in that, firstly, they can be grossed up and subject to independently estimated control totals, and secondly, the 'inner' family and not the household is the basic unit in most social and welfare policy.

3.2.12 *Inland Revenue Data—Pre-War and Historical*

The first paragraph of the introduction of the recent *Inland Revenue Survey of Personal Income 1969–70* [QRL 32] states that: 'Until 1920 the Board of Inland Revenue published an estimated classification every year. However, as a result of the changes in the law introduced in the Finance Act 1920, the work involved became too expensive to undertake.' The aforementioned series began in 1857 with the first Board of Inland Revenue Report [QRL 49]. However the income distributions presented were very different from those in the post-war surveys.

They covered taxable income as broadly defined in the current surveys, but with two notable differences. First the income related to assessment in a given year and not to that accruing in the year. This meant that much of the income classified for a given year was often income accruing in earlier years. This was definitely so for the incomes of self-employed persons and investment income. The second notable difference was that incomes were classified by income range according to the size of each separate source and the numbers of incomes in each source were the number of assessments. In other words an individual with income of varying sizes from four sources would enter the classifications four times. Nowhere would there be any indication of the size of his total income.

These two differences imply that the distributions are of little value. The use of 'assessed taxable income' renders it difficult to predict the effect of changes in tax parameters. Both differences mean that the data are useless for social enquiry. Furthermore it must be remembered that in the middle nineteenth century the proportion of the population subject to income tax was very small. Even by

1910 the distributions covered only cases iv and v of Schedule D and Schedule E. These were broadly the income of persons from businesses, concerns, professions and salaries of employees (other than those in Schedule E) for the Schedule D cases and the salaries of government corporation and public company officials for Schedule E. Practically the whole wage-earning population was not covered by the distributions.

It must not be concluded, however, that all income distributions emanating from the Inland Revenue prior to 1920 were of little value or that the Board did not publish any distributions from 1920 to the 1949–50 survey. The 63rd report ([QRL 50], Cmd. 1083 (1920)) contained a distribution of taxable incomes for the financial year 1918–19 which more closely resembled that of the modern surveys. This distribution requested by the Royal Commission on Taxation [B 96], defined income subject to tax as today and the incomes were classified by the size of total income subject to tax. However the basis was still assessed income as opposed to accrued income. Furthermore only one summary table was produced containing details of total income, income by source and the amount of 'estimated' tax raised. The latter was an estimate inasmuch as the super-tax for 1918–19 incomes would not have been assessed till 1919–20. The summary table also included a row entitled 'other income', which though not classified by ranges was added to the income totals. It amounted to 12 % of total income, three-quarters of which comprised undistributed company profits, the remainder being retained earnings in insurance companies, income distributed to residents not in the United Kingdom and the income of clubs, etc.

This interesting adjoinder illustrates the difference from present-day definitions of personal taxable income which would not include these items. Furthermore undistributed company profits are not even included in the total income of personal sector nowadays. In 1920 however there were no independent estimates of aggregate personal income. In fact cross-checking for deficiencies against independent control totals would have been almost impossible and the Board made no reference to any possible deficiencies. It also gave no information on the method of estimation other than stating that it was based on tax returns. We could conclude that it was probably a total census of these returns.

An identical distribution was made a few years later by the Board for the financial year 1920–1. This appeared in Appendix XIV of the *Report of the Committee on National Debt and Taxation* (the Colwyn Committee) ([QRL 15], Cmd. 2800) which was published in 1927. Again there was no mention of deficiencies and the method of estimation.

The only other pre-war survey by the Inland Revenue was for the financial year 1937–8 which was published in the 83rd report of the Board ([QRL 51], Cmd. 6769) which came out in 1946 and not in 1940 as it should have done. This survey was undoubtedly the 'pioneer' of the post-war surveys. It contained a summary table and five detailed tables. The latter were for income by marital status, income source cross-classified with married units, single males and single females and finally a family classification table.

Unfortunately the explanatory notes with this survey are far from clear. To begin with the Board states that though the survey is for 1937–8 all the income except that of manual workers is actually for 1936–7. That is about 80 % of the total. This implies that the 'assessed' income concept as opposed to 'accrued' income was used though this is never stated. Further only incomes in excess of £200 p.a. were included even though the effective exemption limit was then £125 p.a. Finally no mention is made of any deficiencies nor of the method of estimating. It is generally believed that it was a full census of all four million taxpayers though this has never been officially confirmed. Admittedly however in the 92nd report [QRL 52] the Board did belatedly state that the survey 'suffered from certain defects' and that these had not been 'adjusted for'. At best we can describe the survey as a useful 'pilot study' for subsequent surveys. At worst it remains something of a mystery, to quote Professor A. M. Cartter [B 17].

3.3 Central Statistical Office Data

3.3.1 *Source and Description*

From the first National Income and Expenditure *Blue Book* [QRL 37] in 1952 up to that of 1969, the Central Statistical Office had published data on the distribution of personal income. The distributions were for the calendar years from 1949 up to 1967. After the 1969 *Blue Book*, this source of information temporarily ceased. The CSO explained that the increasing amount of estimation required to produce the distributions was the prime reason for the suspension of the series. However ever-increasing demand for the series to return, particularly since the formation of the Royal Commission on the Distribution of Personal Income and Wealth [QRL 62] coupled with improved estimation procedures has caused the series to be restored in the *National Income and Expenditure 1964–74* [QRL 38] and in the *First Report of the Royal Commission on the Distribution of Personal Income and Wealth* [QRL 62]. A description of these estimates is given in [QRL 62] Appendix E, and a more detailed account is in the August 1975 issue of *Economic Trends* [QRL 20].

The first series of CSO distributions were in fact produced by the Inland Revenue. They were extensions of the latter's survey data to bring in as many of those incomes and income outside the 'taxable income' field as possible. The income recipient in the distributions was defined in exactly the same way as for the Inland Revenue distributions (see sub-section 3.2.3). The survey data was also converted from a financial year to a calendar year basis by extrapolation. This was done so that there could be a link with the other aggregate data on personal income in the *Blue Books* and with the Registrar General's estimates of the mid-year population. This series published distributions for every year from 1949 to 1967 though only those which corresponded to the Inland Revenue surveys, namely for 1949, 1954, 1959 and 1962 onwards can be considered reliable. Those for other years were extrapolations of the above years. The new series differs in that it is now under the auspices of the CSO and avoids the complication of converting the Inland Revenue surveys, which are still the basis of the estimates, to a calendar year equivalent. They will be for financial years.

The amount of information in the distributions was very limited, being equivalent to the Inland Revenue summary tables, that is the aggregate distribution of personal income before and after tax and by pre- and post-tax income ranges. There was no data on the distribution by type of income, region or family size, etc. The new estimates will be likewise restricted.

3.3.2 *Method of Estimation—The Numbers of Incomes*

The models devised formerly by the Inland Revenue and latterly by the CSO in order to build up the control totals of persons in each of the surveys are presented in Table 3.5. The procedures for 1963 and 1972/3 are illustrated as examples. The methods of computation have altered slightly between the old and new series. (For further details of the compilation for the first series see [B 59] Table 1.4, p. 17, and an article in *Economic Trends* [QRL 20] August 1975 for the 1972–3 estimates.)

The basis of the models is the calculated total number of persons over 15 years of age who are residing or have resided in the UK at any time during the year in question. This is item (5) in Table 3.5. The figures for the earlier series are deficient in that net migration as opposed to gross migration was used. From this total the number of married couples, single males and single females during the year are estimated. Item (7)—marriages during the year—is not subtracted, since any female married in the year is counted twice, first as a single person and secondly as part of a married couple. The result is item (10). Again the earlier series computations erred in that they did not take into account the deaths and gross migration of married women during the year. Item (10) is then expanded by those under 15 in receipt of taxable investment income in 1972–3 and in the earlier series by scholarships incomes of minors. This latter category of income is now treated as part of the parents' income. The earlier series finally deducted all incomes below £50 p.a., estimated by the Inland Revenue to constitute 17% of all income units. This was a general rule of thumb based on experience in handling this type of data. The present procedure is to include all such incomes but deduct all pupils over 15 at school, for whom any income received is aggregated implicitly with that of the parents unless covered by item (11).

The main criticism of the models focuses on the treatment of minors' income. The principle in the first series was to enter these as separate income units as far as possible. Unfortunately there were few data available and the coverage was obviously incomplete. The 1972–3 estimates are clearly adopting the principle of aggregation. This, in fact, is closer to a concept of family income. However it is a pity that it has not been possible to aggregate minors' investment income above the exemption limit. The frequent changes in the tax statutes regarding this type of income (see subsection 3.2.3) create further difficulties in devising a consistent series of estimates.

Table 3.5 The Build-Up of the Control Total of Persons and Income Units

Item	*1963 ('000s)*	*1972–3 ('000s)*
1. Total population at end year[(a)]	53,994	55,986
2. Population under 15 at end of year[(a)]	−12,458	−13,400
3. All deaths in population at least 15 during year[(b)]	+627	+657
4. Gross emigration of population during year[(b)]	+12[(c)]	+184
5. TOTAL POPULATION OVER 15 DURING YEAR	42,175	43,427
6. Less all married women at end of year[(a)]	−13,550	−14,127
7. Plus marriages during year[(b)]	+401	+482
8. Less deaths of married women during year [(b)]	n.a.	−95
9. Less gross emigration of married women during year[(b)]	n.a.	−49
10. Total number of males and single females over 15 during year	29,026	29,638
11. Minors with investment income above the effective exemption limit[(d)]	60	+13
12. Pupils over 15 still at school	n.a.	−1,300
13. Minors in receipt of LEA grants[(d)]	154	
14. Less units below £50 p.a.[(e)]	−1962	
15. Total number of units in distributions	27,278	28,351
16. Item (15) rounded off	27,300	n.a.

Sources: n.a.—not available; 1963 from figures provided by the Inland Revenue; 1972–3 ([QRL 62] Table E.4., p. 189).
Notes: (a) For 1963, 31st December; for 1972–3, 6 April 1973; (b) For 1963, 1 January to 31 December; for 1972–3, 6 April 1972 to 5 April 1973; (c) 1963 figures are based on net migration data only; (d) Minors are under 15 years of age; (e) Not deducted in 1972–3

3.3.3 *Method of Estimation—The Amount of Income*

The basis of the estimates is taxable income as defined in the Inland Revenue Surveys (see subsection 3.2.2). In the pre-1967 series they were adjusted by the Inland Revenue to a calendar year equivalent, and the following categories of income incorporated:

1. all units with incomes greater than £50 p.a., but below the effective tax exemption limit;
2. National Assistance grants and benefits paid in the form of non-taxable incomes—for example, unemployment benefits, National Assistance, National Insurance benefits, maternity grants, sickness and injury benefits and the like;
3. scholarships and educational grants paid to persons or paid on their behalf (e.g. university fees);
4. incomes-in-kind of domestic servants and agricultural workers.

These items were all divided between the appropriate income groups, with adjustments being made for incomes which as a result moved into a higher range. The allocation to the various groups was based on information from the public institutions providing national insurance benefits, scholarships, etc. for the items (2) and (3) and from the Ministry of Agriculture and Fisheries (or its equivalent in Scotland and Northern Ireland) for the income-in-kind for agricultural workers. Tax data were used for the income-in-kind of domestic servants. Item (1) was estimated as a residual between total 'taxable income' and total personal income less that not allocated in the distributions. The major proportion of the non-taxable income included in the distributions was allocated to the lowest income range of £50–200 p.a. However with the rise in social security benefits, etc. and the increasing numbers being caught in the 'taxable income' net this proportion was falling. This meant that the scope for avoiding the 'matching' problems of non-taxable and taxable income sources for the same units by using the lowest income range as a residual was being restricted. This in turn implied that much more detailed information was required. This combined with the complexity of the 'matching' processes, one suspects played a dominant part in the Inland Revenue decision to suspend these calculations in 1969.

For the 1972–3 estimates the computation was broadly similar. The National Income Accounts figure for personal income was adjusted to the equivalent financial year and adjustments were made to the Inland Revenue surveys to include as much of this control total as possible and relevant. Incomes below the effective exemption limit were compiled from firstly Inland Revenue returns on such incomes, secondly by reference to the *New Earnings Surveys* to obtain an estimate of employment income for holders of insurance cards without tax deduction cards and finally for National Insurance and occupational pensions below the exemption limit, by reference to the difference between independently estimated control totals and the numbers of these incomes covered by the *Inland Revenue Surveys*. The CSO then states that 'The resulting amount of income and the number of persons were then allocated on the basis of information on tax units extracted principally from the *Family Expenditure Survey*' ([QRL 62], p. 189, para. 6). Family allowances received by incomes below the exemption limits were allocated in a similar manner.

Non-taxable incomes, such as supplementary benefits, unemployment benefits and scholarships (categories 2 and 3 for the earlier series) were also allocated on the basis of information from the FES. The new series makes no adjustment for the income in kind of domestic servants and agricultural workers though an adjustment is made to include the imputed value of luncheon vouchers, again adapting information extracted from the FES. The 'matching' difficulties encountered in the later years of the first series, therefore, have been overcome by an extensive use of the *Family Expenditure Survey*.

The difference between total personal income classified by ranges and total personal income is known as 'unallocatable' non-taxable personal income. 'Classified' total personal income represents the extent of the 'coverage' of the CSO data *vis-à-vis* total personal income: see Table 3.6.

Table 3.6 The Proportion of Total Personal Income classified by Income Ranges (in percentages)

Year	*'Classified' income*	*'Unallocatable' income*
1949	84·8	15·2
1954	85·6	14·4
1959	83·0	17·0
1963	83·5	16·5
1964	81·7	18·3
1965	82·5	17·5
1966	83·5	16·5
1967	83·9	16·1
1972–3	82·1	17·9

Sources: CSO *Blue Book*, various issues; *Royal Commission on the Distribution of Income and Wealth* [QRL 62], Appendix E

'Unallocatable' income, as can be seen from Table 3.6, is quite a large item. Up to and including 1967 it comprised:

1. other non-classified income in kind, e.g. free coal to coal-miners, etc.;
2. non-taxable grants from public authorities, such as milk and welfare foods, industrial services for the disabled, grants to schools and universities;
3. investment income of private non-profit-making bodies, of life assurance companies and superannuation funds;
4. the amount by which the imputed rent of owner-occupied dwellings exceeds the Schedule A valuation (in 1963 the whole of imputed rent as a result of the abolition of Schedule A tax);
5. that part of the income of self-employed persons which is covered by allowances for depreciation;
6. accrued interest on National Savings certificates;
7. post-war credits;
8. incomes of persons receiving less than £50 p.a.;
9. most employers' and employees' contributions to National Insurance and superannuation schemes—this item presumably diminished in importance after 1961–2, since when National Insurance relief has not been deducted from income in the Inland Revenue surveys—less the total of pensions and annuities derived from private superannuation schemes.

The 1972–3 estimates derive and categorize 'unallocatable' income in a different manner. It was defined as the difference between 'allocated' income and the total personal income of individuals and households. This latter figure was derived from total personal income less payments to life assurance and superannuation funds and to private non-profit-making bodies received from outside the personal sector, but plus payments to individuals from these funds. The deductions mainly include employers' superannuation contributions and the investment and property income of life assurance and superannuation funds and charities. There is, however, no allowance made for the transfer of income from private non-profit-making bodies to individuals or the undistributed profit income of unincorporated businesses and agricultural companies. Stock appreciation and capital depreciation are also included. The definition of total personal income of households and individuals is thus not as comprehensive as that computed by Moyle and Reid [QRL 9] (see subsection 2.8.1), where the adjustments resulted in a figure approximately 4% below 'officially' defined total personal income. In this instance the resulting figure was 2·5% lower, implying that the 'unallocated' proportion was effectively 15·7% as opposed to 17·9% given in Table 3.6. Since we argued in subsection 2.8.1 that probably 7 to 8% of personal income as conventionally defined is not the income of households or individuals then both the above figure and those in Table 3.6 considerably overstate the significance of 'unallocated' income.

The 1972–3 categories of income which were not allocated, after the aforementioned adjustment, were classified according to income type, e.g. employment, self-employment, rent, dividends and so on (see Table E3 [QRL 62] for further details).

Exactly half of the 'unallocated' income was accounted for by the imputed rent of owner-occupied dwellings, employers' National Insurance contributions and employees' superannuation contributions. The remainder comprised some adjustment factors, capital allowances, farm self-employment income, income in kind, the undistributed income of private trusts and untaxed interest and investment income. Lump sums payable on death or retirement, marriage gratuities and refunds from life assurance and superannuation funds were also 'unallocated'. Except for these latter lump sum items and bearing in mind the initial adjustment to the definition of total personal income the categories of 'unallocatable' income are broadly comparable with those of the earlier series.

3.3.4 *Criticisms and Developments*

The technical deficiencies of the Inland Revenue surveys, outlined in subsections 3.2.6 and 3.2.7, are very relevant to the CSO distributions. Furthermore the criticisms relating to the definition of the income recipient outlined in subsection 3.2.11 are also relevant, particularly so when we bear in mind that there were no family size cross-classifications accompanying these distributions. The latter point means that the CSO data cannot be used to derive *per capita* or per adult equivalent distributions.

It might be thought that the Inland Revenue survey family classification tables could be readily linked to the CSO distributions and extrapolated to cover all non-taxable income units. Unfortunately one basic defect of the CSO data provides a major obstacle to this exercise. This defect is that some persons are included twice in the CSO distributions. Double-counting arises with respect to marriages, divorces and deaths of husbands in the current year. In each case the female partner was entered twice, first as a single person income unit and, secondly, as part of a married person unit. This implies that the family classification tables could not be 'matched'. The problem is further heightened by the fact that some of the dependents in the family classification tables could also be in receipt of non-taxable incomes and hence part of the CSO distributions (see Stark [B 59] for a detailed description of these problems and an attempt to overcome them).

Another clear deficiency in the data is the 'unallocated' income. Some of this could be classed as either income of households or persons that for certain types of studies ought to be included in the allocation by income ranges. The definition of income is particularly inconsistent by the exclusion of the imputed rent of owner-occupied dwellings (see subsection 3.10.3). The investment income of life assurance companies, superannuation funds, charities and universities and also grants to the latter are items, as argued in subsection 2.8.1, which have little relevance for any area of personal or household income distribution studies. Non-official estimates, incorporating much of the 'unallocated' income into CSO-based income distributions have been made by Stark ([B 59], Chapter 5) and by H. F. Lydall [B 40] for a selected number of years. Stark [B 59] also considers the complex theoretical issues of including both private pensions and superannuation contributions and, adopting similar reasoning as put forward in subsection 2.8.2, incorporates both into the distribution (see subsection 3.10.4 for further discussion on this point). The estimates by Lydall and Stark are naturally speculative but do indicate that these items could have a noticeable effect on the shape of the income distribution.

The CSO distributions were thus of limited value. Nevertheless they did attempt to incorporate a wider range of personal income than the Inland Revenue surveys and could be used as a base for interesting but speculative research by academics, with the attraction that a link to national income and population aggregates was available. This link was particularly useful in providing a control total for family income and incomes below the tax exemption limit. For these reasons it is welcome news that the CSO has restored these distributions in the *National Income and Expenditure 1964–74* [QRL 38].

3.4 Family Expenditure Survey Data

3.4.1 *Introduction*

The *Family Expenditure Survey* (FES) [QRL 28] started at the beginning of 1957. It is a continuing sample survey of the expenditure and income of private households in the United Kingdom. The Cost of Living Advisory Committee had recommended in 1951 that an enquiry into the pattern of expenditure of such households be held as soon as possible and suggested that there should be smaller-scale enquiries at frequent intervals thereafter. The large-scale *Household Expenditure Enquiry* [QRL 46] took place in 1953–4 and provided the basis for the weights used for the Index of Retail Prices (RPI) introduced in 1956.

A main purpose of the smaller-scale enquiries suggested by the Committee was to show whether these weights were becoming unrepresentative of current expenditure patterns and so to indicate when a further large-scale enquiry should be held to provide a basis for revised weights. However it was decided instead that the *Family Expenditure Survey* should be on a continuing basis and that information obtained over a period of three consecutive years should be used as a basis for annual revision of the Index weights. Consequently no further large-scale surveys have been held, but the size of the *Family Expenditure Survey* sample has been enlarged.

Although the primary purpose of these enquiries has been to obtain information on expenditure patterns, they have provided some information, as a by-product, on income distribution. The characteristics of the 1953–5 enquiry differ in some respects from those of the *Family Expenditure Survey* and so that enquiry is considered separately in subsection 3.4.7.

From the beginning, the FES was designed to meet a variety of needs, other than the RPI weights, including estimates of consumers' expenditure in national accounts, demand analysis (i.e. the relationships between the income and the pattern of expenditure of different groups of households) and information on the redistribution of income resulting from direct and indirect taxes on the one hand and from subsidies, social security benefits and some social services on the other.

A volume of detailed results of the 1953–4 enquiry was published in 1957. Reports on the FES have been published annually, except that there was a single report on the first three years 1957 to 1959 and a single report on the next two years, 1960 and 1961. The 1957 survey only covered Great Britain, but was extended to include Northern Ireland from 1958 onwards.

The Department of Employment is responsible for the surveys. The Social Survey Division of the Office of Population Censuses and Surveys carries out the fieldwork. In 1967 a larger survey was begun in Northern Ireland; the Statistics and Economics Unit of the Department of Finance both carries out the survey and is responsible for the data from the province. They in fact publish their own report [QRL 43]. A random sub-sample of the main Northern Ireland sample is included in the sample for the United Kingdom survey (see subsection 3.4.8).

The prime aim is still to provide expenditure weights for the Retail Price Index. Nevertheless the surveys have been widely used by the Central Statistical Office as supplements to data on personal incomes and expenditure and as the main source for work initiated by J. L. Nicholson on the redistributive effects of taxation, both direct and indirect, and government welfare expenditure (see [QRL 10, QRL 20] and subsection 3.4.9.).

The surveys have also been used by academics in the study of income distribution (see Prest and Stark [B 48]) and in the study of poverty, especially by B. Abel-Smith and P. Townsend [B 1] and A. B. Atkinson [B 6].

3.4.2 *Definition of Income*

The basic concept of income is the usual or normal weekly gross cash receipts of the income recipient at the time of interview. This means that most forms of taxable income are included, before the deduction of income tax and National Insurance contributions, as well as social security benefits and scholarships received in cash. On the other hand windfall gains, such as legacies, maturing insurance policies, etc. are omitted as are the gains or receipts from the sale of any financial or tangible asset. These are excluded because they are not considered regular or normal payments. Non-cash receipts of income are generally excluded though the value of luncheon vouchers and rent-free accommodation is included. Cash payments made by persons within the income recipient unit are further omitted, for example lodging charges on boarders since the unit is a household (see subsection 3.4.3). However, cash payments by the household as an employer to a resident domestic servant are taken into account. Finally, unlike the Inland Revenue surveys, mortgage interest payments are not deducted (see subsection 3.10.3). This concept is considered by the Department of Employment as the most relevant income measure for an analysis of consumer expenditure patterns, based on the premise that adjustments in expenditure patterns are only made with respect to 'permanent' changes in income receipts.

The key factor is the concept of the normal or usual receipts. For the standard wage earner it is the amount currently received plus an addition for the value of cash bonuses received during the year. These are converted to a weekly basis. However for other categories of income and income recipient the concept can pose some complex problems.

For an employee away from work social security benefits and grants are the basis for estimating normal income, but only if he or she has been unemployed or sick for thirteen weeks or more. Up to the thirteenth week earnings from the last pay period are considered as the normal income. There is however unpublished data for social security receipts for those unemployed for less than thirteen weeks. Furthermore the thirteen-week convention is only a divide line and not rigidly applied. For investment and self-employed income, the weekly equivalents of the annual amount for the previous twelve months are taken.

The income definition also includes rent income from sub-letting accommodation. The figure adopted is the excess of the rent received over total expenditure on the housing. This implies that if housing expenditure exceeds rent income then a zero rent income is recorded. No attempt is made to apportion housing expenditure to the sub-let accommodation. Furthermore the household expenditure on housing is reduced by the amount of rent received. It is altogether an odd procedure. In addition an imputation is made for those cases where either no rent is paid or where there is owner-occupancy. In those instances the weekly equivalent of the most recent rateable value is adopted but adjusted for increases in rental value by use of the rent component in the General Index of Retail Prices. However from 1975 the adjustment will be related to building society mortgage interest payments less tax allowances, which is in line with the changes recently adopted in the compilation of the Retail Prices Index. Finally the survey interviewers frequently find that though they ask for gross income estimates they often have only net income estimates for investment and self-employment income and for other incomes where tax is paid at source. In these instances imputed tax payments are included.

It can be seen thus that the income concept is only an approximation and that it may or may not if multiplied by fifty-two correspond to actual annual income. This plus the omission of income in kind makes it difficult to link the income totals in the FES reports to independent control totals of personal income. On the other hand, mainly due to lack of resources, there are many unpublished income data derived from the survey and some of them are used by the various government departments and private academic researchers. This material does enable alternative (see [B 20] as an example) and broader definitions of income to be adopted and a closer approximation to actual annual income can be obtained. The SSRC survey archive at Essex University [B 98] holds all the FES data up to 1963–4 and later unpublished data may be obtained by arrangement, for bona fide research workers, from the Government Statistical Service. However it must be stressed that the original source material is not given out by the Department of Employment.

3.4.3 *Definition of the Income Recipient*

All the tables in the FES report adopt a household concept for the income recipient. A household comprises either a single person or a group of persons living at the same address and who share housekeeping and at least one meal per day. The members of the household may or may not be related to each other. The definition implies no family factor, e.g. domestic servants are included.

This is a straightforward definition but problematic elements arise with respect to persons who are only resident part of the time, such as children at boarding-school, husbands away on work or members in hospital. The survey statisticians have their rules for dealing with each type of case. For example in the above cases children under 16 will be regarded as members provided they remain at home during the holidays, or the husband will be included if he is at home at least one night in seven. Interestingly however if the household member is not a marital partner then the criterion steps up to four-nights-in-seven residence. A member in hospital will be considered only if not away for more than one month prior to the beginning of the interview and returning within seven days from the start of record keeping.

There are further minor technical problems that crop up when the household composition changes during the survey interview. The basic principle is generally to omit members leaving and include those joining. Details on these points are given in the *FES Handbook on the Sample, Fieldwork and Coding Procedures* by W. F. F. Kemsley [B 36].

There is clearly a substantial difference between the FES household concept and the Inland Revenue income unit. It is often argued that the household concept is of greater value in low-income and poverty studies since it approximates more closely to actual living arrangements. However much depends on the degree of income sharing. The FES data imply common sharing for food, rent and other regular payments. Furthermore from subsection 3.4.2 we saw that cash transactions within the household are not reported. These factors imply that analysts would have to make their own assumptions with regard to sharing.

The FES data are coded, for some official purposes, using an income unit concept identical to that used in the Inland Revenue surveys though it is sometimes difficult to identify dependent relatives. Unfortunately these data are not published but can be obtained by bona fide researchers. The survey also collects data on the income of the head of the household which are published. A head of household is defined as a member of the household or the husband of the household member who legally owns, or rents or benefits from the house as part of his employment or is the representative of the owner if the latter is not part of the household. If two members have equal claim to this title then either the male is taken or the elder if both are of the same sex.

3.4.4 *Scope of the Data*

Since 1965 the pattern of presentation and the scope of data presented by the FES have been very much standardized. Before 1965 the variation from year to year was quite noticeable. In Table 3.7 we list the income distribution data that are and have been available in the FES reports since 1957.

Most tables refer to household weekly income. The number of single and double cross-classifications is quite substantial. A brief definition of the titles of some of the data in Table 3.7 is essential.

Table 3.7 *Data on Income Distribution Available in the Family Expenditure Survey*

Type of Data	*Years* 74	73	72	71	70	69	68	67	66	65	64	63	62	61	60	59	58	57
(a) Household income by:																		
1. All households	/	/	/	/	/	/	/	/	/	/	/	/	/	/	/	/	/	/
2. Age of head of household	/	/	/	/	/	/	/	/	/	/								
3. Composition of household	/	/	/	/	/	/	/	/	/	/	/	/		/				
4. Occupation of head of household	/	/	/	/	/	/	/	/	/	/	/	/	/					
5. Source of income	/	/	/	/	/	/	/	/	/	/	/	/						
6. Administrative area	/	/	/	/	/	/	/	/	/	/	/	/						
7. Income of head of household	/	/	/	/	/	/	/	/	/	/	/	/						
8. Size of household	/	/	/	/	/	/	/	/	/	/	/	/						
9. Tenure of dwelling	/	/	/	/	/	/	/	/	/	/	/	/						
10. Number of workers per household	/	/	/	/	/	/	/	/	/	/	/	/						
11. Region	/	/	/	/	/	/	/	/	/	/	/	/						
12. Household with working wives	/	/	/	/	/	/	/	/	/	/	/							
13. Car ownership	/	/	/	/														
14. Availability of consumer durables	/	/	/															
15. Numbers of children of working wives	/	/	/	/	/	/	/	/	/	/	/	/						
16. Employment status of head of household	/	/	/															
17. Composition of household and number of workers	/	/	/															
18. Source of income and administrative area											/							
19. Source of income and household composition										/								
20. Source of income and head of household income												/						
21. Source of income and size of household											/							
22. Source of income, age and income of head of household										/								
23. Type of dwelling											/							
24. Rates and rateable value												/						
25. Detailed data on nature of living conditions											/							
(b) Head of household income by age of head										/								
(c) Weekly earnings by individuals						/	/	/	/	/	/							
(d) Alternative definition of household income by all households			/	/	/	/	/											

The composition of a household refers to the number of male and female adults and children whilst the size of a household merely indicates the number of members. There is also a difference between the occupation and employment status of the head of the household. The latter refers to part-time or full-time employment, unemployed or self-employed groupings whilst the former is a division into professional, managerial, teachers, clerical, manual workers and so on. The source of income tables on the other hand divide household income into employment income, self-employment, social security benefits, pensions, etc.

An administrative area classification splits households into an urban or rural grouping with special sections for Greater London and provincial conurbations. The regional tables however refer to the standard geographical regions of the United Kingdom.

Currently there is only one table that gives an

alternative definition of weekly household income. The definition excludes direct taxation and national insurance contributions but includes value-free and concessionary goods. It is published to enable comparison with similar expenditure surveys from other countries. FES reports have head of household income distributions. Data on weekly earnings of individuals were included in past reports, but the *New Earnings Survey* is now a better source for this information (see subsection 3.6.2). Nevertheless there can be no doubt that the scope of the data from these reports is very extensive indeed.

3.4.5 *Method of Estimation*

A detailed and excellent account of the method of sampling for the survey between 1967 and 1974 is to be found in the *FES—Handbook on the Sample, Fieldwork and Coding Procedures* by W. F. F. Kemsley [B 36]. Those who wish for detailed knowledge in this area are advised to consult this source. What follows in this section is a very brief and general description of the method for those who only wish to have a broad idea of the subject.

The sampling for the survey is undertaken by the Social Survey Division of the Office of Population Censuses and Surveys. Each household in the sample is first interviewed and then requested to keep detailed records of expenditure for a period of fourteen consecutive days following the interview. All the information relating to income, household characteristics and some information on expenditure is obtained from the interview. Though the survey is primarily to estimate expenditure, there are no fewer than sixty-five questions on income in the interview questionnaire. A copy of the 1975 income schedule is given in Appendix D.

Since 1967 there have been approximately 2,700 households in Great Britain selected for interview each quarter, giving an annual sample of 10,750. Before 1967 the surveys had been based on 5,000 selected addresses of which between 3,000 and 3,500 responded. In recent years the proportion of households co-operating has varied between 67 and 75%.

The current sampling frame is based on the 1,800 administrative areas of Great Britain, i.e. the London boroughs, county boroughs, municipal boroughs, rural and urban districts for England and Wales and their equivalent for Scotland. These are known as the primary sampling units (PSUs) and are classified by three factors, namely by the fifteen standard geographical regions; the four types of area; and by an economic indicator based on rateable values. The four types of area are the conurbations, other urban, semi-rural and rural.

The first two factors are used to classify unambiguously each of the 1,800 PSUs into theoretically sixty region/type cells (i.e. 15 × 4), though for reasons such as the non-existence of conurbations in the south-west of England or rural areas in Greater London, the actual number of cells is forty-eight. The next stage is to bring in the third stratification factor. This could have been achieved by simply dividing the cells by the number of strata in this factor. However the logistics of the sampling procedure indicated an alternative approach. A basic principle of the sample is that each household should have an equal probability of selection so that the overall sampling fraction is constant. Thus the forty-eight cells are divided into strata of approximately equal population size. The number chosen is actually 168. Therefore the total population is divided by 168 to derive the average population per stratum which is required. This latter figure is then divided into the population of each region/type cell. This determines the number of final strata to be adopted by the economic indicator for each region/type cell. For example if the required average population per stratum is 300,000 persons, and the population of a given cell is 900,000 then the number of final strata for this cell is three. Further, if this cell contained twelve PSUs, these would then be divided into three groups according to the economic indicator. A similar calculation is done for each region/type cell so that the 1,800 PSUs are unambiguously allocated to 168 final strata, which are of equal size but which altogether are representative both geographically and economically. For example the four largest administrative areas, Glasgow, Birmingham, Manchester and Liverpool, each constitute one whole final stratum whereas in certain areas of Scotland a number of region/rural type cells are combined to form one final stratum.

The next step is to select each calendar quarter one PSU from each of the 168 final stratum. This is done randomly with a probability proportional to size of population, thereby preserving the principle of a constant sampling fraction. The final stage is then to select sixteen addresses in each PSU. This is done from the electoral register by first selecting randomly electoral wards, again on the basis probability proportional to size of population, and then randomly picking addresses in the selected ward. The outcome is a sample of 2,688 addresses, concentrated geographically in 168 small areas for the convenience of interviewing. In addition a rota system is introduced whereby each PSU is used four times at intervals of three months and then replaced by another random selection from the same final stratum. Each set of 168 areas selected for a particular quarter is divided into three groups of fifty-six and allocated at random to the three months in a calendar quarter, thus providing an initial monthly sample of 896 addresses. Finally the whole frame has also been designed to allow for changes in the size and distribution of population and in the boundaries of the administrative areas. In the light of the new local government areas introduced in April 1974 there have been corresponding adjustments in the sampling frame for the 1975 survey.

The total sample size used between 1957 and 1966 was smaller than that above and somewhat different in detail. The matrix cross-classified the administrative areas by only three groups for England and Wales, namely the Greater London conurbation, other urban areas and rural areas. For Scotland the areas were divided only into urban and rural. The next stage was to divide the cells into 128 strata from which thirty-nine addresses were finally selected, giving 4,992 addresses in the sample. The 128 primary sampling units, one per stratum, were not in continuous use throughout the year. They were divided into eight sets of sixteen and a set was used for each half quarter of the year. This technique made correct regional representation difficult and as a result the sample was unable to distinguish regional and seasonal variations. Furthermore the response rate was such that only 3,000 to 3,500 addresses co-operated. The data from the sample could only be considered nationally representative for the whole calendar year. It was due to these difficulties that the enlarged sample was introduced in 1967.

3.4.6 *Criticisms and Disadvantages*

A number of the problems of the *Family Expenditure Survey* as a source of income distribution data have already been touched upon in the previous sections. The main problems stem from the definition of income (cf. subsection 3.4.2). The concept of 'normal' income is derived from the Friedman-type permanent income concepts in consumption function studies. Since it excludes so-called 'transitory' income in addition to most incomes in kind and inter-household cash transactions, then it is not an accurate reflection of actual household resources. Thatcher [B 62] has estimated that the average sample household income is 2% below the 'true' population value. These deficiencies are apparent when 'grossed-up' estimates of FES income data are compared to National Income Accounts data. There emerges particularly notable deficiencies in pension, investment and self-employment income. A small proportion of these deficiencies will, of course, result from the exclusion of persons living in institutions in the sample and errors involved in projecting annual data from a weekly reference period. These factors point to the difficulties in cross-checking

FES income with independently estimated control totals.

Another significant criticism of the survey applies to the response rate of the survey. This has varied from 65 to 75% of sampled households. Mogridge [B 43] has argued that the non-respondents are not randomly distributed and that there is a downward bias in the number in the upper income groups. This conclusion is supported by the dramatic fall in the response rates for households with a very high rateable value and those paying a high level of taxes (see Kemsley [B 36], p. 89 for details). Another notable feature is the lack of very high incomes in the surveys. For example in the 1974 survey there were no incomes above £12,000 p.a. on a tax unit definition. Unlike the Inland Revenue surveys there is some cause for caution with the upper tail of the FES distributions. It is also suggested that the combination of non-response and the exclusion of the institutional and homeless population means that the FES distribution is truncated at both ends of the distribution.

There is also considerable regional variation in response rates. The rural response rates are uniformly much higher than the urban centres, with that for Greater London being particularly low. A number of these response problems might be overcome if the sampling technique adopted the quota system as used in the equivalent Irish *Household Budget Enquiries* [B 79]. This system guarantees a given and uniform response rate by demanding a specified number of successfully sampled households in each sampled area. In the FES framework this would require that for each sampled PSU more than sixteen addresses are randomly selected, say thirty, and that the interviewer proceeds randomly through this list until sixteen co-operating households are obtained. Since less than 4% of households promising to co-operate, actually fail to do so, this would lead to considerable standardization of the sample size as well as eliminating bias towards high-response areas. It would also eliminate variations in response rates due to the variation in the skill of interviewers, which in some years have been significant (see Kemsley [B 36], p. 29 for further details).

The overall reliability of the present surveys is very hard to judge. The accuracy of much of the base data will depend on the skill of the interviewers. There is no reason to suspect that this is not generally of the highest quality. The normal statistical indicators, such as standard errors, give a low value of 1% for all income in the survey, with the individual categories of income varying from 1% for employment to 7% or occasionally 10% for self-employed and investment income. A final point is that for some household size/income cells in the very low income groups, the numbers in the sample are so few that very little reliability can be attached to their representativeness. This means that FES-based poverty studies must also be treated with caution.

3.4.7 *The 1953–4 Enquiry*

In 1951 the *Interim Report of the Cost of Living Advisory Committee* [B 80] recommended that there should be a large-scale enquiry into household expenditure as soon as possible and that there should follow smaller enquiries at frequent intervals. The Report was primarily interested in weights for the Retail Price Index. There had been no full-scale enquiry into household expenditure in the UK since 1937–8 [QRL 22], which by 1951 was very clearly out of date.

The outcome was the large 1953–4 *Household Expenditure Survey* [QRL 46] which was published in 1957. As with the *Family Expenditure Survey* the 1,800 administrative areas of the United Kingdom formed the basis of the survey. Of the areas, each of the London boroughs and the seventy most populous urban areas outside London were automatically chosen. Of the remaining areas, 200 smaller urban areas were selected and eighty rural areas. The choice was made randomly but constricted to give a correct regional balance. The next stage was to choose one address per 2,500 persons per area. This sampling fraction was derived from the ratio of the United Kingdom population of 50 million against the desired sample size of 20,000 addresses. As it materialized, 19,881 addresses were selected. The response rate was about 67%, and the number of households that co-operated 13,018.

The households were interviewed over a period from late January 1953 to early 1954. The definition of the household was the same as that used in the *Family Expenditure Survey*. However the definition of income is substantially different. No attempt was made at any concept of 'normal' or regular income as in the *Family Expenditure Survey*, but rather a straight weekly figure of total personal income as conventionally defined. This difference naturally reduces the value of comparisons with the *Family Expenditure Survey* data.

Finally the scope of the data in the survey is extensive. In addition to standard household income distributions there are cross-classifications by household size, occupation of head, type of dwelling, region and type of area (urban, etc.). The data from this enquiry are currently held in the SSRC Survey Archive at Essex University [B 98].

3.4.8 *The Northern Ireland Survey*

Since 1967 the Government of Northern Ireland has published a separate *Family Expenditure Report* [QRL 43] for the province. From 1958 Northern Ireland had been included in the survey for the whole of the United Kingdom, but due to the very small population of the area the number of households sampled was inadequate to provide reliable regional results. Since the separate Northern Ireland Survey began in 1967, a random subsample of approximately one-third of the main sample has been included in the sample for the United Kingdom survey.

The survey is conducted along identical lines to the national one. The sampling frame is based on three broad geographical divisions using local authority areas. The divisions are:

(1) The counties of Fermanagh, Londonderry and Tyrone, including the city of Londonderry,
(2) the counties of Antrim, Armagh and Down, and
(3) Belfast County Borough.

The first two divisions are subdivided into urban and rural areas and a constant sampling fraction based on population is devised such that we have for:

division (1) four urban and eight rural areas with sixteen addresses each;
division (2) six urban and twelve rural areas with twenty-four addresses;
division (3) one area with 288 households.

That is a total of 912 addresses. Cross-checking with census of population data indicates that a correct structure with respect to household size, sex and age is obtained (see [QRL 43], Appendix 1, of the 1970 survey for details). The response rate has to date varied from 75 to 79%, which is noticeably higher than the overall rate for the United Kingdom survey, which, at least to some extent, might be explained by the higher rural/urban mix in Northern Ireland.

The range of data published in the survey is again similar to that in the United Kingdom survey. The only noticeable difference between the two surveys is that the standard errors for the Northern Irish income estimates are appreciably higher. The standard error for all income is 2·7%, with that for individual types of income varying from 4·1% for wages and salaries to 16–20% for investment income, annuities and private pensions. These higher standard errors arise in spite of the higher sampling fraction, since they are primarily a function of the sample size. An effective sample of about 800 households, representing 2,700 persons is a sampling fraction of one person in 500, compared to a rate of one person in 2,500 for the United Kingdom survey. This is, in fact, a good example of a common fallacy, frequently adopted in evaluating sample surveys.

3.4.9 *The Redistribution of Income Studies*

The *Family Expenditure Survey* data are used by the Central Statistical Office to estimate on an annual basis the redistribution of income through taxation and social service benefits. These estimates have been published from time to time, usually once per year since November 1962 in the *Economic Trends* [QRL 20]. The estimates span each year from 1957, with the exception of 1958, to the most recent study for 1974. Similar but less reliable estimates for 1953 from the 1953–4 *Household Expenditure Enquiry* are to be found in J. L. Nicholson's *Redistribution of Incomes in the United Kingdom 1959, 1957 and 1953* [QRL 10]. This work which was published in 1965 contains a detailed account of the author's work at the CSO in this field. Each published study in the *Economic Trends* also gives a comprehensive set of definitions, descriptions and conclusions. A recently published study ([QRL 20], December 1974) contains a summary account of the changes in method and definitions that have taken place since the first estimates. In the main these have been slight and do not impair general comparability over the years. The only major change is in the treatment of employers' National Insurance contributions.

The basic method of the studies, after having converted the *Family Expenditure Survey* data from a weekly to an annual period, is to estimate for each group of households, classified by income, family size, retired and non-retired categories (the latter since 1967); the amounts of direct taxes paid plus those indirect taxes incurred through consumption expenditure on the one hand, and the amounts of direct and indirect social service benefits, including education and health, both in cash and kind, on the other hand.

The definition of income adopted, called original income in the studies, is slightly different from that used for households in the FES reports, in that first, it, includes a broader range of incomes in kind, secondly up to 1969 it included employer contributions for National Insurance, etc. and finally direct cash benefits are excluded. These comprise family allowances, the Family Income Supplements, National Insurance and social security benefits, pensions and grants from the State. Since 1969 employers' contributions for National Insurance have been excluded. The change was made since it was considered that the contributions were indirect taxes on labour utilization akin to the Selective Employment Tax rather than direct taxes on income. Employer National Insurance contributions now enter into the indirect taxation estimates. The CSO estimated for the 1973 study that the change on average reduced original income by about £87 and income after all taxation by about £40. The shift from direct to indirect taxation will not entirely cancel out since some of the incidence now falls on other final consumers such as the government and not just households. It is a matter of opinion how one classifies such contributions. It must be noted that the practice now adopted in these studies and the FES is contrary to the definition of income in the National Income Accounts. Direct cash benefits are excluded from 'original' income as they are part of the redistribution process. To include them would mean that this process could not be gauged against a concept of income which was, in the short run at any rate, independent of the process itself.

The direct tax payments by households, that is income tax, surtax and employee National Insurance contributions are also estimated directly from the returns of the FES. However the remaining items in the redistribution equation, namely direct benefits in kind, indirect taxes and indirect benefits have to be proxied from information received in the sample.

The direct benefits in kind comprise the National Health Service, State education, school health services, scholarships and education grants from the State and school meals, milk and welfare foods. Apart from the receipt of maternity grants, the FES gives no direct indication of the use of the National Health Service by households. The average cost per birth is allocated to each household reporting the receipt of maternity grants. For the other health services, the average cost per service is computed for eight age groups, separately for males and females and then allocated to each individual as appropriate and aggregated for each household. A similar imputation is undertaken for education services, but with the difference in this case that the person to whom the value is imputed actually receives a service, whereas for health they may or may not. The Family Expenditure schedules provide information on the members of households receiving different types of full-time education. The appropriate cost per person per type of education is taken as the value of the benefit.

The only indirect benefit to households computed is the incidence of housing subsidies. The subsidy is estimated separately for each local authority house in the sample. It is defined as the difference between an economic rent and the actual rent paid. The economic rent is calculated 'by marking up the rateable value of the dwelling in the ratio of the total current account expenditure on all dwellings owned by the local authority to the total rateable value of these dwellings' ([QRL 20], November 1972, p. xxi).

Indirect taxes are divided into two categories. First those on consumption expenditure such as Value Added Tax (and formerly purchase tax), Customs and Excise duties on tobacco, petrol, wines, beer, etc. stamp duties, driving licences, the motor vehicle tax, radio and television licences and local rates less rebates. It is assumed that these are borne *in toto* by the households. The incidence per household of VAT and the Customs and Excise duties is estimated by reference to consumption expenditure of each household. The remaining taxes are paid separately by consumers and hence are included in the FES data on household expenditure.

The second group of indirect taxes are those levied on intermediate goods and services. These are, employer National Insurance contributions, rates on commercial and industrial property, duties on hydrocarbon oils, vehicle licences, duties on imported inputs and, formerly, purchase tax on inputs and Selective Employment Tax. Again it is assumed that these taxes are passed on in their entirety to the final purchasers. The National Income input–output tables are used to calculate the ultimate incidence on the products purchased by the household sector.

The basic disadvantages of the estimates are a result of the basic disadvantages within the *Family Expenditure Survey* itself. In our previous sections we have mentioned the problems of bias in the sample response and the under-reporting of investment and self-employment income. Up to 1963 the CSO attempted to adjust for non-response. In addition to these biases it is also known by cross-checking with the National Income Accounts data that there is serious under-reporting of expenditure by households on drink and tobacco in the sample. This could lead to underestimating the incidence of the tobacco and drink taxes. However the incidence estimates are based on adjustments on tobacco and drink expenditure to tie in with known yields of tax. The adjustments are on a *pro rata* basis. Another point is that the direct benefit and direct tax aspects of redistribution policies are formulated with respect to the family unit and not the household. This means that the effectiveness of these particular policies cannot be judged within their formulated terms of reference.

A theoretical purist would probably argue that the assumption of total incidence on the final consumer is theoretically unsound. Consider the diagrams on page 64.

S_1 represents the quantity the suppliers of a specific commodity in a perfectly competitive market wish to supply in a given period of time at each price in order to maximize profits, assuming no consumption taxes. D in case A is the quantity consumers desire to purchase in a given period of time at each price level. The market

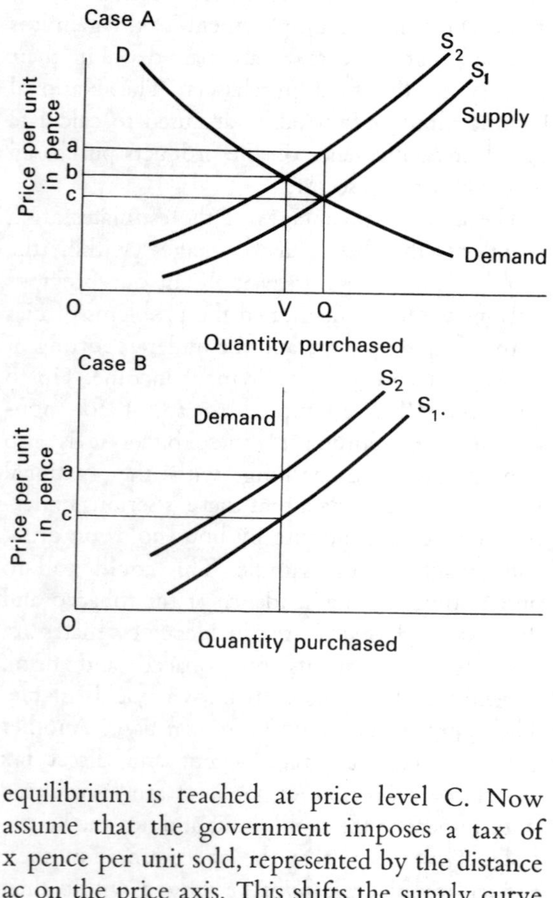

equilibrium is reached at price level C. Now assume that the government imposes a tax of x pence per unit sold, represented by the distance ac on the price axis. This shifts the supply curve to S_2 and the resulting equilibrium price is b. It can be seen in this instance that the full burden of the tax has not been borne by the consumer, only the portion represented by bc/ac. The producer has borne the rest of the burden, represented by the fall in sales from Q to V. Only in case B, where consumer demand is totally insensitive to price, will the consumer pay the full burden. In fact it can be shown that the steeper the slope of the demand curve when the greater the proportion of the tax burden will fall on consumers. However, it is argued that it is unrealistic to assume that all demand curves are as in case B, in fact very few may be. The theoretical arguments are not basically changed by the introduction of monopolistic and dynamic factors. Nevertheless, in the absence of any detailed data on the slopes of demand curves any other assumption of incidence would be as arbitrary as that actually adopted.

A pure theorist would presumably also argue that the value to the consumer of benefits in kind is underestimated by using the cost of the service to the authorities, in that this would be normally less than the price charged were these commodities supplied through the market. Again, there is no obvious practical alternative method of evaluation.

A more significant theoretical cricism concerns the items that are omitted from the redistribution calculation. On the income side capital gains are excluded. Correspondingly all direct capital taxes, such as death duties and capital gains taxes are also excluded. The studies justify these omissions on the grounds that they are in keeping with National Income accounting conventions. This is a weak defence, particularly since they have departed from the convention in respect of employer National Insurance contributions. Furthermore, since rates, essentially a tax on capital, are included, then the aforementioned capital taxes which exist primarily for redistributive reasons should be included. On the other hand the additional questions necessary in the *Family Expenditure Survey* might seriously affect the response rate.

On the benefits side the major omissions are expenditure on policing, prisons, defence, transport, museums, libraries, parks, research and investment grants, etc. These are either considered 'unallocatable' in a statistical sense or not even directly benefiting households. Again from a practical aspect their omission is probably most wise, though it could be argued that some of these items could possibly affect the net redistributive effect such as policing, parks, roads, etc. Certainly earlier pioneering studies on redistribution in the

United Kingdom by Barna in 1938 [B 8] and A. M. Cartter in 1949–50 [B 17] saw fit to include these 'indivisible' benefits.

The above two pioneering studies using Inland Revenue data are very comprehensive and present excellent examples of methodology. However due to very basic defects in the base income distribution data their accuracy is suspect. The Barna study utilized the 1937–8 Inland Revenue income census and Cartter's data for 1949–50 are extrapolations of the above. His work was completed before the 1949–50 census became available. The defects of these income distributions are set out in subsection 3.2. The fact that similar private studies have never been repeated is an indication of the difficulty of research in this field and is a tribute to the work by J. L. Nicholson and the CSO. It is to be hoped that this highly courageous and essentially excellent work will continue.

3.5 The General Household Survey

The *General Household Survey* is a new project sponsored by the Central Statistical Office and produced by the Office of Population Censuses and Surveys. The first survey was published in 1973 and contains data for 1971 [QRL 30], and the second survey with 1972 data was published in early 1976 [QRL 30]. It is intended to publish the surveys regularly but not necessarily every year.

The object is to obtain data on a broad range of social, economic and demographic factors. It will not only be of value to students in these areas but also provide the necessary detailed background information for policy-makers on a wide range of social, educational and environmental problems. In income distribution studies the survey will be of especial interest to those analysts who seek to ascertain the explanation of the distribution of household income by reference to educational factors, e.g. the Human Capital Theories, or by reference to a broader group of environmental and educational factors, such as the theories put forward by Lydall [B 41] and Taubmann [B 61].

3.5.1 *Coverage*

The 1973 *General Household Survey* contained a wide range of income distribution data cross-classified by a number of factors. In Chapter Three, on population, there is a general income classification of households in the survey. This includes cross-classifications by household type, i.e. family size and age of members and source of earnings. This information is contained in three tables.

Chapter Five, on housing, contains tables on tenure (Table 5.15), type of accommodation (Table 5.31), amenities (Table 5.43), all cross-classified by the weekly income of the head of the household. In addition there are further tables on tenure (Table 5.53) and the number of movers in the last five years (also Table 5.53) cross-classified by gross weekly household income. Finally in Chapter Five, Table 5.67 contains data on past movers and potential movers also classified by the weekly income of the head of the household.

Chapter Six, on employment, contains a table on the future work intentions of women with children classified by gross weekly household income. A very important group of tables is in Chapter Seven in Sections 3 and 4 on education. The specific income distribution tables are Table 7.12—type of school by fathers' gross annual earnings from employment; Table 7.13—school or college last attended by gross annual earnings from employment; and finally Table 7.24—full-time employed persons by sex and highest qualification levels attained cross-classified by average annual earnings. This group of data is particularly interesting and should be of value for studies on the human capital factors determining the distribution of earnings. Finally in Chapter Eight, on health, Table 8.15 gives a distribution cross-classifying the incidence of chronic sickness by the weekly income of the head of the household.

3.5.2 *Definitions—The Household and Income*

The income recipient is the household. The definition and usage of this unit is modelled exactly as for the *Family Expenditure Survey* (see subsection 3.4.3).

The definition of income, however, does differ from that of the FES and the number of questions asked on income are fewer. The *General Household Survey* asks each household for gross income over the previous twelve months as opposed to the FES concept of 'normal' income. Gross income comprises earnings from employment and self-employment, pensions, social security and National Insurance benefits, alimonies, annuities, scholarships and transfers from relatives, etc. rent from property and interest income. There is no allowance made for imputed owner-occupied rent, nor are incomes in kind included. Furthermore the inclusion of transfers from other persons would indicate an element of double-counting in aggregation.

3.5.3 *Method of Estimation*

The *General Household Survey* is planned as a continuous survey. It uses the same frame and method as the most recent *Family Expenditure Surveys* (see subsection 3.4.5) except that Northern Ireland is excluded. The two sample surveys are run concurrently and care is taken to ensure that addresses are not duplicated.

Though the frame and method are identical for the two samples the *General Household Survey* adopts a much larger sampling fraction, twenty-two addresses per primary sampling unit as opposed to sixteen in the FES. This produces planned samples of 13,155 households for the *General Household Survey*. In addition there is a supplementary sample of sixty-four primary sampling units in Scotland producing an extra 1,405 addresses. This is done to improve the accuracy of the Scottish estimates for specific use by the Scottish departments. The data for Great Britain as a whole is weighted to allow for this factor.

Chapter Three of the 1973 *General Household Survey* contains a detailed analysis of the statistical issues involved. Particularly interesting and noteworthy are the discussions on the measurement of response rates and its variation by region and area type. The survey as a whole obtained a 71% average response rate for full co-operation only or 83% if partial and proxy replies are included. For the income data the rates are however a little lower. The latter response rate is only 71% of households or 78% of all persons covered for the income questions, although the response rate for these has improved latterly.

The statistics on the pattern of responses are valuable. Very notable are the low responses in the London area and conurbations in general. On the other hand rural communities are replying at a rate over 93% compared to the national average of 83%. Correspondingly Wales and East Anglia are also high response regions. These figures are of some interest to social scientists, though the addition of some social class factor of respondents would enhance their interpretation considerably. These comments, of course, also apply to the *Family Expenditure Survey*.

3.5.4 *Criticisms*

The *General Household Survey* is not designed specifically to produced data on incomes. In fact income information represents only a small fraction of the data output. Furthermore there is no chapter devoted specifically to incomes.

The data contained in the survey is not generally available from the major income distribution sources. In this context the survey is valuable. The avoidance of overlapping between this source and others, particularly the *Family Expenditure Surveys* (see subsection 3.4) is an important design factor. The obvious advantage is the development and expansion of special data sources, without the dangers of overburdening the questionnaires of any particular source. On the other hand the ability to match the *General Household Survey* data with that of other sources is clearly a vital principle. At present, for instance, the survey adopts a wide variety of income definitions. Some of these could be matched with the *Family Expenditure*

Survey data, others possibly with earnings data (see subsections 3.6.1, 2 and 3), but none to the *Inland Revenue Surveys* (see subsection 3.2). A possible future development might be a change in the structure of the questionnaire to permit the presentation of tables adopting as many definitions of incomes as possible. Finally as with most other sources of income distribution data it is difficult to link the results to national aggregates.

3.6 Earnings Data

3.6.1 *Board of Trade and Ministry of Labour Surveys*

Since earnings are intended to be the subject of another review in this series we shall do no more than present a brief outline of sources. Summaries of early surveys of earnings are given in *British Labour Statistics: Historical Abstract 1886–1968* [QRL 16]. This volume in fact contains some data prior to 1886 for a few industries, as early as 1780 for the printing industry.

The first Wages Census was undertaken in the year 1886 by the Board of Trade. It covered all manual workers with the exception of those employed in agriculture, coal-mining, distributive trades and miscellaneous services. The survey produced results on the distribution of earnings of workers in each industry and occupation and by each range of hours worked. The exercise was extensive and expensive and was not repeated till 1906. A detailed account of both of these early 'censuses' is to be found in Bowley [B 13] and Routh [B 50]. Routh [B 50] also contains a detailed analysis of a similar survey undertaken by the Ministry of Labour in 1960. This was the second of such surveys by the Ministry. The first was in 1938 and was similar to that of 1906, except that the distribution of earnings by occupation was excluded (see Ainsworth [B 4] for further details). The 1960 survey was the last of this infrequent series. It covered 5½ million workers, but unlike the others gave no distributions classified by hours worked and occupation and the distributions by industry were restricted to the detail of the minimum list headings of the standard industrial classifications. The results were published in the Ministry of Labour *Gazette* for April and June 1961 [QRL 21]. In all these sources earnings data were restricted to weekly earnings during a given week in the year of the survey.

3.6.2 *The New Earnings Survey*

In September 1968 the Department of Employment and Productivity introduced the *New Earnings Survey*. Initially the survey analysed the results of a sample of 0·5% of all holders of National Insurance cards during a given week in April of each year. The sampling fraction was later increased to 1%, producing an effective sample of 170,000 employees. The survey has been repeated each April since 1970. Analyses of the distribution of weekly earnings are produced for about 120 industries, 190 occupations and ninety national collective agreements and wages councils. The results of all surveys up to 1973 have been published in the Department of Employment *Gazette* [QRL 21] and in the annual reports of the *New Earnings Survey* [QRL 42].

However for 1974 and after the publication details have changed. Some figures will continue to appear in the November issue of the *Gazette* [QRL 21] but the detailed results will come out in six separate booklets at approximately monthly intervals [QRL 41], the first of which appeared in November 1974. The data in the *Gazette* will be restricted to summary tables and key figures for certain national agreements and wages councils, industries, occupations, age-groups and regions.

Another impending change relates to the discontinuance of National Insurance cards in 1975. Consequently from April 1975 onwards the survey will be based on tax deduction cards and the sample will be selected by the Inland Revenue and not as previously by the Department of Health and Social Security from National Insurance card exchanges.

3.6.3 *Department of Health and Social Security Data*
In April 1961 the State Graduated Pension scheme was introduced, in which contributions were payable by employed persons within the PAYE network. These contributions are recorded on deduction cards which are forwarded from the tax authorities to the social security authorities. A sample is drawn from the deduction cards and those selected are matched to the corresponding National Insurance cards.

The Department of Health and Social Security's statistics of earnings are produced from the gross annual earnings recorded on the sampled deduction cards (see F. Whitehead [B 65] subsection 2.28 for further details). The statistics were first produced for 1964–5. The sample is one in every two hundred persons who are 18 or over at the beginning of the year and with at least forty-eight National Insurance contributions either paid or credited and who have not retired, died or attained the age of 70 if male or 65 if female during the year. In addition there are some limited data collected on juveniles.

The statistics are thus restricted to adult full-year employees. The main tables that are produced separately for men and all women by marital status are by age and size of earnings. They relate to Great Britain and are cross-classified by the standard statistical regions, the Greater London Council and the rest of the south-east. There is also some information, but in less detail, for the counties and most large towns. Since 1969–70 the main tables have been reproduced for the eight divisions of the Greater London Council and from 1971/2 additional analyses have been given for Inner and Outer London.

The scope of the statistics is quite extensive and some of the regional figures are published in the *Annual Abstract of Regional Statistics* [QRL 11], the *Scottish Abstract of Statistics* [QRL 64], and some for 1966–7 in an article by A. R. Thatcher [B 62]. However, much of the material is clearly only available on request from the Department of Health and Social Security.

There are a number of limitations to the statistics. As for all tax-based data, earnings below the tax threshold are excluded. Furthermore the sample is unlikely to be representative for women since many are married and working part-time and hence below the tax threshold. Other limitations are technical. The earnings bands extend only up to £5,000 and over per annum. Problems can arise also when the deduction card and National Insurance card fail to match and where the former only records 'net' as opposed to 'gross' earnings. Also the nature of the sample is such that the sampling errors for the smaller sub-regions may be quite large.

The statistics are primarily for the Government Actuary to use in his estimates relating to the National Insurance Fund, but are used extensively by other government departments and local authorities. Unfortunately with the discontinuance of National Insurance cards in April 1975 the data for 1973–4 will be the last of the series. However the Department of Health and Social Security is planning a new and similar series to start for 1974–5. There are no details of these plans to date.

3.7 The Royal Commission on the Distribution of Income and Wealth

3.7.1 *Introduction*
In August 1974 the Royal Commission on the Distribution of Income and Wealth received a Royal Warrant, with extensive powers to obtain evidence and a Standing Reference to report from time to time as requested by the government on the current distribution of personal income and wealth and on the past trends in these distributions. The Standing Reference also stated that the reports should cover a wide range of personal incomes at all levels, both earned and unearned, monetary and non-monetary, capital gains and so on. The Commission is further empowered to consider any other factors, particularly the incidence of taxation, which it may consider relevant.

It is unusual for Royal Commissions to receive a Standing Reference. Effectively the Royal Commission will survive as long as the government wishes. The likely outcome is that over the next few years there could emanate a considerable number of reports on the distribution of income, analysing all aspects of income distribution including the availability of data sources and even the production of new data sources.

To date the Royal Commission has submitted four reports. The first is the *Initial Report on the Standing Reference* [QRL 62], which we consider in subsection 3.7.2 and the second is titled *Income from Companies and its Distribution* [QRL 63] (see subsection 3.7.3). The other reports are No. 3 on *Higher Incomes from Employment* [QRL 75] (see subsection 3.7.4) and the *Second Report on the Standing Reference* [QRL 76]. In addition there have been two background papers [B103, B104] and a collection of submitted evidence for the Initial Report [B105]. It follows that in the short space of a year most of the statistical material published in the reports is derived from the available sources already discussed in this section. Therefore in our discussion we shall concentrate on that data published which is either new or hitherto unpublished.

3.7.2 *Report No. 1—Initial Report on the Standing Reference*

The main statistical contribution of the report is the reconstruction of the CSO *Blue Book* income distributions. These are used for analysis in Chapter Four and compilation of the estimates is outlined in Appendix E (see subsections 3.3.2 and 3.3.3 for further details). The report emphasizes that the matching of the Inland Revenue and FES distributions to produce this data source is a highly valuable exercise and advocates that the CSO repeat the exercise not only for future years but for the missing years since the previous series which ended in 1967. The fourth report in fact, [QRL 76] extended the CSO distributions for 1972–3 and 1974–5 to exclude part-year income units.

The other new statistical contributions are on a much smaller scale. Table E6 in Appendix E publishes the Inland Revenue (called SPI, Survey of Personal Incomes, in the report) summary distribution for 1972–3 incorporating in the published table those income units below the exemption limit for which the Inland Revenue obtains data from its survey. This is a marked deviation from the standard practice by the Inland Revenue. The text of the report, in Chapter Four, also publishes three tables derived from hitherto unpublished data from the *Family Expenditure Surveys*. They are: Table 11, the Distribution of Income for Households and Tax Units (see subsection 3.4.3) for 1972–3; Table 13, the Effect of Including Imputed Rent on the Distribution of Household Income for 1972–3; and finally Table 14, Household Income and Imputed Rent by Tenure Group. Unfortunately Tables 11 and 13 are presented in percentile form as opposed to income ranges, which reduces their adaptability by other researchers.

In addition to much analysis on the nature and trends in the distribution of personal income the report also surveys the major sources of income distribution data in Chapter Four and in Appendix F (for the Inland Revenue, FES, CSO, GHS and CIF) and Appendix H (for the NES and DHSS). Appendix G presents a number of tables analysing the trends indicated by the three main sources, Inland Revenue, CSO and FES (including the redistribution studies—see subsection 3.4.9) and a useful computation in some of these tables is the conversion of the average income of the top 10% of income recipients to 1974 prices.

Chapter Two considers a number of conceptual issues which are covered in our review, including the problem of superannuation contributions (see subsections 2.2.1 and 3.10.4), imputed rent (see subsection 3.10.3) fringe benefit income (see subsection 3.10.2) and the income unit (see subsections 3.2.3, 3.2.11 and 3.4.3). Finally Chapter Six of the report is entitled 'The Gaps in the Coverage of Official Statistics', and this is followed in Chapter Seven by recommendations for future work on and improvements in data sources. There is no doubt that this excellent report is a valuable and necessary addition to the general literature on the distribution of personal income.

3.7.3 *Report No. 2—Income From Companies and Its Distribution* [QRL 63]

The relevant features in this second report are the estimation of the amount of income from companies distributed to the personal sector and its role in the size distribution of personal income. In Appendix M new statistical estimates are published for the years 1963 to 1973 inclusive with respect to the aggregate dividend and other investment income received by individuals, households and private trusts (Table M1) and the estimates of ordinary dividends paid by UK companies and received by (as separate components) superannuation funds, life assurance funds, private non-profit-making bodies and individuals (Table M2). Table M1 is largely an extrapolation based on the work of Moyle and Reid (see [QRL 9], and subsection 2.8.1) while Table M2 is derived from a number of sources including Inland Revenue tax returns from companies and the *Blue Book*. A brief outline of the sources is given in Appendix M of the report.

With respect to the role of company dividend income in the size distribution of incomes most of the statistical material is obtained from the Inland Revenue surveys. The distribution by size of total taxable income is analysed with respect to occupational pensions and dividend and other interest income taxed at source, for both all income units and pensioner tax units. Statistics on these aspects are given in Chapter Three and Appendix K of the report. The data vary slightly from those published in the Inland Revenue surveys in that they incorporate some data on income units below the exemption limit, which had been collected during the surveys. The report notes that the Inland Revenue surveys to date have not separated dividend income from other investment incomes but that this will be undertaken in the 1973–4 survey. In the meantime Appendix J of the report publishes an arbitrary attempt, with assistance from the Inland Revenue, to estimate the distribution of dividend income by taxable income size for 1972–3. The results, however, are presented only in graphical form.

An analysis of the distributional implications of company income would also require data on the distribution of benefits from life assurances. The Commissioners note that no such data exist and proxy the possible effects by analysing the distribution of premiums paid (Tables 21, K5 and K6). These cover the period 1963–4 to 1972–3 and are based on the statistics published in the surveys on life assurance relief claimed, again including some data for income units below the exemption limits. They are in effect a new published data source. Finally the only other relevant new published source is Table 20, which is 'The Contributions of Pension Funds deducted by Employers for Households of different total income levels in 1973', estimated from unpublished data from the *Family Expenditure Surveys*.

3.7.4 *Report No. 3—Higher Incomes from Employment* [QRL 75]

This report is largely based on data compiled from the standard official statistical sources. There are in addition some estimates from a number of salary surveys undertaken by private organizations such as Management Centre Europe, Employment Conditions Abroad, British Institute of Management, AIC/Inbucon plus a special survey commissioned from HAY–MSL, an international management consultancy company. This survey concentrates mainly on international comparisons of executive salaries and is published in detail in a background paper (see [B 103]). Finally Appendix H of the report contains some new material on fringe benefits received by executives. Most of the data in the report spans the period 1969 to 1975.

3.8 Historical Data

3.8.1 *The Oxford Savings Surveys—Source and Coverage*

In April and May 1952 the Oxford Institute of Statistics undertook a sample survey of income for Great Britain (excluding Northern Ireland). The project was led by Professor H. F. Lydall and received considerable assistance from the Central Statistical Office and the Government Social Survey Division which did all the fieldwork and coding.

The initial results of the Survey were published in articles by Professor Lydall in the *Bulletin of the Oxford University Institute of Statistics* between November and December 1952 and July and August 1954 [QRL 7 and QRL 6]. A subsequent and highly detailed account appeared in his book entitled *British Incomes and Savings* [QRL 5] published in 1955.

The data from the survey covered the financial year 1951–2 and Chapter two of Lydall's book contains all the basic material on the income distributions that emerged from the survey. In addition to the usual summary distributions there were numerous multi-cross-classifications between income and occupation, source of income, age, sex, family size, residence, pre- and post-tax and manual and non-manual workers. There were also distributions on children's earnings and comparisons with the corresponding Inland Revenue data for that year, which in fact was no more than an extrapolation of the 1949–50 Income Census.

In later chapters there are further cross-classifications with respect to the holdings of liquid assets, stocks and shares and savings. Savings in the survey were estimated as the change in the value and holdings of personal wealth as opposed to the residual between income and consumption which is the method adopted in the National Income Accounts.

The 1952 survey was followed by three other surveys in the summers of 1953, 1954 and 1955, each providing data for the financial years 1952–3, 1953–4 and 1954–5. All but the last of these surveys were conducted by the Central Statistical Office using though the same sampling frame and definitions as the others. The results of these surveys, plus discussions on the methodology and results are published in five articles in the *Bulletin of the Oxford University Institute of Statistics* in 1955 and 1958. The articles are:

(i) The Saving Survey 1953: Response Rates and Reliability of the Data, by T. P. Hill, L. R. Klein and K. H. Straw, February 1955 [B 33].
(ii) Income, Savings and Net Worth: The Savings Survey of 1952–4, by T. P. Hill, May 1955 [QRL 3].
(iii) Patterns of Savings: The Surveys of 1953 and 1954, by L. R. Klein, May 1955 [B 38].
(iv) The Savings Survey and Official Sources, by K. H. Straw, August 1958 [B 60].
(v) The 1955 Savings Survey, by M. J. Erritt and J. L. Nicholson, May 1958 [QRL 1].

As the titles suggest the preoccupation of the studies was savings. Nevertheless there resulted much useful information on income distributions as a by-product, though nowhere to the same extent or detail as contained in Professor Lydall's book for the first survey.

The bulk of the data on income distribution for 1952–3 and 1953–4 are published in T. P. Hill's [QRL 3] and L. R. Klein's [B 38] articles. Klein's article in particular provides some interesting data on savings, classified by type, e.g. contractual, etc. in relation to income by size and age. It also contains interesting estimates of trying to separate 'personal' savings from business savings for self-employed incomes (see subsection 2.8.1).

The Erritt and Nicholson article [QRL 1] is the sole source for the 1954–5 survey. The data on income distribution is very limited, comprising a basic summary distribution plus a number of cross-classifications between savings by type and income.

3.8.2 *Definition of Income and the Income Recipient*
The surveys are unique inasmuch as they adopted the Inland Revenue's concept of the 'income unit' as their definition of the income recipient (see subsection 3.2.3).

The income concept used, called Gross Income in the surveys, comprised all cash receipts but excluded most forms of income in kind. The 1951–2 survey excluded in fact all income in kind, though the others did include imputed owner-occupied rent and the 1954–5 survey also included imputed farm produce consumed by owners of farms. This definition means that a number of incomes not assessable for income tax are included. The obvious case is incomes below the effective exemption limit, but less obvious and more difficult to adjust for comparison with the Inland Revenue data is the fact that tax-deductible allowances such as Schedule A expenses, mortgage interest, private allowances from relatives and legitimate expenses of employment borne by the employee are included in the concept. Surprisingly though, income from boarders was not included in the 1951–2 survey, though it was included in the later surveys as was mortgage interest.

The definition of income thus did not readily correspond to any official definition of personal income. The outcome was that a notable proportion of the survey literature centred on the problem of comparison with official data.

3.8.3 *Method of Sampling*
Though the income recipient was defined as an 'income unit', the sample extracted information on units by sampling persons living in private households, but not those in institutions. The sampling frame was designed to obtain approximately 3,500 addresses. The frame was quite similar to that subsequently used by the first *Family Expenditure Survey* (see subsection 3.4.5). It was based on local administrative areas with provisions to obtain a correct balance with respect to regional distribution, administrative type of area and the degree of industrialization. Sixty-nine local administrative areas in Great Britain were selected proportional to its population size. These areas are equivalent to the 'Primary sampling units' of the *Family Expenditure Surveys*. Roughly fifty addresses were apportioned to each area, randomly selected from registered ratepayers for the first two surveys and the electoral register for the latter two. A detailed account of the method is given in Chapter seven of Professor Lydall's book [QRL 5].

There were minor revisions to the sample and questionnaire each in the light of results. The main problems confronting the first survey were the lower response rates of the upper income groups and the underestimation of unearned income (see subsection 3.8.4). In the 1952–3 surveys the sampling fraction was increased for the upper income groups to deal with this, but with little success. This survey also severely underestimated self-employment income. These problems remained for the other two surveys though the results were slightly improved by more experienced interviewing.

3.8.4 *Reliability*
It is generally accepted that the first survey is much more reliable than the others. This ties in well with the higher response rate for that survey (see Table 3.8 below). All surveys suffered from a much lower response rate for the upper income households, though this defect did partially improve in the last two samples (see Table 3.8). However some of this improvement probably resulted in a changed definition of an upper strata from a rate-

Table 3.8 Overall Response Rates for the Oxford Savings Surveys

	All Households	*Upper Strata Households*
1951–2	75·1	57·5
1952–3	66·1	47·2
1953–4	67·2	62·0
1954–5	71·1	63·0

Source: Erritt and Nicholson [QRL 1], p. 125

able value basis to jury service. The latter could considerably reduce the numbers eligible for this group since certain categories of professional persons are exempt from jury service.

Another check on reliability undertaken by Erritt and Nicholson [QRL 1] was to compare the grossed-up income totals with those independently estimated for the National Accounts with appropriate adjustments where possible to approach perfect comparability. Table 3.9 indicates a considerable weakness in each survey with regard to unearned income and to self-employed income in all but the 1951–2 study.

Table 3.9 Survey Estimates as Percentage of the CSO 'Blue Book' Estimates (adjusted)

	1951–2	*1952–3*	*1953–4*	*1954–5*
Employment Income	98·1	96·9	97·5	98·2
Self-Employment Income	98·1	64·9	84·3	54·2
Unearned Income	48·3	43·5	55·2	65·2
Government Transfers	87·7	106·3	97·7	95·5
Total Personal Income	92·5	88·4	91·7	89·9

Source: Erritt and Nicholson [QRL 1], Table VII

Control total and structural checks with respect to population generally indicated that this aspect of the sampling was satisfactory. However further checks against Inland Revenue income distribution data by Erritt and Nicholson [QRL 1] again showed up a marked underestimation of the numbers of incomes above £2,000 p.a.

3.8.5 *Concluding Remarks*

Though the results of the surveys must be treated with caution, as indicated in the previous section, it must not be forgotten that they were essentially pioneering studies from which considerable experience was gained. Furthermore they are still today our best source of data for the relationship between income distributions and personal wealth distributions.

3.8.6 *Other Historical Data*

In addition to the historical Inland Revenue sources listed in subsection 3.2.12, there have been numerous diverse private studies dating as far back as 1436. The reliability of all these studies is extremely poor and to discuss and compare them in detail is beyond the scope of this chapter. In Table 3.10 below we present a comprehensive list of published material.

Table 3.10 A Summary of Unofficial Estimates of Aggregate Personal Income Distribution for the United Kingdom

Year	*Author*	*Reference*	*Region*	*Type of Data*	*No. of persons covered (millions)*
1913	A. L. Bowley	[B 12]	UK	Wages data plus Inland Revenue	20·7
1910	A. L. Bowley	[B 12]	UK	Wages data plus Inland Revenue	19·9
1904	L. G. Chiozza-Money	[B 19]	UK	Board of Trade Wages Census plus Inland Revenue data	19·0
1880	A. L. Bowley	[B 12]	UK	Wages data plus Inland Revenue	14·8
1867	R. Dudley Baxter	[B 9]	GB and Ireland	Wages data plus Inland Revenue	13·7
1812	P. Colquhoun	[B 25]	GB and Ireland		4·4
1801–3	P. Colquhoun	[B 24]	England and Wales		2·2
1688	G. King	[B 37]	England and Wales		1·3

The first four studies are a combination of Inland Revenue and wages data. Basically the procedure is to subtract the number of taxable incomes from the estimated working population and assume that these were all incomes below the effective tax exemption limit. This group would also include those incomes assessed for tax but exempt, some of which may be slightly in excess of the exemption limit. The procedure is very rough and ready and the main conclusion we can draw is that in spite of a very low effective exemption limit—e.g. £160 p.a. in 1913—the proportion of total incomes subject to tax is remarkably small, 5·75% in 1913 and 4·2% in 1880.

The 1867 estimates of R. Dudley Baxter [B 9] are computed in a similar manner, though they do provide a more detailed breakdown by income size for those with taxable incomes. However, as we pointed out in subsection 3.2.12, the Inland Revenue data prior to 1920 is really quite unsuitable for income distribution analysis.

The remaining three distributions in Table 3.10 are of quite a different nature from those discussed so far. Broadly Gregory King [B 37] attempted to estimate the annual income and number of families by social class group. He chose twenty-six classes ranging from Temporal Lords through Freeholders right to vagrants, beggars, etc. The feudal system of records probably meant that for a large number of these classes his estimates were reasonably accurate, though in the absence of reliable census of population his figures for the lowest three or four classes must be no more than an inspired guess. Nevertheless they are interesting estimates and Phylis Deane [B 26] used them as the basis for her estimates of national income for 1688.

Colquhoun's data for 1801–3 and 1912 are estimated in a similar manner to that of King's. He added many more classes, many resulting from the 'Industrial Revolution'. His estimates of national income are not too different from those by Deane and Cole [B 27] for the same years.

The only other estimates of note for early years are first an estimated Schedule D income for 1801 contained in the Parliamentary Accounts and Records for 1801–2 [B 91]. These are of limited value, particularly in view of the high degree of tax evasion that is generally accepted to have occurred. A second and final source are estimates by H. L. Gray in 1934 [B 30] of the number of families and incomes of the six highest social classes in 1436. A valuable account and use of many of the above sources is made by L. Soltow in an excellent article on the 'Long-Run Changes in British Income Inequality' [B 56].

3.9 Forthcoming Data

There are two sources of data in the pipeline which when they appear could be very useful additions to the stock of aggregate data which we have covered in this section.

3.9.1 *The 1971 Census of Population Income Follow-Up* [B 75]

In 1972 the Office of Population Censuses and Surveys attempted an exciting new venture in the collection of income distribution statistics. A postal and voluntary questionnaire was sent to all private households and persons living in institutions who had been selected for the 1% summary tables published from the 1971 decennial census of population. The method used to select this 1% is outlined in the explanatory notes to these summary tables [B 76]. The original intention was that the income follow-up would be within three months of the actual census. However it was delayed by one year.

Respondents were requested to supply some income details for the year ending 5 April 1972. The questionnaire is reproduced in Appendix E. Useful inclusions are the questions on student incomes, pension schemes outside the state system and the extensive questions on social security benefits received and the number of weeks for which they were received. A cross-classification between total income and other census characteristics, such as age, occupation and educational factors, will be provided by this source. There may be also the possibility of valuable matching with the other major sources of income distributions (see subsection 5.1).

The questionnaire is directed at persons and not specifically households or families. There are no questions relating to dependency, etc. However, the returns are collected for each person over 15 in every 1 % sampled private household and for 1 % of all persons over 15 living in institutions. These are then collated, as is clearly indicated by the Secretary of State's preamble to the questionnaire, with the household size, education and housing data collected from the census of population for the same households and persons. Though there may be a few minor problems resulting from the one-year lag, there is technically possible a wide range of valuable information contained in this follow-up. An extensive number of cross-classifications can be envisaged, for example by household income and/or head of household income to household size, education, tenure, as well as by type of income and the number of weeks worked, etc. available from the income questionnaire. It may be even possible to cross-classify household and family income data. Apart from the omission of tax details in the questionnaire this data source is potentially as close to that ideally required by income distribution analysts as any other source. The obvious link to the essential control total of population is also a clear advantage.

The Office of Population Censuses and Surveys is still processing the results of the sample. It is intended to publish some results in 1977. Whether the potential of the source is realized or not will depend heavily on the response rate and bias and the accuracy and honesty of respondents. The latter can be gauged probably by reference to the relevant National Income Aggregates. The response rate was 45 % but as yet there is no information on bias. The extent to which the Office publishes the results of the sample will probably depend heavily on its assessment of response bias and other factors influencing reliability. One development that might be possible in this manner is the addition of one or two questions on personal wealth, providing a much needed bridge, albeit flimsy, between income and wealth data for persons.

3.9.2 *The Essex Poverty Study* [B 2]

In 1968 Professors Brian Abel-Smith and Peter Townsend, with the University of Essex, undertook a sample survey of approximately 2,500 households throughout the United Kingdom. The sample was designed to cover all income level, though with the emphasis on poverty there was naturally a greater level of sampling at the lower end of the income scale.

The results of the survey have not yet been published though Atkinson and Harrison [B 7] in a companion review in this volume do give some details. They point to a 75 % response rate and a very large questionnaire with a substantial number of questions on both income and wealth, again indicating a useful development in this area. Atkinson and Harrison include in their review a useful discussion on the need for joint distributions on income and wealth.

Though the survey has not been published, the results of a number of pilot studies connected with the project are available. These focus predominantly on poverty and low incomes and are briefly listed in subsection 4.3 of this work.

3.10 Concluding Thoughts

3.10.1 *Omitted Incomes—Capital Gains*

In line with National Income Accounting conventions capital gains are omitted from all income distribution estimates. It can be argued though that capital gains do provide a command over consumer resources or more generally represent a nominal increase in the stock of personal economic power and if this is so then capital gains ought to be included as they have implications for welfare and equity.

This was clearly the view taken by the Minority Report of the 1956 United Kingdom Royal Commission on Taxation [B 97]. It is also a view which concurs with the widely accepted definition of income of H. Simons ([B 54], see also subsection 2.8.2) which is that personal income is the algebraic sum of (1) the market value of rights exercised in consumption and (2) the change in the value of the store of property rights between the beginning and the end of the period. There is also no doubt that the Minority Report above was influential in the subsequent introduction of a capital gains tax in the United Kingdom.

There is, however, a substantial difference between the tax concept of capital gains and that implied by the theoretical definitions of personal income. The latter refer to the appreciation in value of the capital stock of an individual over a period. The part of this appreciation that cannot be accounted for by saving or dissaving is thus a capital gain. Whether the gain is realized or not is irrelevant in this instance. The tax concept of gains on the other hand focuses solely on realized gains and also covers gains which once realized may have been accumulated over a number of periods. The amounts involved in the two different types of estimates vary substantially. For example between 1969–70 and 1971–2 taxable capital gains (net of deductible losses) charged to individuals and trustees by the Inland Revenue varied from £371m to £502m, whereas Stark's [B 59] estimates of capital appreciation for the period 1954 to 1963 fluctuated from £603m to £4055m. Some of the difference will be attributable to the exclusion of owner-occupied houses and other exemptions in taxable capital gains. Nevertheless the major portion reflects the quantitative difference between the two definitions.

Neither of these definitions is entirely satisfactory. The 'appreciation' concept attaches equal weight to unrealized and realized gains and this is clearly an area for debate. A possible solution could be the choice of an appropriate weighting system if this could ever be found. A weighting or discounting system would also have to be devised if the tax concept of gains were adopted to offset the fact that the value of gains will vary misleadingly as the rate of realization changes and consequently the average time length of a gain.

These basic conceptual problems are quite minor in comparison to the general lack of any useful data on capital gains. The Inland Revenue does publish data on capital gains, both by size of net chargeable gains and by size of their largest components cross-classified by size of net chargeable gains (see IRS [QRL 32] 1974, Tables 107 to 111). The Inland Revenue also has tables linking capital gains returns to the Inland Revenue Surveys of Personal Incomes, though these are as yet unpublished. All other existing attempts to compute personal capital gains have come from non-official sources. They fall into two categories. The first adopts the 'appreciation' concept mentioned above. There have been three such estimates. Two of these, J. C. R. Dow's publication [B 28] and the *Minority Report of the Royal Commission on Taxation* [B 97] estimate the aggregate value only. The third by Stark ([B 59], Ch. 1.4) goes further and allocates gains to various income groups. This was achieved by 'marrying' the personal income and wealth distributions via investment income, using a modification of methods first put forward by Barna [B 8] and Cartter [B 16]. The method is far from satisfactory and involves many arbitrary assumptions and serves mainly to illustrate the necessity for joint income and wealth distributions (see Atkinson and Harrison [B 7]).

Cartter and Barna represent our second category of estimates of capital gains. These authors assumed that undistributed company profits could be adopted as a proxy for share prices and capital gains. There is neither any sound theoretical nor empirical justification for such an assumption.

3.10.2 *Omitted Incomes—Fringe Benefits*

Fringe benefits are defined as those benefits provided by employers for their employees which are not included as part of taxable income. These benefits comprise free or reduced-price availability of factory products, recreational and educational facilities, subsidized meals, company cars, expense accounts, etc. None of the sources of income distribution statistics in the UK include such benefits, though the *Family Expenditure Surveys* do include the value of luncheon vouchers. There can be no doubt that they do enhance the living standards of the beneficiaries and therefore ought to be included in the income distributions. Furthermore the value of luncheon vouchers in the *Family Expenditure Surveys* is more relevant to low income households and here could be a bias in the distribution as a result.

Information on all possible fringe benefits is simply unavailable. There are, though, a number of various sources which can be used to make approximate estimates. The most significant of these are the periodic *Labour Cost Surveys* undertaken by the Department of Employment [QRL 24, QRL 33, QRL 34] covering the years 1955, 1964, 1968, 1973, 1974 and 1975. These official studies can be supplemented by a private but highly comprehensive survey of fringe benefits in 1960 by Reid and Robertson [B 49] of Glasgow University. There have been a number of other useful but less detailed private surveys. The most notable are by W. Durham [B 29] of the Industrial Welfare Society for 1957, and by R. Harris and M. Solly [B 31] of the Institute of Economic Affairs for 1958. All of these studies restrict themselves to benefits that accrue largely to non-salaried employees. The scope and coverage of the benefits even within this narrow frame is restricted even further in some instances. Nevertheless with a certain degree of imagination they can be utilized to supplement income distributions (see Stark [B 59], Ch. 5 for example).

Estimates of the more esoteric benefits for the higher-paid employees are even more difficult to come by. Stark [B 59] attempted to evaluate the benefit from company cars. The British Institute of Management in 1965 published a survey of fringe benefits for executives [B 78]. Similar studies have been undertaken by the Challoner Management Appointments Limited [B 77] and Hay-MSL [B 32]. The three above sources however are either restrictedly or privately circulated though some of this type of survey work is published in Report No. 4 of the Royal Commission on the Distribution of Income and Wealth ([QRL 75] and see subsection 3.7.4).

This vital area therefore is not statistically fruitful. This, of course, diminishes the relevance of the theoretical problems of valuation. However, briefly these are that valuation at the cost of the provision of the benefits, which would be a highly tempting measure to adopt, would greatly underestimate the real value to the recipient on two scores. First it will be less than the market price and secondly it does not take into account tax-savings incurred by receiving income under the guise of company expenditure. On the other hand it would overestimate by the extent to which the restriction in choice implied by payment-in-kind diminishes utility in comparison to that from a payment in cash.

3.10.3 *A Theoretical Issue—Interest Payments*

In the National Income Accounts interest payments by the personal sector are deducted from the gross receipts of rent, dividends and interest (see Table 2.2). This is a practice that would be demanded by any definition of income. However the treatment of both interest receipts and interest payments varies considerably in the income distribution statistics analysed in this section. For example the Inland Revenue and CSO distributions deduct mortgage interest payments and other interest payments over a certain limit per annum (currently £40), though between 1969–70 and 1972–3 no other interest deductions were permitted. On the other hand since 1963 the Inland Revenue Surveys and the CSO have excluded the Schedule A evaluation of imputed rent income from owner-occupancy as part of interest and property income. The FES distributions, however, include an imputed rent for owner-occupiers but make no deductions for mortgage and other interest payments, while the GHS neither include the imputation nor make the deduction.

Therefore, there is inconsistency in the treatment of this particular category of income, particularly that section referring to the net income from house-ownership. This inconsistency is further confused by arguments such as that the exclusion of mortgage interest payments leads to an underestimation of the share of personal income by owner-occupiers (see [QRL 62], p. 38, para. 109). This confusion can be increased if it is argued that the income of renting householders is underestimated by the extent of the subsidies of local government-provided housing or private rent-free accommodation. Confusions of this nature are likely to arise if statistics are presented without an underlying concept of the meaning of income.

The ideal state of affairs is that for owner-occupancy the imputed rent factor should be included and the mortgage interest payments deducted. This gives a true picture of net flow of income or the command over resources resulting from the ownership of property. With respect to rented accommodation, since the property is not owned by the householder there can be no concept of property income. However a subsidized rent represents a type of fringe benefit (see subsection 3.10.2) and ought to be treated accordingly. There are no published distributions which comply with the rule regarding house-ownership and only the FES-based redistribution studies (see subsection 3.4.9) regarding rented accommodation.

There are, of course, many practical difficulties involved in computing the imputed rent of owner-occupation. A less ideal solution would be to assume the benefits are reflected in the mortgage interest payments. This is a procedure implicit in the GHS. However to deduct those payments and exclude imputed rent, as in the Inland Revenue and CSO, or include both as in the FES, makes no sense at all.

3.10.4 *A Theoretical Issue—Transfer Incomes*

In the course of this chapter we have occasionally come across the problem of transfer incomes, particularly those within the personal sector, which introduces the possibility of double-counting. Let us put the problem formally by accepting as a starting point H. Simons' definition of income (see subsection 3.10.1).

This definition requires that all additions to personal wealth be included and deductions subtracted. Thus incomes such as pensions, which are deductions or dissavings, should be netted out of income distribution statistics and presented as non-existent, symptomatic of a zero command over resources. However official statistics either include pensions and contributions to them both as income (cf. FES and GHS) or include the pension element and exclude contributions in opposition to the dictates of the Simons definition. The latter is the case with the pre-1961 Inland Revenue and CSO data where all contributions to private and state schemes were excluded. Since 1961 the employee contributions to the state pension scheme have been included. This is quite an inconsistent mixture. The inconsistency appears even more marked if we consider all social security benefits on the same basis as pensions and taxation as the equivalent of contributions. In all statistics both of these items are included.

The solution to these problems is to draw a fine but important distinction with respect to forced and contractual saving between that which increases property rights on the one hand and that which does not on the other hand. The latter category includes all direct taxation and National Insurance contributions. These contributions cannot be recouped at will nor do they form part of personal wealth. Thus since these do not increase property rights, then there is no case for deducting the pensions and benefits received from forced contributions to the State. They do not constitute a double-counting in the aggregate estimates as the transfers operate via the public sector. A similar argument can be made with respect to employer contributions to private pension schemes, which invariably do not include employee withdrawal rights and on the same basis involve no increase in property rights. Furthermore in this instance the company sector can be likened to the public sector's role for state schemes. The problematic item is employee contributions to private schemes. To include both Pension and contribution is double-counting, but to exclude the former as the Simons definition would have it, would clearly produce misleading statistics. The living standard, or consumption possibilities of pensioners in relation to other groups would be totally understated. Likewise if the contributions were excluded, then misleading comparisons would result, e.g. we would have spurious equality between two persons with identically reported incomes but one in addition making an unreported private pension contribution. Furthermore practical complications arise since the pension outgoings at any one time are invariably in excess of the corresponding contributions, not merely by the extent of employer contributions but also by the profits gained in investing the funds. To allow for this factor in any calculations to avoid double-counting would be complex to say the least.

The essence of the problem is that the same part of a current income can benefit two different persons simultaneously, first as current consumption (the pensioner) and secondly as future consumption (the contributor). Three solutions spring to mind. The first is to exclude the contributions as income but include them as part of the stock of personal wealth, perhaps estimated at its net present value to put all estimates on a flow basis. The second solution is to construct an age-weighted life-cycle income distribution. Both of these solutions unfortunately involve data that are not currently available, nor are likely to be in the foreseeable future. It seems therefore that users of income distribution statistics must choose to tolerate at present this theoretical double-counting and include both sides of the transfers, and in the absence of a household sector as opposed to a personal sector (see subsection 2.8.1), also tolerate the problems that arise in estimating a control total of incomes for the personal sector.

4 Special Data Sources

In this section we will list a number of sources on income data relating to specific groups of persons or categories of income. These sources do not present data on the aggregate picture, though they may well act as useful supplements to those intending to use or manipulate such data. Because of the diversity of the statistics we shall not discuss each source in the same detail as the major sources in Chapters 2 and 3.

4.1 Data on Specific Occupations and Professions

4.1.1 *National Board of Prices and Incomes Reports* [QRL 36]

This is by far the most prolific source for income information on specific occupations, etc. The Board operated between October 1966 and March 1971. It was part of the mechanism for implementing a national incomes policy. One of its prime aims was to assemble statistics necessary for decisions on pay, conditions, etc. This frequently entailed undertaking samples and detailed research.

During its five years the Board produced 170 reports and conducted some 150 statistical surveys of incomes and earnings. Table 4.1 contains a summary of the output of the statistics branch. The volume and speed of the output was indeed remarkable. The Board set new and high standards in obtaining information. It also pioneered improved sampling techniques.

A list of the reports published by the Board is given in Appendix F. A further description of the Board's work is contained in *Statistical News*, No. 13, pp. 6–13 [B 102] in an article by R. F. Burch, former Chief Statistician of the NBPI.

4.1.2 *Technological Manpower Studies*

To date, there have been three studies in this series. The first two, *The Survey of Professional Engineers 1968* [QRL 72] and *The Survey of Professional Scientists* [QRL 73] also for 1968, were published jointly by the Ministry of Technology, the

Table 4.1 Summary of Statistical Surveys Carried Out by NBPI, Statistics Branch, 1967–71

Year	All Surveys Questionnaires Number of Surveys	Issued	Usable returns	Response rate %	Earnings surveys only Questionnaires Number of Surveys	Issued	Usable returns	Response rate %	Workers Number in sample 000s	Total number covered 000s	Average sampling fraction
1967	32	27,821	16,531	59·4	12	5,480	3,473	63·4	139·9	2,647·2	5·3
1968	61	48,244	28,812	59·7	14	12,532	8,530	68·1	47·4	1,367·8	3·5
1969	30	18,718	13,431	71·8	16	5,487	4,170	76·0	29·9	734·2	4·1
1970	15	8,204	5,614	68·4	9	2,306	1,513	65·6	36·6	650·5	5·6
1971	13	12,000	5,306	44·2	4	1,392	925	66·5	35·0	377·0	9·3
Total	151	114,987	69,694	60·6[1]	55	27,197	18,611	68·4	288·8	5,776·7	5·0

[1] Based on the ratio of total usable returns to questionnaires issued. The unweighted average of the response rates for each survey was 72%. Either figure understates the true response rate for reasons explained in the tests.
Source: [B 102] p. 13.

Council of Science and Technical Institutes and the Council of Engineering. Both contain data on pay and deployment plus some very useful and unique comparative information. A similar survey of engineers, but prior to the new series, was undertaken by the same bodies in 1966, i.e. *The Survey of Professional Engineers 1966* [QRL 71]. The third publication in the series produced in 1973 now jointly by the Department of Trade and Industry and the Council of Science and Technology Institutes is a *Survey of Professional Scientists 1971* [QRL 74]. Similar surveys are under way for professional engineers in 1971 and 1973 but so far have not been published.

4.1.3 *Other Government Studies*

(a) *Doctors and Dentists*

The *Report of the Royal Commission on Doctors and Dentists 1957–60* [QRL 61] recommended in 1960 that a Review Body on Doctors' and Dentists' Remuneration be set up. This recommendation was implemented in 1962. From then till 1971 the Review Body published twelve reports [QRL 58], which are listed in Appendix G. These reports periodically contained statistical material. The Royal Commission also provided some data on pay and income. In 1971 the Review Body was made independent and became partially connected with two other Review Bodies formed at the same time, on Top Salaries (in the public sector) and the Armed Forces. Since 1971 the new Review Body has published four reports [QRL 59] with two supplements to the third. These occasionally also incorporate data on pay and income. They are listed in Appendix G.

(b) *Armed Forces*

As mentioned in section (a) above there has been an independent Review Body on Armed Forces Pay [QRL 57] since 1971. This body reviews pay of all members of the forces up to the equivalent army rank of brigadier. Ranks higher than this come under the Review Body on Top Salaries. The Review Body has published to date four reports plus a supplement to the second report on the Pay of Service Medical and Dental Officers. These are listed in Appendix G. Before the Review Body was set up, data on Armed Forces pay could be obtained in the National Board of Prices and Incomes Standing Reference [QRL 66] and the periodic publications by the Ministry of Defence on Pay, Charges and Pensions, references for which can be obtained from the lists of command papers [B 74]. The Inland Revenue Income Distribution Surveys also include separate tables on forces' pay (see subsection 3.2).

(c) *Top Salaries*

This was the third Review Body formed in 1971. Its terms of reference extend to public sector industries, including the Civil Service and Armed Forces. Though it has to date published six reports, only the sixth contains statistical material. This report [QRL 60] contains two surveys, undertaken by the Office of Manpower Economics. The first, in Appendix J, is a Survey of Salaries at the Bar for the years 1969–70 and 1971–2 and was carried out in July 1972. The second, in Appendix L, was conducted over the period September 1971 to September 1973 and is a general Survey of Top Salaries in private and nationalized industries for the years 1971–2 and 1972–3. The latter survey contains particularly useful data on bonuses and superannuation contributions classified by salary size. In addition the sixth report includes a comparative study of top salaries within the EEC countries. Finally since 1971 the government has published Lists of Members of Public Boards of a Commercial Character as at 1 April of each year [B 82]. These state salaries together with lists of those holding more than one appointment.

(d) *The Pay Board*

The Pay Board is largely an advisory body and only one of its publications so far could be classified as a data source. This publication is the *Special Report on the Relative Pay of Mineworkers*

[B 100] which came out in March 1974 at the height of the miners' strike of that year.

Recent industrial action, of which the miners' strike of 1974 is a prime example, has indicated that pay relativities and income distribution are becoming major political issues. These factors were doubtless instrumental in the setting up of the Royal Commission on the Distribution of Income and Wealth (see subsection 3.7).

(e) *Committee of Inquiry Reports*
In recent months the government has set up Committees of Inquiry into pay and conditions for specific types of occupation. Each contains some statistical survey material resulting from studies undertaken by the relevant government department and the Office of Manpower Economics. To date there have been three published reports in this category, namely the *Report of the Committee of Inquiry into the Pay and Related Conditions of Service of Nurses and Midwives* [QRL 54], published in September 1974 with a *Supplement* in 1975, the *Report of the Committee of Inquiry into the Pay and Related Conditions of Service of the Professions supplementary to Medicine and Speech Therapists* [QRL 55], published in January 1975, and finally the *Report of the Committee of Inquiry into the Pay of Non-University Teachers* [QRL 56]. The last has a particularly valuable statistical appendix.

4.2 Official Social Security Data

In the last ten years the administrative structure of the social security departments of the British government has changed substantially. Today we have the Department of Health and Social Security (DHSS) which is an amalgam of the former Ministries of Health and Social Security. The Ministry of Social Security in turn was formed in 1967 out of the Ministry of Pensions and National Insurance and the National Assistance Board. In this section we shall review the relevant material of all these bodies other than the former Ministry of Health. This material comprises three special surveys, the statistical report series of the DHSS and the standard array of regular annual statistics. We shall conclude by listing the sources of regional data.

4.2.1 *An Enquiry into the Financial and Other Circumstances of Retirement Pensioners, 1966* [QRL 26]

In 1966 the Ministry of Pensions and National Insurance published the results of an extensive survey on the financial circumstances of old age pensioners in Great Britain (see subsection 4.2.6 for Northern Ireland). The report, which was spawned by the political discontent with the efficiency of the social security system, largely as a result of the academic poverty studies such as those carried out by Professors Abel-Smith and P. Townsend [B 1], had a powerful impact and undoubtedly added significant political ammunition for the changes in the social security structure that took place in 1967 and subsequently.

The aim of the survey was basically to discover how many pensioners were eligible for National Assistance and how many of these in fact did not receive benefits and why. The data were obtained from a sub-sample of the Ministry's standing sample of all persons receiving state retirement pensions.

The standing sample is a random selection drawn from all pensioners whose code numbers end in 4. The code number is that allotted by the Ministry's Central Office and gives information on sex, age, size of benefit in addition to a serial number. It is a continuing population with numbers being withdrawn on death and new ones added when retirement age is reached. The sample covers approximately 5% or 150,000 of all retirement pensioners. It forms the source for the regular statistics on retirement pensions (see subsection 4.2.5).

The sub-sample was designed to produce 10,000 pensioner households from the standing sample. Systematic sampling was undertaken as it was felt that the standing sample under-represented the very old and would have produced twice as many married couple households as was appropriate. It was also designed to exclude pensioners living abroad, permanently in hospitals, prisons, or those who were married to a person not of pensionable age. There was also a minor problem related to married pensioners with separate pensions. Wives of such couples were discarded in order to avoid double representation. The object was to include only single and married male pensioners. Further details of the sample are given in Appendix II of the report [QRL 26].

Eventually 10,018 households were chosen and contacted during May and June 1965. Information was gathered entirely by interviewing. The questionnaire was long and complex, undoubtedly beyond the ability of many old-aged persons. There was a very high response, in the region of 85%, and there was no obvious bias or pattern amongst the non-respondents. The age structure of the sub-sample when compared to the Registrar General's data appeared satisfactory. Since there are no income data for the 'old' apart from the standing sample, it was not possible to compare the survey with independent control totals covering all old-aged persons. In other words it had to be assumed that those in receipt of state pensions are representative of the 'retired' in the community.

The report produced considerable income data, the bulk of which are contained in Chapters II and III and Appendices IV and V. There are data on the size distribution of the total incomes of pensioners, plus cross-classifications by age, marital status and household status. In Appendix V there are also data on the size distribution of occupational pensions. One notable omission however is the paucity of data on National Assistance payments. There are aggregate figures naturally, but no cross-classifications between size of payment and size of non-National Assistance income, though these might be inferred from the many tables indicating the gap between 'resources' and needs, but only after a number of complex manipulations (needs are defined as the maximum statutory National Assistance payments). This means that the report is limited in its potential to provide information as to the allocation of National Assistance by income size. This type of information could be very helpful to those intending to extend the Inland Revenue income distributions to cover all total personal income, as used to be the case with the recently reinstated CSO distributions (cf. subsection 3.3). On the other hand with respect to its objective of analysing the efficiency of the National Assistance system the report provided valuable information, which has been extensively used by academic researchers (see A. B. Atkinson [B 6]).

4.2.2 *An Enquiry into the Circumstances of Families, 1967* [QRL 25]

The aim of this enquiry was akin to that of the previous section, namely to obtain information on the resources of families in relation to their requirements and to what extent National Assistance was bridging the gap for low-resource families. There is reason to believe that the instigators of the report, the National Assistance Board, had intended a survey of comparable scale with that for retirement pensioners [QRL 26]. However, the amalgamation of the Board with the Ministry of Pensions and National Insurance to form the Ministry of Social Security, who subsequently published the report in 1967, plus the introduction of the earnings-related benefits, meant that the survey had to be rushed and reduced in scale.

The outcome was an in-depth interview survey of 2,409 families, of which 2,331 produced sufficient information for detailed income data. The sample was drawn as a sub-sample from the Ministry's standing sample of all families receiving family allowances. It was a stratified sub-sample to allow for the increase in standard errors as family size increased. It was designed to produce 2,684 families and the interview of 2,409 families in June and July of 1966 gave an 89% response rate, representing approximately 3·3 million families out of 3·9 million receiving family allowances.

Details of the sample are given in Appendix I of the report [QRL 25].

Most of the income data is contained in Chapters IV and V, the latter being a special section on fatherless families and families with sick and unemployed fathers. There are income distribution data on the net earnings of fathers and mothers cross-classified by family size and minimum requirements. In fact there is a wealth of information with regard to wives' earnings, family types, housing, savings and requirements. There is also information on the number of families receiving National Assistance, but as in the previous report (cf. subsection 4.2.1), no size distributions of assistance payments by family size and 'non-assistance' income, though this information was available from the questionnaires.

The report is thus of limited value for those seeking a back-up to aggregate data. Even as a source for specific data on families it must be used with caution. The sample was small and the sampling errors are large, specially for two-children families. There was however no obvious response bias and as far as possible the Ministry cross-checked data from the questionnaires against its own records. Again as with the survey of the retirement pensioners the information has been valuable to researchers, particularly in the poverty field (see A. B. Atkinson [B 6]).

4.2.3 *Families and their Needs with Particular Reference to One-Parent Families, 1973* [QRL 4]

This massive survey, by Audrey Hunt, Judith Fox and Margaret Morgan, which takes up two volumes, was published under the auspices of the Department of Health and Social Security. Its main objective was to provide information for the Finer Committee on One-Parent Families [B 94] (see subsection 4.2.4).

The sample, undertaken by the Social Survey Division of the Office of Population Censuses and Surveys, comprised detailed interviews of three types of families in five selected areas, namely Dorset, Dundee, Glamorgan, Halifax and Haringey. About 5,000 families were interviewed.

Though the report does contain much information on income it cannot be used to provide quantitative national estimates. Its value applies to the 'casework' level of the social security system with the consequent implications for the rates of social security and their implementation.

4.2.4 *Finer Committee Report on One-Parent Families* [B 94]

Appendix 2 in Volume 2 of this report published in July 1974 outlines and summarizes the research and statistical enquiries conducted by the Committee in producing this very extensive report under the chairmanship of Sir Morris Finer. The report was the culmination of five years' study and research.

Some of the enquiries listed in Appendix 2 were published previously and are included in other sections of our study, such as those on One-Parent Families [QRL 4] in subsection 4.2.3, on Families Receiving Supplementary Benefits by Rosalind Marshall [QRL 8] and on Financial Circumstances of Two-Parent Families by J. R. Howe [B 34] in subsection 4.2.5. These surveys in fact represent the major sources for income distribution data in the report. The additional surveys referred to in Appendix 2 are largely of a highly specialized nature, dealing with the social administrative problems of one-parent families.

4.2.5 *DHSS Statistical Report Series*

Up to 1971 the Department of Health and Social Security produced a Statistical Report Series. Since 1972 the name of the series, plus numbers, was changed to the Statistical and Research Report Series. There have been two publications to date in these series which have some relevance for income analysis. The first was a study of low-income families, their resources and needs by J. R. Howe in 1971. This was No. 14 in the Statistical Report Series and entitled *Two-Parent Families: A Study of their Resources and Needs* [B 34].

This work attempted to estimate for the years 1968, 1969 and 1970 the numbers of families with incomes at or below the social security assistance levels. The base data were the FES for those years. The FES, which are described in detail in subsection 3.4, have formed the basis of two previous estimates of low incomes or poverty, one the famous private study by P. Townsend and B. Abel-Smith for 1953–4 and 1960 [B 1] and the other an official enquiry published in the *Report of an Inquiry into the Impact of Rates on Households* [QRL 47] for 1964. Naturally any evaluation of these data sources depends on the evaluation of the base data which we considered in subsections 3.4.6 and 3.4.7.

The second work, *Families Receiving Supplementary Benefit* [QRL 8] by Rosalind Marshall, was published in 1972 and was the first in the new Statistical and Research Report Series. In fact it was an in-depth study of 348 families, classified into six equal categories, e.g. unmarried mother, mother divorced, fathers unemployed, etc. which attempted to compare the social and economic characteristics of fatherless families with two-parent families. The families were restricted to those receiving supplementary benefits. The field-work, undertaken by the Survey Division of the Office of Population Censuses and Survey, was completed during May and September 1969.

The enquiry was carried out for the Committee on One-Parent Families [B 94] set up in 1969. The sample was clearly very small-scale, such that the results are quite unsuitable for aggregation. Again like the survey described in subsection 4.2.3, for which this sample was a forerunner, it must be noted that the prime purpose of the exercise was not to produce income or even aggregate poverty data. These reports are of considerable potential value to social administrators.

4.2.6 *Social Security Statistical Series—National*
A detailed account of social security statistics is given in Review 4 in Volume II in this series by F. E. Whitehead [B 65]. We shall only give a brief outline of these sources relevant to personal income analysis.

There are two readily available regular sources of United Kingdom or Great Britain basic annual social security data. These are the *Annual Abstract of Statistics* [QRL 13] and the Central Statistical Office's recent *Social Trends* [QRL 65], now in its fifth year. Monthly data on some items is also published in the *Monthly Digest of Statistics* [QRL 35]. In the Quick Reference List we list the data available from these sources.

Current detailed information on all aspects of the above data can be obtained from the *Annual Reports of the Department of Health and Social Security* [B 71] for the period 1969 to 1972, and for 1973 onwards in the new *Social Security Statistics* [B 99] published by the Department. The relevant data formerly in the *Annual Reports* has been transferred to this new source. Prior to the formation of the Department of Health and Social Security the same information was published in the annual reports of the Ministry of Social Security, and prior to 1966 in the annual reports of the National Assistance Board and Ministry of Pensions and National Insurance. These sources also give an outline of the sampling and estimation techniques for each of the data series. They comprise well over fifty tables. We shall not list the data available in these volumes as they are largely a finer breakdown of those presented in the Quick Reference List.

It is also possible to obtain very highly detailed data on pensions and widows' benefits from the *Abstract of Retirement Pensions and Widows' Benefits* [B 66]. This is an annual production, but is only available on request from the Chief Statistician at the Department of Health and Social Security. Similarly detailed data on war pensions is available annually in the *Reports on War Pensions* [B 95] and in the First (1958), Second (1966) and Third (1968) *Government Actuary Surveys on Occupational Pensions* [B 90, QRL 44, QRL 45] for occupational pensions.

Finally, it should be noted that all the tables in

the above sources, which give the number of recipients of benefit income, etc. refer to the number of recipients receiving on one particular date within the period concerned, usually 31 December for annual data but on some occasions dates in other months are adopted. Users of the data should beware of this feature, especially since expenditure estimates refer to amounts arising during a whole period of time.

4.2.7 *Social Security Statistics—Regional*
A detailed account of regional social security statistics is given in Review 4 in Volume II of the present series by F. E. Whitehead [B 65].

Regional data on social security payments are published in the major regional statistical sources, namely the *Digest of Welsh Statistics* [QRL 19], the *Statistical Digest of Northern Ireland* [QRL 18] and the *Digest of Scottish Statistics* [QRL 17] to 1970 and the *Scottish Abstract of Statistics* [QRL 64] thereafter. Each source gives data on the numbers of retirement pensions, war pensions, monthly data on the new claims for injury and sickness benefits by broad type of invalidity, annual figures on regular weekly numbers in receipt of supplementary benefit by type of benefit (including estimates on the number of wage-stopped males) and finally numbers in receipt of family allowances by family size and age of child.

The Scottish and Irish statistics provide additional information on National Insurance benefits, including some monthly data, and the Northern Irish digest alone gives figures on family income supplements, guardians' allowances, orphans' pensions, children's allowances and attendance allowances. The Scottish Abstract is the only source which publishes details on the method of collection and sampling for each series. However for Northern Ireland very detailed information for both method and data is available in the *Annual Reports of the Northern Ireland Supplementary Benefit Commission* [B 73].

Finally for Northern Ireland, the Stormont Ministry of Health and Social Services published a report in 1966 on the *Financial and other Circumstances of Retirement Pensioners in Northern Ireland* [QRL 27]. The report was identical in lay-out and the type of data provided to that produced simultaneously for the rest of the United Kingdom [QRL 26] (see subsection 4.2.1). The sample technique was also similarly stratified, but with higher sampling fractions applied to the smaller population in order to produce a total sample size which would yield acceptable sampling errors. In all 1,300 pensioners were selected and there was a 90% response rate.

4.3 Unofficial Data on Low Incomes and Poverty

There have been numerous very small-scale surveys done on the characteristics and resources of low-income families. These surveys are generally localized with no pretence at being representative nationally. Furthermore most are undertaken by social administrators where the aim of producing nationally representative statistics is of minimal importance. Many in fact are so small that they are not even statistically significant for the small local areas from which they are drawn. Finally it is impossible to trace all the surveys that have been undertaken. There is undoubtedly a need for a national register of such works and the recent Archive for Income Surveys undertaken by the SSRC and the University of Essex [B 98] is a very important development in this area. In this section we shall only list a small proportion of the total which has been brought to the author's attention.

4.3.1 *The Pilot Surveys for the Essex Poverty Study* [B 1]
In subsection 3.9.2 we pointed out that a forthcoming publication will be the Essex Poverty Study under the auspices of Professors Brian Abel-Smith and Peter Townsend. There have been four pilot studies in connection with this massive study. These are: *The Poor and Out of Work in Shields* by Adrian Sinfield [B 55]; *A Study*

of the Chronic Sick by John Viet-Wilson [B 64]; *Large Families in London* by Hilary Land [B 39] and *Mothers Alone* by Dennis Marsden [B 42]. [B 55, B 39 and B 42] are all published but [B 64] is an unpublished paper.

The first two studies do not contain any relevant income data. The third survey was based on a sample of 150 large families selected from the family allowance records of the former Ministry of Pensions and National Insurance. A large family was defined as one with five or more children and the sample was designed to produce equal numbers of families with five, six, seven and eight or more children. The sampling fraction therefore varied with family size.

The interviewing took place in two stages between Spring 1965 and Spring 1966. There was an overall response rate of 57%, which varied quite noticeably with family size. The largest families were far more responsive. The income data published comprised a distribution of regular weekly income by households. Regular weekly income was defined as basic wages, state cash benefits, overtime earnings plus mothers' earnings and children's contributions. There was also some additional data on welfare and educational benefits, valued at cost, and miscellaneous irregular income and income in kind.

Dennis Marsden's survey interviewed 116 families in 1965 living on National Assistance. The sample was divided between a northern and a southern town, both of which were given fictitious names. The results did contain some income data, but no information on the distribution of total income by family size or the amounts of total income by source. The author interestingly emphasizes that the sample is not nationally representative and to be so would have required a sample of 100,000 cases.

4.3.2 *Other Surveys*

One of the best-known independent studies was that by Ken Coates and Richard Silbern of Nottingham University. These authors surveyed between 1966 and 1968 over 400 households in the St Ann's district of Nottingham. Details of the first 176 interviews were published in *Poverty, Deprivation and Morale* [B 22] in 1967. A descriptive report of all the surveys is in *Poverty: The Forgotten Englishmen* [B 23] published in 1970. This latter source however does not provide any tables or data.

The income data from most independent surveys is rarely as detailed or useful as can be obtained from the *Family Expenditure Surveys* and invariably less statistically reliable. This is certainly the case with surveys such as that by the Child Poverty Action Group of Northern Ireland in *Poverty in Downpatrick* [B 92]. Probably the most important independent studies are those that were undertaken before the emergence of reasonable official data in the 1960s. In those days they were the only source of data, the most significant being the studies of poverty in York in 1936 by Seebohm Rowntree [B 51, B 52, B 53] which played such an important role in planning the modern British social security system. An excellent summary of surveys before 1945 is given by D. Caradog Jones in his book *Social Surveys* [B 35] and for the immediate post-war years in PEP's *Poverty Ten Years after Beveridge* [B 93] published in 1952.

5 Concluding Thoughts

5.1 The Linking of Data Sources

We have seen in this review that both the definitions of income and of the recipient and moreover the coverage of income distribution surveys vary quite considerably from one source to another. This variation reflects partly the main purpose of the data, which is rarely to collect data on income distribution, and partly the fact that the different requirements of income distribution analysis necessitate different definitions. However in spite of the need for a degree of variation, the present means of attaining this diversity sadly limits the collective value of the sources.

There are currently six official published sources of data for income distribution analysis. We can add to this the forthcoming Census Income Follow-Up (CIF). Of these seven sources two adopt a household definition (FES and GHS), two a tax unit definition (CSO and Inland Revenue) and the remaining three (NES, DHSS and possibly CIF) relate to the individual. The definitions of income adopted also vary considerably ranging from annual taxable income plus certain benefit incomes and non-taxable incomes in the CSO distributions to main-source weekly earnings in the NES. The methods of obtaining the data for the distributions again vary, from large random samples utilizing official information collected by the operation of the Income Tax and National Insurance systems to voluntary samples which with the exception of the CIF are on a much smaller scale.

The characteristics cross-classified by income size in each of the sources are also very varied. Apart from an after-tax summary the CSO distributions present no further characteristics. The others to some degree give detailed data on marital status, sex, income sources, tax deductions, residence by region and smaller areas, occupation, age, expenditure and some other general household characteristics. In no instance however are all these characteristics covered by any one particular source.

It follows that if all the sources could be 'matched' or linked to produce a distribution embodying all these main characteristics and be capable of grossing-up, providing an extensive coverage with respect to the aggregate personal income of households and individuals and with respect to total population, then we would have indeed a valuable stock of data for analysis. The benefits of linking are not unrecognized in official circles. There exists already an inter-departmental committee formed by the CSO to consider means of supplementing the Inland Revenue Surveys and DHSS earnings distributions with data from the FES and GHS and from statistics on social security benefits. The Royal Commission in its first report ([QRL 62], para. 363) has requested that the CSO report on the linking of various sources.

At present there is some linking undertaken on a small scale between the Inland Revenue Surveys and the FES to produce the CSO distributions. The linking is restricted to the expansion of the Inland Revenue Surveys by the inclusion of some non-taxable incomes and income units with wholly non-taxable income. The procedure adopted is to estimate, by reference to control totals, the amounts of income and units not covered by the Inland Revenue data and to allocate and attach as much as possible of these using patterns indicated by the FES suitably converted to a tax unit basis. However the CSO does not attempt to incorporate other characteristics from either of the base distributions. There is some evidence (see Stark [B 59]) that the family circumstance data in the Inland Revenue Surveys could be linked and perhaps the FES in conjunction with benchmark control totals from the Censuses of Population could be used to expand family size classification to incomes below the tax exemption limit.

It may be possible to project other patterns from the 'converted' FES data on to the Inland Revenue and subsequent CSO distributions. For example the classifications by age in the FES, again in conjunction with control totals from population data, would be an exercise worthy of consideration. However it would not be possible to project the FES expenditure patterns since expenditure data is only classified according to a household recipient unit. The study of income redistribution for the time being appears to be restricted to data solely from the *Family Expenditure Survey*.

The FES and GHS employ virtually identical concepts and sampling methods. The scope for 'matching' these two sources is considerable. The two sources could be linked by the use of the micro-data synthesizing techniques developed in the USA by the Bureau of Economic Analysis and the Brooking Institute (see [B 15] and [B 45] for further details). Briefly this would entail matching households from both surveys which display a high element of similarity with respect to variables common to both surveys and by doing so create a composite or synthetic file for the two particular households in which the characteristics available in each of the surveys would be included. The joint files would then become the basis of a new set of data comprising the whole range of characteristics. The matching of the households would be achieved by random selection, with replacement for non-selection, of the sample returns, suitably converted to preserve the anonymity of households. Selection for matching would be upheld only if the returns reached or surpassed a pre-defined level of identity with respect to such factors as size, income on a comparable basis and perhaps age of household head and area of residence.

One of the major limitations of micro-data synthesizing is that the size of the synthetic distribution is restricted at the maximum to the size of the smallest survey, assuming all households in it can be 'matched'. In our example this would be the FES. This restriction could weaken the value of the resulting additional characteristics since the expansion of cross-classifications increases the number of household category cells and with a small initial sample size, such as in the FES, the standard errors of some of these cells may become very large and untolerable. Given also that both the FES and GHS display some notable deficiencies when grossed-up, then it may be that the patterns derived from matching may be biased and unsuitable for projection on to a source, like the Inland Revenue Surveys, which can be and is grossed-up. Thus micro-data synthesis in this area may be a limited development. Finally the relative smallness of the FES or GHS surveys would restrict the usefulness of matching with the Inland Revenue Surveys by micro-data synthesis. The deficiency of the FES and GHS with respect to higher incomes would also present many problems. The present system of 'projecting patterns' between these sources seems a more valuable exercise.

The above arguments might suggest that matching by micro-data techniques has a greater chance of success if large samples are linked. In the UK there are four samples in excess of 100,000 returns which theoretically is sufficiently large to permit a very large number of cells. The sources are the Inland Revenue Surveys, NES, DHSS and the forthcoming CIF. The first three sources do have common features which it would be thought might facilitate matching, such as main source earnings, area of residence, sex and marital status. However the differing techniques of classification and definition certainly prevent any matching or linking between the DHSS and NES earnings data and one suspects that there would be no scope for matching the NES with the Inland Revenue Surveys.

With respect to a DHSS and Inland Revenue Survey link it might be worth considering which characteristics the former may bring to the latter. The DHSS provides cross-classifications by age and some occupational variables for fully employed PAYE earners. The details were collected from a sample of tax deduction cards and their matched National Insurance cards. Since all deduction cards contain information on the National Insurance number and the number of weeks employed by the employer, a direct administrative link of deduction cards and the Inland Revenue Survey sample Form X (see Appendix B) might be a more useful line of attack. An anonymous link between Form X and the National Insurance records via the insurance number could provide data on age, whilst the classification of the employer and weeks paid could provide some data on employment by activity and by industry. Clearly there would arise a number of problems with respect to employees whose employment practices were subject to numerous changes. There is also a possibility that the extra administrative burden may be cost-prohibitive.

Even if a development of this type were feasible there still remain the considerable problems of finding similar data on incomes outside the tax deduction card area. The simplest solution of all however to obtaining age and occupation data for the Inland Revenue Surveys would be to request specifically such information on the tax returns. The tax authorities however may be reluctant to request information which is not required by the statutory arrangements of the tax system.

A development on which we can only speculate is the 'matching' capabilities of the CIF. If we presume that the sampled returns can be directly linked with the Census of Population returns, then the cross-classification between income and other characteristics is potentially extensive. The main census asks over thirty questions, twenty-four on specific individual characteristics and others on household factors such as tenure, rooms, the provision of amenities and so on. The individual questions cover age, occupation and employment, educational qualifications and the relationship between members of a household and the head of the household (n.b. provision is made also for those living outside households). The last factor could facilitate classification on an inner family and unrelated individuals basis similar to the tax unit or on a household basis if required.

The Census Income Follow-Up is a large sample involving some 400,000 persons. The micro-data synthesizing of this source with the Inland Revenue Surveys would be a valuable step. Though it is impossible to consider the technique in depth a broad plan might be usefully outlined. The plan of approach would be to divide the CIF data into two categories:

(A) Those likely to have taxable income;
(B) Those unlikely.

Micro-data filing could proceed, as previously described, between group (A) and the Inland Revenue Surveys. The 'matching' features might be:

(i) Family size;
(ii) Age, over or under 65;
(iii) Place of residence;
(iv) An income indicator, perhaps based on main source income or relative position in the two distributions.

The object of the exercise would be to use the Inland Revenue data regarding taxable income and all other characteristics, including non-taxable income from the CIF. The family size, age and residence matching should be exact. Persons in group (B) could then be incorporated into the composite distribution, perhaps utilizing information from the FES. The whole exercise would be subject of course to appropriate income and population control totals. Naturally these are only tentative suggestions and in no way imply that the process would be fraught-free both technically and computationally. Nevertheless the potential appears immense and the only sad prospect is that there is no possibility of another CIF until at least 1981 unless the authorities can be persuaded to re-introduce the five-year 5% population sample survey.

It is clear from the foregoing analysis that there are many problems and difficulties in attempting to match sources. In fact one is tempted to conclude that the value of 'matching' is unlikely to be high unless there are some changes made in the methods of collecting data, specifically to facilitate matching or data expansion, such as a much larger FES or more regular Census of Population data or additional questions on the tax returns and so on.

5.2 Other Gaps in Statistics

There are three noticeable gaps in the present array of available statistics. These are data on the income–wealth link, for longitudinal studies and finally for inter-generational studies.

5.2.1 *The Income–Wealth Link*

There can be little quarrel with the statement that the relative well-being of individuals, families or households cannot be wholly represented by the distribution of either income or wealth. A low income level is not a sufficient condition for a low standard of living. The balance between the income and expenditure flows is linked via the residual of savings to the stock of wealth. This balance may well display specific patterns related to age and inheritance, in addition to income levels. Thus an overall picture would require a joint distribution of income and wealth. Furthermore it would enable us more accurately to apportion those non-monetary flows from the ownership of property such as imputed rent and capital appreciation.

As Atkinson and Harrison state in our companion review [B 7] the data on wealth statistics are far from satisfactory. There are however no official data whatsoever on the joint distribution of income and wealth. Tentative estimates have been made by academics using investment income as the link (see Stark [B 59]) but these are generally unsatisfactory. The only viable solution to this deficiency is a Wealth Survey with an income variable to enable matching to one of the main income distribution sources.

5.2.2 *Longitudinal Data*

The term longitudinal is used to indicate a sample of observations at the same point over a number of periods of time. In the income distribution field this would enable analysis of income changes for a given group of recipients over a number of years. It is a matter of considerable importance with respect to the interpretation of the standard 'static' income distributions whether the incomes at the extremes represent over time the same group of recipients. Available evidence in other countries and from the two-year longitudinal data occasionally published by the Inland Revenue (see sub-section 3.2.4) suggest that incomes at the extremes are highly unstable, indicating that the degree of dispersion over a longer period of time may be much less than normally indicated. Furthermore longitudinal information would be specifically valuable in studying the long-term policy requirements with respect to low incomes and poverty, particularly if information on age, employment and education were simultaneously available. The present data from this point of view is insufficient. There is a clear need for at least a five-yearly continuous sample survey of two to four thousand families or households for this purpose.

The extremes in longitudinal analyses of course are life-cycle income data. It is unlikely that a continuous life-cycle sample, which is sufficiently representative of the community, is feasible. A more likely source is the administrative records of tax payments such as the study by Soltow [B 57] for the Norwegian city of Sarpsborg. At present there are no life-time income data in the United Kingdom, nor are there any plans, to our knowledge, to collect such data. The current viewpoint is that age-income size cross-section data should suffice to analyse the probable life-time pattern of incomes. There is scope here for controversy.

5.2.3 *Inter-generational Studies*

This group of analyses attempts to trace the relative income class relationships between parents and children. The analysis of economic mobility and the long-term effects of the income-cum-class structure are the motivating factors in undertaking studies of this type. There are no published data in the UK on inter-generational incomes, though there are plans by a team led by Professor A. B. Atkinson to trace some of the children of those sampled in Rowntree's 1950 survey of incomes in York [B 52]. With regard to official sources the FES and GHS sources could be adapted by selecting each year a specific number of children in some households to be interviewed a generation later. The long fruition period for this type of data makes it imperative that plans be drawn up as soon as possible.

5.3 Improvements in the Presentation of Statistics

There are a number of changes in the presentation of current official statistics that could reduce the difficulties in interpreting and expanding these sources. The first and most obvious is the need to redefine aggregate personal income to refer solely to the income of households/families and individuals. This, as we have discussed (see subsection 2.8.1) is already under way.

It may also be useful to present official summary income distribution data separating households/families and unrelated individuals. This undoubtedly aids interpretation and could be incorporated readily into the Inland Revenue Survey and CSO data. The detailed tables of the Inland Revenue Surveys in effect do this by the division between single and married tax units. It would also be valuable in the CSO and Inland Revenue sources to adjust for part-year incomes. These generally lead to an artificially larger number of low incomes. The main part-year incomes are those arising from the deaths of single persons and married males, the marriage and divorce of females with independent incomes, and school leavers. A suggestion may be to extract deaths, adjust school leavers to an annual basis if possible, and combine the income of newly married females whilst single with that of their husbands and the opposite for divorced females.

Further suggestions for presenting data may be to produce *per capita* and equivalent adult distributions and possibly the regular estimation of incomes at or below the supplementary benefit levels in the Family Expenditure Surveys which could be interpreted as an official indicator of poverty. In addition it would be a considerable convenience if all official data were published in one annual source.

A final point relates to the time lag in publishing the results of surveys, particularly those with an immediate policy value such as the FES-based redistribution studies (see subsection 3.4.9). In the main the process is fast but nevertheless inadequate for providing data for current policy decisions. The only solution is the construction of simulation models designed to forecast the present state of affairs. A recent paper by Boreham and Semple [B 11] indicates that the government statisticians are clearly thinking along these lines among other improvements in data on redistribution. It may be hoped that such models, when they emerge, also will be published.

Quick Reference List—Table of Contents

Quick Reference List

Type of Data	Breakdown	Area	Frequency	Publication	Text Reference
Personal Income, 1938, 1946–					
Aggregate Personal Income	By type	UK	Annual	[QRL 37]	2.1
	By type	UK	Quarterly	[QRL 35]	2.1
				[QRL 29]	2.1
				[QRL 20]	2.1
Aggregate Personal Income from Employment	By type	UK	Annual	[QRL 37]	2.2.1
		UK	Quarterly	[QRL 35]	2.2.1
				[QRL 20]	2.2.1
				[QRL 29]	2.2.1
Wages and salaries in cash and kind		UK	Annual	[QRL 37]	2.3.1, 2.3.2
			Quarterly	[QRL 35]	2.3.1, 2.3.2
				[QRL 29]	2.3.1, 2.3.2
				[QRL 20]	2.3.1, 2.3.2
Pay in cash and kind—HM Forces		UK	Annual	[QRL 37]	2.3.3
			Quarterly	[QRL 35]	2.3.3
				[QRL 20]	2.3.3
				[QRL 29]	2.3.3
Employers' contributions—National Insurance		UK	Annual	[QRL 37]	2.3.4
			Quarterly	[QRL 35]	2.3.11
Employers' contributions—others		UK	Annual	[QRL 37]	2.3.4
			Quarterly	[QRL 35]	2.3.11
Occupational pension schemes	By type	UK	Annual	[QRL 44]	2.3.4
				[QRL 45]	2.3.4
Occupational pension schemes	No. of employees covered	UK	Annual	[QRL 21]	2.3.4
Aggregate Personal Income from Self-Employment	By type	UK	Annual	[QRL 37]	2.3
			Quarterly	[QRL 35]	2.3.11
				[QRL 29]	2.3.11
				[QRL 20]	2.3.11
Income of professional persons		UK	Annual	[QRL 37]	2.3.5
			Quarterly	[QRL 35]	2.3.11
				[QRL 20]	2.3.11
				[QRL 29]	2.3.11

Income of farmers		UK	Annual	[QRL 37]	2.3.6
				[QRL 14]	2.3.6
			Quarterly	[QRL 35]	2.3.11
				[QRL 20]	2.3.11
				[QRL 29]	2.3.11
Income of other sole traders and partnerships		UK	Annual	[QRL 37]	2.3.7
			Quarterly	[QRL 35]	2.3.11
				[QRL 20]	2.3.11
				[QRL 29]	2.3.11
Aggregate Personal Income from Property		UK	Annual	[QRL 37]	2.2.1
			Quarterly	[QRL 35]	2.3.11
				[QRL 20]	2.3.11
				[QRL 29]	2.3.11
Income from rent, net interest and dividends of life assurances and superannuation funds		UK	Annual	[QRL 37]	2.3.8
			Quarterly	[QRL 35]	2.3.11
				[QRL 20]	2.3.11
				[QRL 29]	2.3.11
Receipts, property income, by rest of personal sector		UK	Annual	[QRL 37]	2.3.8
Receipts by rest of personal sector		UK	Quarterly	[QRL 35]	2.3.11
				[QRL 20]	2.3.11
				[QRL 29]	2.3.11
Rent of owner-occupied dwellings		UK	Annual	[QRL 37]	2.3.8
			Quarterly	[QRL 20]	2.3.11
				[QRL 35]	2.3.11
				[QRL 29]	2.3.11
Accrued interest on National Savings Certificates		UK	Annual	[QRL 37]	2.2.1
			Quarterly	[QRL 35]	2.3.11
				[QRL 20]	2.3.11
				[QRL 29]	2.3.11
Aggregate Transfer Incomes in the Personal Sector	By type	UK	Annual	[QRL 37]	2.3.9
					2.3.10
	By type	UK	Quarterly	[QRL 35]	2.3.11
				[QRL 20]	2.3.11
				[QRL 29]	2.3.11
Current transfers to charities from companies		UK	Annual	[QRL 37]	2.3.9
			Quarterly	[QRL 35]	2.3.11
				[QRL 20]	2.3.11
				[QRL 29]	2.3.11
Aggregate National Insurance benefits and other current grants from public authorities	By type	UK	Annual	[QRL 37]	2.3.9
			Quarterly	[QRL 35]	2.3.11
				[QRL 20]	2.3.11
				[QRL 29]	2.3.11

Type of Data	*Breakdown*	*Area*	*Frequency*	*Publication*	*Text Reference*
Retirement pensions, widows' benefits, etc. non-contributory pensions		UK	Annual	[QRL 37]	2.3.9
			Quarterly	[QRL 35]	2.3.11
				[QRL 20]	2.3.11
				[QRL 29]	2.3.11
Grants to private non-profit-making bodies		UK	Annual	[QRL 37]	2.3.9
			Quarterly	[QRL 35]	2.3.11
				[QRL 20]	2.3.11
				[QRL 29]	2.3.11
Other grants from public authorities		UK	Annual	[QRL 37]	2.3.9
			Quarterly	[QRL 35]	2.3.11
				[QRL 20]	2.3.11
				[QRL 29]	2.3.11
Pensions and benefits from life assurance and superannuation schemes		UK	Annual	[QRL 37]	2.3.10
			Quarterly	[QRL 35]	2.3.11
				[QRL 20]	2.3.11
				[QRL 29]	2.3.11
Personal disposable income	Aggregate	UK	Annual	[QRL 37]	2.4.1
			Quarterly	[QRL 35]	2.4.1
				[QRL 20]	2.4.1
Personal real disposable income	Aggregate	UK	Annual and Quarterly	[QRL 29]	2.4.2
				[QRL 20]	2.4.2
Personal income in Northern Ireland	Aggregate	NI	Annual	[QRL 18]	2·5
Personal Income, 1938–45					
Aggregate personal income—official	By type	UK	Annual	[QRL 12]	2.6.1
	By type	UK	Annual	[QRL 39]	2.6.1
	By type	UK	Annual	[QRL 67]	2.6.1
	By type	UK	Annual	[QRL 2]	2.6.1
Income from employment		UK	Annual	[QRL 2]	2.6.4
Income from farming		UK	Annual	[QRL 2]	2.6.4
Employers' National Insurance contributions		UK	Annual	[QRL 2]	2.6.4
Non-farm self-employment income		UK	Annual	[QRL 2]	2.6.4
Transfer incomes from the public sector		UK	Annual	[QRL 2]	2.6.4
Personal Income, 1920–38					
Aggregate personal income		UK	Annual	[QRL 2]	2.6.5
Income from employment		UK	Annual	[QRL 2]	2.6.5
Income from self-employment		UK	Annual	[QRL 2]	2.6.5
Rent, dividends and net interest		UK	Annual	[QRL 2]	2.6.5
National Health and Insurance contributions		UK	Annual	[QRL 2]	2.6.5
Grants to persons from public sector		UK	Annual	[QRL 2]	2.6.5

Personal Income, 1855–1920					
Wages and salaries		UK	Annual	[QRL 2]	2.6.6
Farmers' income		UK	Annual	[QRL 2]	2.6.6
Forces' pay in cash and kind (since 1900)		UK	Annual	[QRL 2]	2.6.6
Employers' National Insurance and Health contributions (since 1912)		UK	Annual	[QRL 2]	2.6.6
Household and Non-Household Income in the Personal Sector					
Income of households		UK	Annual	[QRL 20]	2.8.1
Income of non-profit-making bodies		UK	Annual	[QRL 20]	2.8.1
Income of life assurance companies and superannuation funds		UK	Annual	[QRL 20]	2.8.1
Distribution of Personal Income					
Taxable Income					
Net taxable income of tax units	Before and after tax deductions, marital status, source of income, family circumstances, region, countries, conurbations	UK	Annual since 1962/3 and before that for 1949–50, 1954–5, 1959–60	For 1949–50 to 1966–7 see [QRL 53] For 1967–8 see [QRL 32]. Also for 1969–70, 1970–1, 1972–3. See [QRL 68, QRL 69, QRL 70]	3.2.1–3.2.11
Net taxable income of tax units by component items by size of components		UK	1959–60, 1964–5,	[QRL 53]	3.2.1–3.2.11
			1969–70	[QRL 68]	
			1970–1	[QRL 69]	
			1972–3	[QRL 70]	
Net taxable income of tax units by region and family size		UK	1949–50	[QRL 53]	3.2.4
			1970–1	[QRL 69]	
Net taxable income of tax units and range of life insurance relief		UK	1954–5	[QRL 53]	3.2.4
			1967–8	[QRL 32]	3.2.4
			since then	[QRL 68, QRL 69]	
Benefits from life insurance by net taxable income		UK	1963–4 to 1972–3	[QRL 63]	3.7.3
Net taxable income of tax units after tax by net taxable income before tax		UK	1964–5	[QRL 53]	3.2.4
			1969–70	[QRL 68]	3.2.4
			1970–1	[QRL 69]	3.2.4
Proportionate changes in taxable wages and salaries over two tax years		UK	1959–60	[QRL 53]	3.2.4
Dividend income by net taxable income of tax units		UK	1972–3	[QRL 63]	3.2.4

Type of Data	*Breakdown*	*Area*	*Frequency*	*Publication*	*Text Reference*
Assessed taxable income of tax units 1857–1920	Source of income	UK	Annual	[QRL 48]	3.2.12
Assessed taxable income of tax units 1918–19	Source of income and tax raised	UK	Annual	[QRL 50]	3.2.12
Assessed taxable income of tax units 1920–1	Source of income and tax raised	UK	Annual	[QRL 15]	3.2.12
Assessed taxable income of tax units 1937–8	Marital status, source of incomes family circumstances	UK	Annual	[QRL 51]	3.2.12
Aggregate Personal Income					
Aggregate personal income of tax units and equivalent	Before and after tax	UK	Annual to 1969 Annual	[QRL 37] [QRL 38] [QRL 62] [QRL 20]	3.3.1–3.3.4
	Less part-year income units before tax	UK	1972–3, 1973–4	[QRL 76]	3.7.2
Household Income					
Gross weekly 'normal' income by households	Age of head, composition and size of household, occupation of head, source of income, tenure, region, consumer durables, children of working wives, etc.	UK	Annual	[QRL 28]	3.4.1–3.4.6 See Table 3.7 for details of breakdown
Gross 'weekly' income by households 1953–4	Size of household, occupation of head, type of dwelling, region and type of area, age of head, source of income	UK	Annual	[QRL 46]	3.4.7
Gross 'weekly' normal income in Northern Ireland by households	Same as UK	NI	Annual	[QRL 43]	3.4.8
Redistribution of gross 'annual' income by households	Type of taxation and benefit, family size, retired and non-retired	UK	Annual	[QRL 20] For 1959, 1957 and 1953 see [QRL 10]	3.4.9

Gross annual income by households	Family size, sex, age of members, source of income, tenure, type of accommodation, past and potential movers, work intentions of women, some educational factors, earnings, education, and sex	GB	Annual	[QRL 30]	3.5
Contributions to pension funds deducted by employers by gross annual income of households		UK	1972–3	[QRL 63]	3.7.3
Earnings					
Weekly earnings (1886, 1906, 1938, 1960)	Hours worked, occupation and industry	UK	Annual	[QRL 16]	3.6.1
Weekly earnings (1968 and since 1970)	Industry, occupation	UK	Annual	[QRL 41]	3.6.2
				[QRL 21]	3.6.2
Annual earnings	Sex, age, marital status, regions and large towns	UK	Annual	[QRL 11]	3.6.3
				[QRL 64]	3.6.3
Gross Income					
Gross income by tax units or equivalent (1951–2, 1952–3, 1953–4, 1954–5)	Before and after tax, age, sex, marital status, source of income, savings and types of savings, residence, occupation, manual and non-manual workers, children's earnings	GB	Annual	[QRL 5]	3.8.1
		GB		[QRL 3]	3.8.1
		GB		[QRL 1]	3.8.1 [QRL5] in much more detail than others
Gross weekly income by households and tax units		UK	1972–3	[QRL 62]	3.7.2
Other Types of Personal Income					
Capital gains of persons	Type of gain	UK	Annual	[QRL 32]	3.10.1
Fringe benefits from employment (1955, 1964, 1968, 1973, 1974, 1975)	Aggregate totals for specific industries only	GB	Annual	[QRL 24]	3.10.2
		GB	Annual	[QRL 33]	3.10.2
		GB	Annual	[QRL 34]	3.10.2
Fringe benefits with managerial salaries		UK	1973–5	[QRL 75]	3.7.4

Type of Data	*Breakdown*	*Area*	*Frequency*	*Publication*	*Text Reference*
Personal Incomes by Occupation					
Income and earnings in specific occupations		UK	Annual	[QRL 36]	4.1.1
Earnings of professional engineers		UK	Annual	[QRL 72]	4.1.2
Earnings of professional scientists		UK	Annual	[QRL 73]	4.1.2
			Annual	[QRL 74]	4.1.2
Earnings of doctors and dentists		UK	1957–60	[QRL 62]	4.1.3
		UK	Annual	[QRL 58]	4.1.3
		UK	Annual	[QRL 60]	4.1.3 (a)
Earnings of Armed Forces		UK	Annual	[QRL 57]	4.1.3 (b)
		UK	Annual	[QRL 66]	4.1.3 (b)
Top salaries in industry and the civil service		UK	Annual	[QRL 60]	4.1.3 (c)
Earnings of nurses and midwives		UK	Annual	[QRL 54]	4.1.3 (e)
Earnings of professions supplementary to medicine and speech therapy		UK	Annual	[QRL 55]	4.1.3 (e)
Earnings of non-university teachers		GB	Annual	[QRL 56]	4.1.3 (e)
Higher incomes from employment		UK	1969–75	[QRL 75]	3.7.4
Social Security and Pension Incomes					
Regular Income Series:					
National Insurance					
Receipts of funds, including industrial injuries		UK	Annual	[QRL 13]	4.2
Numbers of contributors by type of contribution, by type of benefit		UK	Annual	[QRL 13]	4.2
Numbers receiving benefits by type of benefit		UK	Annual	[QRL 13]	4.2
				[QRL 65]	4.2
Numbers of retirement pensions by sex and age		GB	Annual	[QRL 13]	4.2
Numbers of retirement and widows' pensions, recipients of unemployment benefit, injured persons absent from work by type of injury and new claims for benefit by type of benefit		GB	Monthly from 1971	[QRL 35]	4.2
Family Allowances					
Expenditure and numbers receiving by family size		GB	Annual	[QRL 13]	4.2
				[QRL 65]	4.2
Numbers receiving by family size		GB	Monthly from 1971	[QRL 35]	4.2
Estimated number of one-child families		GB	Annual	[QRL 65]	4.2
Family Income Supplement					
Numbers receiving by type of family and by family size		GB	Annual	[QRL 13]	4.2
				[QRL 65]	4.2

Supplementary Benefits (and National Assistance)				
Numbers receiving non-contributory pensions, number of cases of supplementary benefits (and National Assistance)	UK	Annual	[QRL 13]	4.2
Amount paid in non-contributory pensions, benefits and assistance	UK	Annual	[QRL 13]	4.2
Average weekly benefits by type of benefit	UK	Annual	[QRL 13]	4.2
Number of beneficiaries by type of benefit	UK	Annual	[QRL 13]	4.2
			[QRL 65]	4·2
Number receiving by characteristics of beneficiaries, numbers receiving long-term, exceptional circumstance benefits and attendance allowances by age	UK	Annual	[QRL 65]	4.2
Other Data				
Income distribution of persons over retirement age by gross weekly income	UK	Annual	[QRL 65]	4.2
Numbers receiving occupational pensions by marital status, sex, manual and non-manual	UK	Annual	[QRL 65]	4.2
Numbers receiving war pensions, grants and allowances, and amounts paid	UK	Annual	[QRL 13]	4.2
Numbers receiving sickness and invalidity benefits by age, sex and cause of incapacity	GB	Annual	[QRL 13]	4.2
Regular Incomes Series—Regional	Wales	Annual	[QRL 19]	4.2.7
	NI	Annual	[QRL 18]	4.2.7
	Scotland	Annual	[QRL 17]	4.2.7
	Scotland	Annual	[QRL 64]	4.2.7
Special Income Series				
Income of retired pensioners	GB	1966	[QRL 26]	4.2.1
Income of retired pensioners	NI	1966	[QRL 27]	4.2.1, 4.2.7
Income of low-resource families	UK	1973	[QRL 25]	4.2.2
Income of one parent families	GB	Annual	[QRL 1]	4.2.3
Impact of rates on households	GB	1972	[QRL 47]	4.2.5
Families receiving supplementary benefit	GB		[QRL 8]	4.2.5

Quick Reference List Key

Reference Number	*Author/Organization Responsible*	*Title*	*Publisher*	*Frequency or Date*	*Remarks*
[QRL 1]	Erritt, M. J. and Nicholson, J. L.	'The 1955 Savings Survey' in *Bulletin of the Oxford University Institute of Statistics*, **20**, 2	Basil Blackwell, Oxford	May 1958	
[QRL 2]	Feinstein, C. H.	*National Income, Expenditure and Output of the United Kingdom 1855–1965*. Studies in the National Income and Expenditure of the United Kingdom, Vol. 6	Cambridge University Press, Cambridge	1972	
[QRL 3]	Hill, T. P.	'Income, Savings and Net Worth: The Savings Surveys of 1952–54' in *Bulletin of the Oxford University Institute of Statistics*, **17**, 2	Basil Blackwell, Oxford	May 1955	
[QRL 4]	Hunt, A., Fox, J. and Morgan, M. Department of Health and Social Security	*Families and their Needs with Particular Reference to One-Parent Families.*	HMSO, London	1973	Two volumes
[QRL 5]	Lydall, H. F.	*British Incomes and Savings*	Basil Blackwell, Oxford	1955	
[QRL 6]	Lydall, H. F.	'The Methods of the Savings Survey' in *Bulletin of the Oxford University Institute of Statistics*, **16**, 7 and 8	Basil Blackwell, Oxford	July/Aug. 1954	
[QRL 7]	Lydall, H. F.	'The National Survey of Personal Incomes and Savings' in *Bulletin of the Oxford University Institute of Statistics*	Basil Blackwell, Oxford	Nov/Dec 1952	
[QRL 8]	Marshall, Rosalind	*Families Receiving Supplementary Benefit.* Department of Health and Social Security, Statistical and Research Report Series, No. 1	HMSO, London	1972	
[QRL 9]	Moyle, J. and Reid, D. J.	'Private non-profit making bodies serving persons' in *Economic Trends*, No. 259	HMSO, London	May 1975	
[QRL 10]	Nicholson, J. L.	*Redistribution of Income in the United Kingdom in 1959, 1957 and 1953*	Bowes and Bowes	1965	
[QRL 11]	CSO	*Abstract of Regional Statistics*	HMSO, London	Annual	
[QRL 12]	White Paper	*An Analysis of the Sources of War Finance and An Estimate of the National Income and Expenditure in 1935 and 1940*, Cmd. 6261	HMSO, London	1941	
[QRL 13]	CSO	*Annual Abstract of Statistics*	HMSO, London	Annual	

[QRL 14]	White Paper	*Annual Review and Determination of Guarantees*	HMSO, London	Annual	Formerly *Annual Review and fixing of farm prices* (1951–2). After 1972 *Annual Review of Agriculture*
[QRL 15]	Committee on National Debt and Taxation (Colwyn Committee)	*Appendices to the Report of the Committee on National Debt and Taxation* (Appendix XIV)	HMSO, London	1927	
[QRL 16]	Department of Employment	*British Labour Statistics: Historical Abstract 1866–1968*	HMSO, London	1971	
[QRL 17]	Economics and Statistics Unit, St Andrew's House	*Digest of Scottish Statistics*	HMSO, Edinburgh	Twice yearly	From 1971 *Scottish Abstract of Statistics*
[QRL 18]	Northern Ireland Department of Finance	*Digest of Statistics*	HMSO, Belfast	Biannual	
[QRL 19]	Welsh Office	*Digest of Welsh Statistics*	HMSO, Cardiff	Annual	
[QRL 20]	CSO	*Economic Trends*	HMSO, London	Monthly	
[QRL 21]	Department of Employment	*Department of Employment Gazette*	HMSO, London	Monthly	Formerly the *Employment and Productivity Gazette* and the *Ministry of Labour Gazette*
[QRL 22]	Ministry of Labour	*Employment Gazette*, 'Enquiry into Household Expenditure 1937–38'	HMSO, London	Dec. 1940, Jan. and Feb. 1941	
[QRL 23]	Department of Employment and Productivity	*Employment Gazette*, 'Survey of Labour Costs in Northern Ireland, 1968'	HMSO, London	Oct. 1970	In 1970 *Employment and Productivity Gazette*
[QRL 24]	Department of Employment and Productivity	*Employment Gazette*, 'Wages and Related Elements of Labour Costs'	HMSO, London	Aug 1957	
[QRL 25]	Ministry of Social Security	*An Enquiry into the Circumstances of Families*	HMSO, London	1967	
[QRL 26]	Ministry of Pensions and National Insurance	*An Enquiry into Financial and Other Circumstances of Retirement Pensioners*	HMSO, London	1966	
[QRL 27]	Northern Ireland Ministry of Health and Social Security	*An Enquiry into Financial and Other Circumstances of Retirement Pensioners in N.I.*	HMSO, Belfast	1966	
[QRL 28]	Department of Employment	*Family Expenditure Survey*	HMSO, London	Annual	1957–9 and annual since 1961
[QRL 29]	CSO	*Financial Statistics*	HMSO, London	Monthly	

Reference Number	Author/Organization Responsible	Title	Publisher	Frequency or Date	Remarks
[QRL 30]	Office of Population Censuses and Surveys	*General Household Survey*	HMSO, London	1973, 1975, 1976	
[QRL 31]	Board of Inland Revenue	*Inland Revenue Statistics*	HMSO, London	Annual	
[QRL 32]	Board of Inland Revenue	*Inland Revenue Statistics Survey of the Distribution of Personal Incomes*: 1970 for 1967/8; 1971 for 1968/9; 1972 for 1968/70; 1973 for 1970/1; 1974 for 1971/2; 1975 for 1972/3	HMSO, London	Annual	
[QRL 33]	Department of Employment and Productivity	*Labour Costs in Great Britain in 1964: Manufacturing Industries*	HMSO, London	1968	Also *Gazette*, Dec. 1966 and March 1967
[QRL 34]	Department of Employment and Productivity	*Labour Costs in Great Britain 1968*	HMSO, London	1971	Also *Gazette*, Aug., Oct. 1970 and Jan. 1971
			not published as yet	Labour Costs in Great Britain 1973: Industry; Labour Costs in Great Britain 1974: Distribution, Banking and Insurance; Labour Costs in Great Britain 1975: Industry	
[QRL 35]	CSO	*Monthly Digest of Statistics*	HMSO, London	Monthly	
[QRL 36]	National Board for Prices and Incomes	*National Board for Prices and Incomes Reports*	HMSO, London	Occasional	See Appendix F
[QRL 37]	CSO	*National Income and Expenditure*	HMSO, London	Annual	
[QRL 38]	CSO	*National Income and Expenditure 1964–1974*	HMSO, London	1975	
[QRL 39]	White Paper	*National Income and Expenditure of the United Kingdom 1938–1945*, Cmd. 6784	HMSO, London	1946	
[QRL 40]	White Paper	*National Income and Expenditure of the United Kingdom 1938–1946*, Cmd. 7099	HMSO, London	1947	
[QRL 41]	Department of Employment	*New Earnings Survey Booklets*	HMSO, London	Annual	
[QRL 42]	Department of Employment and Productivity	*New Earnings Survey 1968*	HMSO, London	1970	
[QRL 43]	Northern Ireland Department of Finance	*Northern Ireland Family Expenditure Survey*	HMSO, Belfast	Annual	
[QRL 44]	Government Actuary's Department	*Occupational Pension Schemes: A New Survey by the Government Actuary*	HMSO, London	Occasional from 1966	

[QRL 45]	Government Actuary's Department	*Occupational Pension Schemes: A Third Survey by the Government Actuary*	HMSO, London	1968	
[QRL 46]	Ministry of Labour and National Service	*Report of an Enquiry into Household Expenditure in 1953–54*	HMSO, London	1957	
[QRL 47]	Command Paper	*Report of an Inquiry into the Impact of Rates on Households*, Cmnd. 2582	HMSO, London	1965	
[QRL 48]	Board of Inland Revenue	*Report of the Commissioners of HM Inland Revenue*, Command Papers	HMSO, London	Annual	
[QRL 49]	Board of Inland Revenue	*Report of the Commissioners of HM Inland Revenue, 1st*, Cmd. 2199	HMSO, London	1857	
[QRL 50]	Board of Inland Revenue	*Report of the Commissioners of HM Inland Revenue, 63rd*, Cmd. 1083	HMSO, London	1920	
[QRL 51]	Board of Inland Revenue	*Report of the Commissioners of HM Inland Revenue, 83rd*, Cmd. 6769	HMSO, London	1946	
[QRL 52]	Board of Inland Revenue	*Report of the Commissioners of HM Inland Revenue, 92nd*, Cmd. 8052	HMSO, London	1950	
[QRL 53]	Board of Inland Revenue	*Reports of the Commissioners of HM Inland Revenue, Surveys of the Distribution of Personal Incomes*: 94, 95 for 1949–50, Cmd. 8436, 8726 99, 100, 101 for 1954–5, Cmnd. 54, 341, 628 105, 106 for 1959–60, Cmnd. 1906, 2283 107 for 1962–3, Cmnd. 2672 108 for 1963–4, Cmnd. 2876 109, 110 for 1964–5, Cmnd. 3200, 3508 110 for 1965–6, Cmnd. 3508 111 for 1966–7, Cmnd. 3879	HMSO, London	Various	
[QRL 54]	DHSS	*Report of the Committee of Inquiry into Pay and Related Conditions of Service of Nurses and Midwives*	HMSO, London	Sept. 1974	Also *Supplement*, Feb. 1975
[QRL 55]	DHSS	*Report of the Committee of Inquiry into the Pay and Related Conditions of Service of the Professions supplementary to Medicine and Speech Therapists*	HMSO, London	Jan. 1975	
[QRL 56]	Command Paper	*Report of the Committee of Inquiry into the Pay of Non-University Teachers*, Cmnd. 5848	HMSO, London	Dec. 1974	
[QRL 57]	Command Papers	*Reports of Review Body on Armed Forces' Pay*	HMSO, London	Annual	See Appendix G
[QRL 58]	Command Papers	*Reports of Review Body on Doctors' and Dentists' Remuneration*	HMSO, London	Annual	See Appendix G
[QRL 59]	Command Paper	*Review Body on Doctors' and Dentists' Remuneration*	HMSO, London	1971	See Appendix G
[QRL 60]	Command Papers	*Review Body on Top Salaries: Reports*	HMSO, London	Annual	See Appendix G

Reference Number	*Author/Organization Responsible*	*Title*	*Publisher*	*Frequency or Date*	*Remarks*
[QRL 61]	Command Paper	*Royal Commission on Doctors' and Dentists' Remuneration 1957–1960*, Cmnd. 939	HMSO, London	1960	
[QRL 62]	Command Paper	*Royal Commission on the Distribution of Income and Wealth, Report No. 1, Initial Report on the Standing References*, Cmnd. 6171	HMSO, London	1975	
[QRL 63]	Command Paper	*Royal Commission on the Distribution of Income and Wealth, Report No. 2, Income from Companies and its Distribution*, Cmnd. 6172	HMSO, London	1975	
[QRL 64]	Scottish Office	*Scottish Abstract of Statistics*	HMSO, Edinburgh	Annual	
[QRL 65]	CSO	*Social Trends*	HMSO, London	Annual	
[QRL 66]	National Board for Prices and Incomes	*Standing Reference on Forces' Pay*	HMSO, London		See Appendix G
[QRL 67]	CSO	*Statistical Digest of the War*	HMSO; Longmans, Green & Co.	1951	Now out of print
[QRL 68]	Board of Inland Revenue	*Survey of Personal Incomes, 1969–1970*	HMSO, London	1972	
[QRL 69]	Board of Inland Revenue	*Survey of Personal Incomes, 1970–1971*	HMSO, London	1973	
[QRL 70]	Board of Inland Revenue	*Survey of Personal Incomes, 1972–1973*	HMSO, London	1975	
[QRL 71]	Ministry of Technology	*Survey of Professional Engineers, 1966*	HMSO, London	1967	
[QRL 72]	Ministry of Technology	*Survey of Professional Engineers 1968*, Studies in Technological Manpower, 1	HMSO, London	1970	
[QRL 73]	Ministry of Technology	*Survey of Professional Scientists 1968*, Studies in Technological Manpower, 2	HMSO, London	1970	
[QRL 74]	Department of Trade and Industry	*Survey of Professional Scientists 1971*, Studies in Technological Manpower, 4	HMSO, London	1974	
[QRL 75]	Command Paper	*Royal Commission on the Distribution of Income and Wealth, Report No. 3, Higher Incomes from Employment*, Cmnd. 6383	HMSO, London	1976	
[QRL 76]	Command Paper	*Royal Commission on the Distribution of Income and Wealth, Report No. 4, Second Report on the Standing Reference*, Cmnd. 6626	HMSO, London	1976	

Bibliography

[B 1] Abel-Smith, B. and Townsend, P., *The Poor and and the Poorest*, Occasional Papers in Social Administration, No. 17, Bell & Sons, London, 1965.

[B 2] Abel-Smith, B. and Townsend, P., *The Poverty Survey*, Essex University (forthcoming).

[B 3] Abraham, W. I., *National Income and Economic Accounting*, Prentice-Hall, New Jersey, 1969.

[B 4] Ainsworth, R. B., 'Earnings and Working Hours of Manual Wage-Earners in the United Kingdom in October 1968', *Journal of the Royal Statistical Society*, Series A, Vol. 112, Part 1, p. 35, 1949.

[B 5] Atkinson, A. B., *Economics of Inequality*, Clarendon Press, Oxford, 1975.

[B 6] Atkinson, A. B., *Poverty in Britain and the Reform of Social Security*, Cambridge University Press, Cambridge, 1969.

[B 7] Atkinson, A. B. and Harrison, A. J., *Reviews of UK Statistical Sources*, Vol. VI, no. 10, Pergamon Press, Oxford, 1977.

[B 8] Barna, T., *The Redistribution of Incomes through Public Finance in 1937*, Oxford University Press, London, 1945.

[B 9] Baxter, R. Dudley, *National Income, the United Kingdom*, Macmillan, London, 1868.

[B 10] Bellerby, J. R., 'Agricultural Income', *Journal of the Royal Statistical Society*, Series A, Vol. 118, Part 3, p. 336, 1955.

[B 11] Boreham, A. J. and Semple, M., 'Future Development of Work in the Government Statistical Service on the Distribution and Redistribution of Household Income', Paper presented to the Royal Economic Society Conference on the Personal Distribution of Income and Property, Lancaster, July 1974.

[B 12] Bowley, A. L., *The Change in the Distribution of National Income 1880–1913*, Oxford University Press, London, 1920.

[B 13] Bowley, A. L., *Wages and Income in the United Kingdom since 1860*, Cambridge University Press, Cambridge, 1937.

[B 14] Bowley, A. L. and Stamp, Sir Josiah, *The National Income 1924*, Clarendon Press, Oxford, 1927.

[B 15] Budd, E. C. 'The Creation of a Microdata File for estimating the Size Distribution of Income,' *Review of Income and Wealth*, p. 317, Dec. 1971.

[B 16] Cartter, A. M., 'A new method of relating British capital ownership and estate duty liability to income groups', *Economica*, Vol. 120, p. 247, August 1953.

[B 17] Cartter, A. M., *The Redistribution of Income in Post-War Britain*, Yale University Press, New Haven, 1955.

[B 18] Chapman, A. L. (assisted by Rose Knight), 'Wages and Salaries in the United Kingdom', *Studies in the National Income and Expenditure of the United Kingdom*, Vol. 5, Cambridge University Press, Cambridge, 1952.

[B 19] Chiozza-Money, L. G., *Riches and Poverty*, Methuen, London, 1906.

[B 20] Churchill, R. C. (DHSS), 'Expenditure patterns of retired persons at or immediately above the Supplementary Benefit Level in October 1972', *Economic Trends*, No. 254, p. lxxx, December 1974.

[B 21] Clarke, Colin, *National Income and Outlay*, Macmillan, London, 1937.

[B 22] Coates, Ken and Silbum, Richard, *Poverty, Deprivation and Morale*, Department of Adult Education, The University of Nottingham, 1970.

[B 23] Coates, Ken and Silbum, Richard, *Poverty: The Forgotten Englishmen*, Penguin Press, Harmondsworth, 1970.

[B 24] Colquhoun, P., *A Treatise on Indigence*, J. Hatchard, London, 1806.

[B 25] Colquhoun, P., *A Treatise on the Wealth, Power and Resources of the British Empire*, J. Mawman, London, 1814.

[B 26] Deane, P., 'The implications of early national income estimates for the measurement of long-term economic growth in the United Kingdom', *Economic Development and Cultural Change*, Vol. 4, p. 3, 1955–6.

[B 27] Deane, P. and Cole, W. A., *British Economic Growth 1688–1959*, Cambridge University Press, Cambridge, 1967. Also in *Abstract of British*

Historical Statistics by B. R. Mitchell and P. Deane, Cambridge University Press, Cambridge, 1962.

[B 28] Dow, J. C. R., *The Management of the British Economy 1945–60*, Cambridge University Press, Cambridge, 1964.

[B 29] Durham, W., *The £.s.d. of Welfare in Industry*, Industrial Welfare Society, London, 1958.

[B 30] Gray, H. L., 'Incomes from land in England in 1436', *English History Review*, Vol. 49, p. 607, 1934.

[B 31] Harris, R. and Solly, M., *A Survey of Large Companies*, Institute of Economic Affairs, London, 1959.

[B 32] Hay–MSL, *United Kingdom Salary Guide for Management*, 1966 (private circulation).

[B 33] Hill, T. P., Klein, L. A. and Straw, K. H., 'The Savings Survey 1953: Response Rates and Reliability of Data', *Bulletin of the Oxford University Institute of Statistics*, Vol. 17, Part 1, p. 89, February 1955.

[B 34] Howe, J. R., *Two parent families: A Study of their Resources and Needs*, DHSS Statistical Report Series, No. 14, HMSO, London, 1971.

[B 35] Jones, D. Caradog, *Social Surveys*, Hutchinson, London, 1949.

[B 36] Kemsley, W. F. F., *Family Expenditure Survey: Handbook on the Sample, Fieldwork and Coding Procedures*, HMSO, London, 1969.

[B 37] King, G., *Two Tracts*, ed. G. Barnett, John Hopkins Press, Baltimore, 1936.

[B 38] Klein, L. R., 'Patterns of Savings: The Surveys of 1953 and 1954', *Bulletin of the Oxford University Institute of Statistics*, Vol. 17, p. 173, 1955.

[B 39] Land, Hilary, *Large Families in London*, Occasional Papers in Social Administration, No. 32, Bell & Sons, London, 1969.

[B 40] Lydall, H. F., 'The Long Term Trend in the Size Distribution of Income', *Journal of the Royal Statistical Society*, Series A, Vol. 122, Part 1, p. 1, 1959.

[B 41] Lydall, H. F., *The Structure of Earnings*, Clarendon Press, Oxford, 1968.

[B 42] Marsden, Dennis, *Mothers Alone: Poverty and the Fatherless Family*, Allen Lane, The Penguin Press, London, 1969.

[B 43] Mogridge, M. J. H., *Planning, Incomes and Increasing Prosperity*, Centre for Environmental Studies, Working Paper, London, 1969.

[B 44] Ojala, E. M., *Agriculture and Economic Progress*, Oxford University Press, London, 1952.

[B 45] Okner, B. A., 'Constructing a new Data Base from Existing Microdata Sets, The 1966 Merge File', *Annals of Economic and Social Measurement*, 1/3, p. 325, 1972.

[B 46] Peacock, A. T. and Wiseman, J., *The Growth of Public Expenditure in the United Kingdom*, National Bureau of Economic Research, Princeton, 1961.

[B 47] Prest, A. R., 'Feinstein, C. H., National Income, Expenditure and Output of the UK 1855–1965', Review article, *Economic Journal*, Vol. 83, p. 580, June 1973.

[B 48] Prest, A. R. and Stark, T., 'Some Aspects of Income Distribution in the UK since World War II', *The Manchester School*, XXXV, September 1967.

[B 49] Reid, G. L. and Robertson, D. J. (eds.), *Fringe Benefits, Labour Costs and Social Security*, Allen and Unwin, London, 1965.

[B 50] Routh, G., *Occupation and Pay in Great Britain 1906–1960*, Cambridge University Press, Cambridge, 1965.

[B 51] Rowntree, B. S., *Poverty and Progress*, Longmans, London, 1941.

[B 52] Rowntree, B. S. and Lavers, R., *Poverty and the Welfare State*, Longmans, London, 1951.

[B 53] Rowntree, B. S. and Lavers, G. R., *Poverty and the Welfare State. A Third Social Survey of York dealing only with Economic Questions*, Longmans, London, 1951.

[B 54] Simons, H. C., *Personal Income • Taxation*, University of Chicago Press, Chicago, 1938.

[B 55] Sinfield, Adrian, 'Poor and Out of Work in Shields', *The Concept of Poverty*, ed. P. Townsend, Ch. 13, Heinemann, London, 1970.

[B 56] Soltow, L., 'Long-run changes in British income inequality', *Economic History Review*, Vol. 21, p. 17, 1968.

[B 57] Soltow, L., *Toward Income Equality in Norway*, University of Wisconsin Press, Madison, Milwaukee, 1965.

[B 58] Stamp, J., *British Incomes and Property*, King and Son, London, 1916.

[B 59] Stark, T., *The Distribution of Personal Income in the United Kingdom 1949–1963*, Cambridge University Press, Cambridge, 1972.

[B 60] Straw, K. H., 'The Savings Surveys and Official Sources', *Bulletin of the Oxford University Institute of Statistics*, Vol. 17, p. 283, August 1955.

[B 61] Taubmann, P. J., 'Personal Characteristics and the Distribution of Earnings', Paper to the Royal Economic Society Conference on the Personal Distribution of Incomes and Property, Lancaster, 1974.

[B 62] Thatcher, A. R., 'The Distribution of Earnings of Employees in Great Britain', *Journal of the Royal*

Statistical Society, Series A, Vol. 130, Part 2, p. 133, 1968.
[B 63] Titmuss, R. M., *Income Distribution and Social Change*, Allen and Unwin, London, 1962.
[B 64] Viet-Wilson, John, *A Study of the Chronic Sick*, Unpublished.
[B 65] Whitehead, F., 'Social Security Statistics', *Reviews of United Kingdom Statistical Sources*, ed. W. F. Maunder, Vol. II, no. 4, Heinemann Educational Books, London, 1974.
[B 66] Department of Health and Social Security, *Abstract of Retirement Pensions and Widows' Pensions*, HMSO, London. Available only from the Chief Statistician, Department of Health and Social Security.
[B 67] House of Commons, *Accounts of the National Insurance Funds*, HMSO, London, 1920–38 (annually).
[B 68] House of Commons, *Accounts of the Treasury Pensions Account*, HMSO, London, 1920–38.
[B 69] House of Commons, *Accounts of the Unemployment Fund*, HMSO, London, 1920–38.
[B 70] Ministry of Health, *Annual Local Taxation Returns*, HMSO, London, 1915/16 to 1932/3.
[B 71] Department of Health and Social Security, *Annual Reports*, HMSO London, 1969–72.
[B 72] Scottish Department of Health, *Annual Reports*, HMSO, Edinburgh.
[B 73] Northern Ireland Department of Health and Social Security, (formerly Ministry of Health and Social Service), *Annual Reports of the Supplementary Benefits Commission*, HMSO, Belfast.
[B 74] HMSO, *Catalogue (formerly 'List') of Government Publications*, HMSO, London, annual.
[B 75] Office of Population Censuses and Surveys, *Census of Population 1971: Income Follow-Up*, HMSO, London, forthcoming.
[B 76] Office of Population Censuses and Surveys, *Census 1971, Great Britain Summary Tables* (1% Sample), HMSO, London, 1973.
[B 77] Challoner Management Appointments Ltd., *Executive Salary Development—Report of a Survey*, London, 1966. Restricted circulation.
[B 78] British Institute of Management, *Fringe Benefits for Executives*, Information Summary 120, December 1965. Private circulation only.
[B 79] Central Statistics Office, *Household Budget Inquiry 1965–66*, Prl. 266, Stationery Office, Dublin, 1969.
[B 80] *Interim Report of the Cost of Living Advisory Committee*, Cmnd. 7077, HMSO, London, 1947.
[B 81] Life Offices Association, The Associated Scottish Life Offices and the Industrial Life Offices Association, *Life Assurance in the United Kingdom*, Life Offices Association, London, annual.
[B 82] *Lists of Members of Public Boards of a Commercial Character*, Cmnd. 4611, HMSO, London, 1971; Cmnd. 4876, HMSO, London, 1972.
[B 83] Ministry of Health, *Local Government Financial Statistics*, HMSO, London, annual from 1933/4.
[B 84] Northern Ireland Ministry of Home Affairs. *Local Taxation Returns*, HMSO, Belfast, annual.
[B 85] *National Accounts Statistics: Sources and Methods* (ed. Rita Maurice), HMSO, London, 1968.
[B 86] *National Income and Expenditure of the United Kingdom 1945–1948*, White Paper, Cmd. 7649, HMSO, London, 1949.
[B 87] *National Income and Expenditure of the United Kingdom 1946–1949*, White Paper, Cmd. 7933, HMSO, London, 1950.
[B 88] Central Statistical Office, *National Income Statistics: Sources and Methods*, HMSO, London, 1956.
[B 89] Central Statistical Office, *New Contributions to Economic Statistics*, Third Series, HMSO London, 1964.
[B 90] Government Actuary's Department, *Occupational Pension Schemes*, A Survey by the Government Actuary, HMSO, London, 1958.
[B 91] House of Commons, *Parliamentary Accounts and Records for 1801–2*, Vol. 4.
[B 92] Child Poverty Action Group of Northern Ireland, *Poverty in Downpatrick*, Belfast, 1970.
[B 93] Political and Economic Planning, 'Poverty Ten Years after Beveridge', *Planning*, Vol. XIX, No. 344, 1952.
[B 94] Department of Health and Social Security, *Report of the Committee on One Parent Families* (Finer Report), Cmnd. 5629, HMSO, London, 1974.
[B 95] *Reports on War Pensions*, HMSO, London, annual.
[B 96] *Royal Commission on Income Tax*, Cmd. 615, HMSO, London, 1920.
[B 97] *Royal Commission on Taxation. Final Report*, Memorandum of Dissent, Cmd. 9474, HMSO, London, 1955.
[B 98] *Social Science Research Council Archive*, University of Essex.
[B 99] Department of Health and Social Security, *Social Security Statistics*, HMSO, London, 1973 and after.
[B 100] Pay Board, *Special Report on the Relative Pay of Mineworkers*, Cmnd. 5567, HMSO, London, 1974.
[B 101] Central Statistical Office, 'Developments in

British Official Statistics', *Statistical News*, No. 17, HMSO, London, May 1972.

[B 102] Central Statistical Office, 'Developments in British Official Statistics', *Statistical News*, No. 13, HMSO, London, May 1971.

[B 103] *Royal Commission on the Distribution of Income and Wealth. Background Paper No. 2 Analysis of Managerial Renumeration in the United Kingdom and Overseas.* A report HAY–MSL Limited. HMSO, London, 1976.

[B 104] *Royal Commission on the Distribution of Income and Wealth. Background Paper No. 1. The Financing of Quoted Companies in the United Kingdom* (by Geoffrey Weeks and Geoffrey Whittington) HMSO, London, 1976.

[B 105] *Royal Commission on the Distribution of Income and Wealth. Selected evidence submitted to the Royal Commission for Report No. 1: Initial Report of the Standing Reference.* HMSO, London, 1976.

Appendices

1975-76 DEDUCTION CARD

Employee's National Insurance No. | Employee's Surname *(Enter in BLOCK CAPITALS)* | First two forenames

CODE † | Amended code † | Week/Month No. in which applied | Employer

District | Employer's reference

Works No., Branch, Dept., Contract, etc.

Make entries from 6 April 1975 to 5/6 December 1975 overleaf

This space is for employer's use	National Insurance Contributions: Total of Employee's and Employer's Contributions (1a)	National Insurance Contributions: Employee's Basic Contributions (1b)	Month number	Week number	Pay in the week or month (2)	Total pay to date (3)	Total free pay to date as shown by Table A (4)	Total taxable pay to date (5)	Total tax due to date as shown by Taxable Pay Tables (6)	Tax deducted or refunded in the week or month (Mark refunds "R") (7)
	£	£	B.F. from Mth. 8	B.F. from Wk. 35	£	£	£	£	£	£
			6 Dec. to 5 Jan.	36						
				37						
				38						
			9	39						
			6 Jan. to 5 Feb.	40						
				41						
				42						
			10	43						
			6 Feb. to 5 Mar.	44						
				45						
				46						
			11	47						
			6 Mar. to 5 Apr.	48						
				49						
				50						
N.I. Cont'n. Table Letter				51						
			12	52						
				§						

SPECIMEN

‡

N.I. LETTER AND TOTALS
‡ Enter letter identifying contribution table used when making first entry on card and on change of table.
Cols. 1a and 1b: Enter separate contribution totals for each table used.

TOTALS Previous employment(s)

This employment *(Mark net refund "R")*

Date of leaving (if before 5.4.1976) Enter in figs.

DAY	MTH.	YEAR

Employee's Widows and Orphans/Life insurance contributions in this employment £

Holiday pay paid but not included in column (2) £

Payment in Week 53: you must include pay and tax in totals above and complete this box — "X" in this box

DIRECTORS AND CERTAIN EMPLOYEES: A return on form P11D or P11D(a) is required.

OTHER EMPLOYEES: A return on form P9D is required only where payments of the nature described on the form have been made.

For Official use

† *If amended cross out previous code*
§ *Complete this line if pay day falls on 4 or 5 April 1976. (See Week 53 instructions on the BLUE CARD)*

For Official use

P9D	P11D				

P11 (1975)

CODE†	Amended code†	Week/Month No. in which applied

Follow the instructions on the BLUE CARD
WEEKS 1–35, 6 APRIL 1975 TO 6 DECEMBER 1975
MONTHS 1–8, 6 APRIL 1975 TO 5 DECEMBER 1975

National Insurance Contributions: Total of Employee's and Employer's Contributions (1a)	National Insurance Contributions: Employee's Basic Contributions (1b)	Month number	Week number	Pay in the Week or Month (2)	Total pay to date (3)	Total free pay to date as shown by Table A (4)	Total* taxable pay to date (5)	Total tax due to date as shown by Taxable Pay Tables (6)	Tax deducted or refunded in the week or month (Mark refunds "R") (7)
£	£	6		£	£	£	£	£	£
		Apr.	1						
		to 5	2						
		May	3						
		1	4						
		6 May	5						
		to	6						
		5 Jun.	7						
		2	8						
		6 Jun.	9						
		to	10						
		5 July	11						
			12						
		3	13						
		6 July	14						
		to	15						
		5 Aug.	16						
		4	17						
		6 Aug.	18						
		to	19						
		5 Sep.	20						
		5	21						
		6 Sep.	22						
		to	23						
		5 Oct.	24						
			25						
		6	26						
		6 Oct.	27						
		to	28						
		5 Nov.	29						
		7	30						
		6 Nov.	31						
		to	32						
		5 Dec.	33						
			34						
		8	35						
Totals carried forward									

SPECIMEN

This space is for employer's use

This box may be used to record the National Insurance Table Letter in use during Weeks 1–35 (Months 1–8). Enter in pencil in case of change.

† *If amended cross out previous code.*
* *If in any week/month the amount in col (4) is more than the amount in col. (3), make no entry in col. (5).*

P11(1975)

G.B.R. Ltd. 52-8..

Part A — INCOME SURVEY 1974-75

(See Notes overleaf)

a. District number   b. Section letter   c. Serial number

a. Control List number
b. *(To be completed*
c. *in all cases including R.U.s.)*

NOTE: If section letter is G or H fill in items a, b, c, 03, 14, 15, 16, 17, 18 and send to G.C.D. to complete form.

d. Area reference ... ... d.

OR

e. Place in which taxpayer resides ....
and
County in which taxpayer resides ....

f. ENTER "PLACE OF ISSUE" NUMERAL; viz.

1. for Sch. D Register or New Case Record
2. For Claims folder
3. For Sch. E: Concard or Incard or HR/S Register *(excluding cases at 4)*
4. For Sch. E: where wife's concard is place of issue

SPECIMEN

Part B — Allowances etc. for 1974-75

g. P.A.: enter "1" for A.S. (Male)
enter "2" for A.S. (Female)
enter "3" for A.M. (Full)
enter "4" for A.M. (Reduced)
enter "5" for "Wife's Earnings Election" case
(only one entry at g) g

h. If taxpayer (or wife) is known to be over 65 in 1974–75 enter "1" ... h

i. If taxpayer is known to be a widow in 1974–75 enter "1" i

CHILDREN

Enter number of children for whom C.A. (full restricted or apportioned) is due

j. Not over 11 years old ... ... j
k. Over 11 not over 16 ... ... k
l. Over 16 years l

Part D — Schedule E income for 1974-75

INCOME FOR WHICH DEDUCTION CARD ISSUED
(including D.P. cases)

Amount to nearest £ only

Main source *(Other than wife's income)*

09. Pay, etc. (including expenses payments, benefits etc. treated as pay on Deduction Card) ... ... [09]
10. Pensions ... ... [10]

Subsidiary source *(Other than wife's income)*

11. Pay, etc. (including expenses payments, benefits etc., treated as pay on Deduction Card) ... ... [11]
12. Pensions ... ... [12]

Main and subsidiary

13. Expenses payments, benefits etc. *(excluding wife's)* not treated as pay on Deduction Card ... ... [13]

Complete in all cases

Wife's income *(Excluding any income before marriage)*

14. Pay, etc. (including expenses payments, benefits, etc., whether OR NOT treated as pay on Deduction Card) ... [14]
15. Pensions ... ... [15]

If marriage took place in 1974–75 AND Section letter G or H complete items 16 and 17

Wife's income before marriage

16. Pay, etc. (including expenses payments, benefits etc., whether OR NOT treated as pay on Deduction Card) ... [16]
17. Pensions ... ... [17]

INCOME FOR WHICH DEDUCTION CARD *NOT* ISSUED
(including D.C. cases)

18. Wife's N.I. Retirement Pension by virtue of her own contributions ... ... [18]
19. N.I. Retirement Pension *(including wife's not entered at item 18)* or Widow's pension ... ... [19]
20. Any other pension ... ... [20]
21. Family allowance ... ... [21]
22. Wife's earnings *(including wife's wages from husband's business)* ... ... [22]
23. Any other Schedule E source ... ... [23]

m. Enter number of children INCLUDED AT ITEMS j, k, or l for whom restricted or apportioned C.A. is due ... ... m

n. D.R. *Enter number of dependants*
n. for whom full allowance due ... ...n
o. for whom restricted allowance due ... ... o

p. H.K.: If due enter "1"
ADDITIONAL P.A.: If due enter "2" ... ...p

q. BLIND P.A. if one allowance is due enter "1"
if two allowances due enter "2"
DAUGHTER'S SERVICES: If due enter "3" ... ... q

Nearest £ only

01. LIFE INSURANCE: Enter amount of allowable premiums *(NOT amount of tax relief)* 01

Part C — Deductions for 1974-75 *Enter gross amount*

SPECIMEN

02. TOTAL Sch. E expenses *(other than wife's)* including allowances against expenses payments *(item 13)* 02
03. TOTAL Sch. E expenses *(wife's)* 03
04. Retirement annuity relief *(amount allowed – NOT amount due)* 04
05. Charges *(enter gross amount allowable)* 05
06. B.S.I. allowable 06
07. Other deductions i.e. interest paid, small maintenance payments etc. ... 07
08. Family allowance deduction 08

**TO: Inland Revenue (E), Statistics Division,
A.D.P. Centre, WORTHING
Via I.R. Sorting Centre**

INCOME SURVEY FORM X

Part E — Schedule D Cases I and II income 1974-75

Income other than wife's
24. Profit *(total from all sources)* 24
25. Trade Classification for item 24 *(see notes)* 25
26. Losses and capital allowances set against profit at item 24 or any other income for 1974–75 26

Wife's income
27. Profit *(total from all sources)* 27
28. Trade Classification for item 27 *(see notes)* 28
29. Losses and capital allowances set against profit at item 27 or any other income for 1974–75 29

Part F — Other income for 1974-75

30. Schedule D Case III *(excluding exempt Savings Bank interest)* 30
31. Schedule D Cases IV to VI *(excluding pension shown at item 32)* 31
32. Schedule D Case V pension ranking as earned income 32
33. Schedule A rents, etc. 33
34. B.S.I. received NET 34
35. Dividends from U.K. Coys. – amount received *(do not add in tax credit)* 35
36. Any other income taxed before receipt – *GROSS amount* 36

REMARKS: If any apparent inconsistency in figures as reported please explain.
REPORT UNNECESSARY: If R.U. please state reason.

4614302 12.74. E.P. 400 M

Appendix C

[INCOME SURVEY 1972–3]

Section	*Type of case*	*Sampling Fraction*
D	Main source of income is within Schedule D	1 in 50
F	Main source of income is chargeable under PAYE: larger cases (generally those over £2,000) in the live range	1 in 100
G	Married woman's employment income chargeable under PAYE: cases in the live range	1 in 400
H	Married woman's employment income chargeable under PAYE: cases in leaver range	1 in 400
L	Main source of income is chargeable under PAYE: cases in leaver range	1 in 400
P	Main source of income is chargeable under PAYE: smaller cases in the live range	1 in 1200
R	Cases where a repayment of tax deducted at source has been claimed and which are not sampled elsewhere	1 in 100
S	Surtax payers not chosen under Section T	1 in 20
T	Surtax payers whose income for the previous year	
	(a) exceeded £100,000	1 in 1
	(b) exceeded £20,000 but did not exceed £100,000	1 in 4

Taxpayers who might have been chosen under Sections S and T are excluded when choosing the samples for the other sections.

The leaver range consists of taxpayers who during the year have ceased to have income chargeable under PAYE, including those who have died, together with those who changed jobs shortly before the end of the year and whose papers have not yet been transferred to the District dealing with their affairs in their new jobs. All other PAYE cases are in the live range.

Information supplied by Inland Revenue.

Family Expenditure Survey

S 825B

Area	Ser.	Hld.

INCOME SCHEDULE

START FRESH CARD TYPE 4 FOR EACH PERSON

IN CONFIDENCE

TO ALL

1. Are you doing any kind of paid work at present?
(PROBE AND CODE ONE ONLY FOR EACH PERSON).

		Per. No.	Per. No.	ASK
WORKING	an employee*	1	1	Q.3
	self employed or employer	2	2	Q.4
INTENDING TO WORK	out of employment but seeking work	3	3	Q.3(b1)
	out of employment because of sickness or injury but intending to seek work	4	4	Q.3(b1)
NOT WORKING	sick or injured but <u>not</u> intending to seek work	5	5	Q.28
	retired	6	6	Q.2
	none of these	7	7	Q.28

*EMPLOYEE INCLUDES
ALL WORKING FOR AN EMPLOYER IRRESPECTIVE OF HOURS.
INCLUDE PERSON ABSENT DUE TO HOLIDAYS, STRIKES, SICKNESS, INJURY OR TEMPORARILY LAID OFF AS LONG AS HE HAS JOB TO RETURN TO.
INCLUDE STUDENT 16 OR OVER IF WORKING AT PRESENT.

Per. No.	Per. No.
....	....
£	£
A201	A201

TO ALL RETIRED (CODED 6 AT Q.1)

2. In what year did you retire? Year .... IF LESS THAN 2 YEARS AGO ASK (a) & (b)

IF LESS THAN 2 YEARS AGO

(a) What was the exact date of your retirement? → A206 A206

(b) How much did you earn from your job (before tax) in the 12 months just before you retired? £ .... NOW ASK Q.28 302 8 302 8

TO ALL EMPLOYEES (CODED 1 AT Q.1.)

3. Are you away from work now (that is for more than the last 3 working days)?

No X X ASK Q.4

IF YES

(a) What is the reason for your absence?

illness or accident	1	1	
holiday	2	2	
strike	3	3	
other, SPECIFY	4	4	

A207 A207

(b) Are you receiving

full pay from your employer?	1	1	ASK (b1)
part pay or made up pay?	2	2	ASK (b1)
no pay?	3	3	ASK (b1)

A209 A209

TO ALL CODED 3 OR 4 AT Q.1 AND ALL ANSWERING YES TO Q.3

(b1) How many weeks have you been away from work? → .... A208 .... A208

ASK Q.4.

Per. No.	Per. No.
....	....

TO ALL CODED 1-4 AT Q.1

		Per. No.		
4.	Do you have more than one job (for pay or profit)?	.....	.....	
	one job only.........	X	X	ENTER DETAILS AT (a)
	more than one job...	Y	Y	ENTER DETAILS AT (a) AND THEN (b)

LIST ALL JOBS AT WHICH SUBJECT IS CURRENTLY WORKING.
IF ABOUT TO CHANGE JOBS OR UNEMPLOYED OR NOT YET PAID GIVE DETAILS FOR LAST JOB NOTING IF THIS DIFFERS FROM USUAL OCCUPATION.

a) **MOST REMUNERATIVE – LAST JOB IF SEEKING WORK**

Per. No. ....

Occupation A210

....

Industry A211

....

Per. No. A210

Occupation A211

....

Industry ....

....

SPECIMEN

Employee.....................	X	X	ASK Q's 5-19
Self-employed	Y	Y	ASK Q. 27

A212

b) **SUBSIDIARY**

Per. No. ....

Occupation ....

Industry .... employee .... X ASK Q's 20-23 / self-employed Y ASK Q. 27 — A214, A212

....

Per. No. ....

Occupation ....

Industry .... employee .... X ASK Q's 20-23 / self-employed Y ASK Q. 27 — A214

....

TO ALL EMPLOYEES WORKING OR INTENDING TO SEEK WORK CODED X AT Q.4(a)

MOST REMUNERATIVE JOB

	Per. No.		Per. No.	Per. No.
			£	£
5. On what date were you last paid a wage or salary? → IF MORE THAN A YEAR AGO NO FURTHER DETAILS REQUIRED. GO TO NEXT JOB OR Q.28.			A250	A250
6. What was your wage/salary, including overtime, bonus, commission or tips after all deductions, the last time you were paid? →			303	303
7. How long a period did your last wage or salary cover?				
week	1	1		
fortnight	2	2		
four weeks	4	4		
calendar month	5	5		
some other period SPECIFY				
8. Did this include a refund of income tax? No	X	X ASK Q.9		
IF YES (a) How much was the refund? →			304	304
9. How much was deducted for income tax under PAYE? →			305	305
IF NO PAYE TAX DEDUCTED (a) Do you usually pay any tax? Yes	Y	Y		
No	X	X		
10. How much was deducted as: (a) National Insurance contribution? →			306	306
(b) Graduated Pension contribution? →			307	307

SPECIMEN

11. Were there any other deductions from your wage/salary such as sports club, subscriptions to hospitals and charities, superannuation or private pension funds? ITEMISE COMPOSITE DEDUCTIONS.

Per No.	Type of deduction	£	

318	318
308	308

ENTER GROSS WAGE OR SALARY FROM PAY SLIP

INTERVIEWER TO CODE

Pay Slip:		
seen by interviewer	1	1
consulted by informant	2	2
not consulted	3	3

Per. No.	Per. No.
£	£ ....

EMPLOYEES - MOST REMUNERATIVE JOB (CONTINUED)

ASK WEEKLY PAID ONLY (CODED 1 AT Q.7)

12. For how many actual hours' work (excluding meal intervals but including paid overtime) were you paid in the weekly pay you quoted before? → NOW ASK Q.14 — A216 | A216

ASK ALL OTHER PAY PERIODS (CODED 2 TO OTHER AT Q.7)

13. How many hours a week (excluding meal intervals but including overtime) did you work during the (GIVE PERIOD AT Q.7) for which you have given me the details of your pay? → NOW ASK Q.14 — A218 | A218

ASK ALL PAY PERIODS

14. How many hours a week (excluding meal intervals but including overtime) do you usually work? → A220 | A220

IF 8 HOURS OR MORE CONTINUE WITH Q's 15-19.
IF LESS THAN 8 HOURS, GO TO NEXT JOB OR Q.28.

IF Q.14 (OR Q.15) CANNOT BE ANSWERED BECAUSE OF THE IRREGULAR NATURE OF THE JOB, SPECIFY — A234 | A234

....

SPECIMEN

ASK ALL

	Per. No.		
15. Do you usually receive the wage/salary* you mentioned before? Yes ...	1	1	ASK Q.16

*SEE Q.6 ON PREVIOUS PAGE — A254 | A254

IF NO

(a) What do you usually receive each time you are paid after all deductions? → 329 | 329

IF PAY VARIES A GREAT DEAL GIVE AVERAGE PAY RECEIVED *AND* before all deductions? → 315 | 315

(b) How often are you usually paid?

week	1	1
fortnight	2	2
four weeks	4	4
calendar month	5	5
some other period ..	0	0

........................(SPECIFY AT LEFT)
NOW ASK Q.16 — 330 8 | 330 8

16. Do you ever get an occasional addition to pay such as Christmas or quarterly bonus or an occasional commission? No. ...	X	X	ASK Q.17

312 8 | 312 8

IF YES

(a) What payments of this kind have you had in the last 12 months? PLEASE ITEMIZE BELOW

Per. No.	Description	Amount in last 12 months	ASK: Is this amount given: Before tax?	After tax?	No tax payable?	D.K.	IF NO AT Q.15 ASK: Did you include the bonus you just mentioned in your usual/average pay? Yes - How much was included? £	No
......	....	£..........	1	2	3	4	....	X
......	....	£..........	1	2	3	4	....	X
......	....	£..........	1	2	3	4	....	X
......	....	£..........	1	2	3	4	....	X
......	....	£..........	1	2	3	4	....	X
......	....	£..........	1	2	3	4	....	X

EMPLOYEES – MOST REMUNERATIVE JOB (CONTINUED)

	Per. No.			Per. No.	Per. No.
17. Do you receive any of the following benefits from your present/last employer:	....	....		£	£
PROMPT EACH					
(a) Luncheon vouchers? No...	X	X			
Yes – no. used in last 7 days →	....	....			
value of each voucher →	..........p	..........p		316 1	316 1
(b) Meals supplied free? No...	X	X			
Yes – meals in last 7 days →	....	....		317 1	317 1
(c) Any other food supplied free, e.g. milk, potatoes? No...	X	X			
IF YES, SPECIFY WITH QUANTITIES RECEIVED SINCE A MONTH AGO	Quantity	Quantity			
....	....	....			
....	....	....			
....	....	....			
....	....	....		320 5	320 5
(d) Free or subsidized housing such as a company house, subsidized rent or special help with house purchase? No...	X	X	ASK Q. 19	A241	A241
IF YES – SPECIFY AND ASK (d1)					
....					
(d1) Is your tenancy dependent on your job? Yes...	1	1			
No...	X	X			
19. Has Inland Revenue allowed you, or will you be claiming tax relief for expenses incurred as a result of your employment such as overalls, clothing, tools, subscriptions to professional societies? No...	X	X			

SPECIMEN

IF YES SPECIFY BELOW

Per. No.	Description of expenses claimed as tax relief	Period	Amount of tax relief £			
....	....	....	....	....		
....	....	....	....	....	370 8	370 8

GO TO NEXT JOB OR Q.28

NOTE: No Q.18

DETAILS OF JOB FOR SUBSIDIARY EMPLOYMENT AS EMPLOYEE

	Per. No.	Per. No.	Per. No.
		£	£
20. On what date were you last paid a wage or salary? →		A255	A255
21. What was your wage or salary, including overtime, bonus, commission or tips after all deductions the last time you were paid? →		309	309
22. How long a period did this cover? →		310	310
23. Were any deductions made from this pay before you received it? No...	X X	311	311

IF YES SPECIFY BELOW

Per. No.	Type of Deduction	£			
				313	313
				314	314
				319	319

SPECIMEN

NOTE: NO QUESTIONS 24 to 26

TO ALL SELF EMPLOYED - DETAILS OF JOB(S) CODED Y AT Q.4

		Per. No.	Per. No.
27. (a) How much net profit before tax did you get in the last 12 months from the business or profession, after deducting all expenses and wages (but including money drawn for your own use)? NOTE IF LOSS GIVEN RATHER THAN PROFIT		£........ ASK (a1)	£........ ASK (a1)
	D.K.	X ASK (b)	X ASK (b)
Dates of most recent 12 months for which figures are available		....	....
		£ 326 8	£ 326 8
		327 2	327 2
		328 8	328 8
IF NET PROFIT GIVEN ASK: (a1) Are you the sole owner of your business or are you in partnership with someone else?	Sole owner ...	X SEE*	X SEE*
	In partnership	Y ASK (i)	Y ASK (i)
IF IN PARTNERSHIP ASK: (i) Have your partner's shares been included in the net profit you gave me?	No ...	X SEE*	X SEE*
IF YES: (1) How much was included?		....	....
FOR REGULAR JOBS, SUCH AS MAIL ORDER AGENTS, BABY SITTERS, ASK: ALTERNATIVE WORDING TO Q.27(a): How much did you earn in the last 12 months?		....	....
IF D.K. TO (a) ASK: (b) Do you draw sums of money regularly from the business for your own use?	No ...	X ASK (c)	X ASK (c)
IF YES (b1) How much on average do you usually take out?		....	....
	D.K..	X ASK (c)	X ASK (c)
(b2) How often is this?	Period	....	....
(b3) After deducting the amount you withdrew and other expenses, how much profit, before tax, did your business yield in the most recent 12 months for which you have figures?	SEE Q.28	....	....
	D.K..	X ASK (c)	X ASK (c)
GIVE DATES		....	....
IF NO TO (b) OR D.K. TO (b1) OR (b3) ASK: (c) What was the total turnover of the business during the most recent period of 12 months for which you have figures?		....	....
GIVE DATES		....	....

SPECIMEN

TURNOVER IS TOTAL RECEIPTS FROM SALES AND REMUNERATION FOR SERVICES, LESS ANY DISCOUNT ALLOWED

*IF NO SUBSIDIARY JOB ASK Q.28.

IF SUBSIDIARY JOB AS EMPLOYEE GO BACK TO Q.20.

IF SUBSIDIARY JOB AS SELF-EMPLOYED ASK Q.27 USING MARGIN AT LEFT FOR ANSWERS.

TO ALL (NOTE: FOR MOST EMPLOYEES ANSWER IS AVAILABLE AT Q.10)

Question		Per. No.	Per. No.		Per. No.	Per. No.
28. Do you pay a National Insurance contribution?	No..	X	X	ASK Q.29	£	£
IF YES; (a) How much is it? (b) How long a period does this cover?					336	336
TO ALL Are you *at present* receiving any of the following State benefits? EXCLUDE ANY SUPPLEMENTARY BENEFIT FROM Qs 30 TO 37						
PROMPT EACH 29. Family allowances	No..	X	X	YES WEEKLY RATE	337 1	337 1
30. National Insurance retirement pension or Old Age Pension	No..	X	X	YES WEEKLY RATE	338 1	338 1
31. N.I. Widow's benefits	No..	X	X	YES WEEKLY RATE	339 1	339 1
32. Industrial Injury disablement pension or War Disability pension or allowance from the State	No..	X	X	YES WEEKLY RATE	340 1	340 1
TO ALL In the *last 12 months* have you received any of the following State benefits? PROMPT EACH 33. Invalidity pension, Invalidity Allowance and Attendance Allowance?	No...	X	X	YES TOTAL NO OF WEEKS RECEIVED	A258	A258
				AND LAST FULL WEEKLY PAYMENT AND ASK (a)	369 1	369 1
(a) Are you receiving benefit at present?	Yes.. No...	1 X	1 X		A259	A259
34. N.I. Unemployment benefit (INCLUDE EARNINGS-RELATED SUPPLEMENT)	No..	X	X	YES TOTAL NO. OF WEEKS RECEIVED	A222	A222
				AND LAST FULL WEEKLY PAYMENT AND ASK (a)	362 1	362 1
(a) Are you receiving benefit at present?	Yes.. No..	1 X	1 X		A223	A223
35. N.I. Sickness benefit or Industrial Injury benefit (INCLUDE EARNINGS-RELATED SUPPLEMENT)	No..	X	X	YES TOTAL NO. OF WEEKS RECEIVED	A224	A224
				AND LAST FULL WEEKLY PAYMENT AND ASK (a)	363 1	363 1
(a) Are you receiving benefit at present?	Yes.. No..	1 X	1 X		A225	A225

TO ALL		Per. No.			Per. No.	Per. No.
In the *last 12 months* have you received any of the following? PROMPT EACH		....	....		£	£
36. Family Income Supplement	No...	X	X	YES TOTAL NO. OF WEEKS RECEIVED → *AND*	A256	A256
				LAST FULL WEEKLY PAYMENT → AND ASK (a)	368 1	368 1
(a) Are you receiving benefit at present?	Yes.. No...	1 X	1 X		A257	A257
37. N.I. Maternity Grant or Allowance	No...	X	X	YES 12 MONTHS TOTAL →	371 8	371 8
38. Supplementary Benefit (INCLUDING SUPPLEMENTARY PENSION AND SUPPLEMENTARY ALLOWANCE)	No...	X	X	YES TOTAL NO. OF WEEKS RECEIVED → *AND*	A228	A228
				LAST FULL WEEKLY PAYMENT → AND ASK (a)	365 1	365 1
(a) Are you receiving benefit at present?	Yes.. No...	1 X	1 X		A229	A229
40. Any other N.I. or State benefit SPECIFY	No...	X	X	YES TOTAL NO. OF WEEKS RECEIVED → *AND*	A232	A232
				LAST FULL WEEKLY PAYMENT → AND ASK (a)	367 1	367 1
(a) Are you receiving benefit at present?	Yes.. No...	1 X	1 X		A233	A233
41. N.I. Death Grant	No...	X	X	YES 12 MONTHS TOTAL →	372 8	372 8
42. Redundancy payment under Redundancy Payments Act	No...	X	X	YES 12 MONTHS TOTAL → AND ASK (a)	356 8	356 8
(a) How many years were you working with the firm?	Yrs..	....	....		357 8	357 8
43. (a) Any other lump sum payment from the State SPECIFY	No...	X	X	YES 12 MONTHS TOTAL →	398 8	398 8
(b) Special Christmas payment	No...	X	X	YES 12 MONTHS TOTAL →	364 8	364 8
44. Trade Union sick pay or strike pay, Friendly Society benefits, benefits under private sickness scheme, accident insurance, hospital savings scheme.	No...	X	X	YES TOTAL NO. OF WEEKS RECEIVED → *AND*	A230	A230
				LAST FULL WEEKLY PAYMENT → AND ASK (a)	366 1	366 1
(a) Are you receiving benefit at present?	Yes.. No...	1 X	1 X		A231	A231

NOTE: No Q.39

TO ALL
PENSIONS – INCLUDE ONLY IF BY VIRTUE OF OWN (OR SPOUSE'S) FORMER EMPLOYMENT

PROMPT EACH

Are you *at present* receiving: Pension from:	Per. No.	IF NO RING	Own pension / Spouse's	Last payment £	Period	Was tax deducted at source? NO	IF YES How much? £	Was 'last payment' before tax?	after tax?
45. Central or Local Govt. or Armed Forces?	....	X	3 4	....	....	X	....	Y	X
	....	X	3 4	....	....	X	....	Y	X
46. Other previous employers? SPECIFY INDUSTRY									
....	....	X	3 4	....	....	X	....	Y	X
....	....	X	3 4	....	....	X	....	Y	X
47. Annuity?	....	X		....	....	X	....	Y	X
	....	X		....	....	X	....	Y	X
48. Payment from trust or covenant?	....	X		....	....	X	....	Y	X
	....	X		....	....	X	....	Y	X

SPECIMEN

CONTINUE PROMPT

49. Pension as a member of a Trade Union or a pension from a Friendly Society? No.. X X
IF YES
(a) How much was the last payment? →
(b) How long a period did it cover? →

50. Allowances from someone in Armed Forces or Merchant Navy? No.. X X
EXCLUDE HUSBAND TEMPORARILY NOT A MEMBER OF HOUSEHOLD. SEE Q.61
IF YES
(a) How much was the last payment? →
(b) How long a period did it cover? →

51. Regular allowance from a friend or relative outside the household or from an organization; or alimony or separation allowance? No.. X X
IF YES
(a) How much was the last payment? →
(b) How long a period did it cover? →

52. An allowance for a foster child? No.. X X
IF YES
(a1) Local Authority Grant: last payment →
(a2) Other source: last payment →
(b) How long a period did it cover?

Per. No.	Per. No.
£	£
342	342
343	343
A236	A236
344	344
345	345
A237	A237
346	346
347	347
348	348
349	349
350	350
351	351
352	352
353	353
352	352

TO ALL

	Per. No.			Per. No.	Per. No.
In the *last 12 months* have you received or been credited with any of the following:-	....	....	IF YES TO ANY ENTER 12 MONTHS TOTAL	.... £	.... £
PROMPT EACH					
Interest on:					
53. National Savings Bank or Trustee Savings Bank deposits? No...	X	X	→	373 8	373 8
54. Co-operative Society shares and deposits or dividends on purchases? No...	X	X	→	375 8	375 8
55. Building Society shares and deposits? No...	X	X	→	376 8	376 8
56. Defence Bonds, National Development Bonds, War Loan or British Savings Bonds? No...	X	X	→	377 8	377 8
57. Other Savings Accounts or bank deposits? No...	X	X	→	374 8	374 8
Interest and dividends on:					
58. Stocks, shares, bonds, debentures, any other securities after deduction of tax at source? No...	X	X	→	378 8	378 8
Rent from:					
59. Property (excluding the part of your accommodation you sub-let which you told me about earlier)? No...	X	X	ASK Q. 60		
IF YES (a) How much did you receive in the last 12 months before deducting income tax but after deducting all allowable expenses?			→	360 8	360 8
60. In the last 12 months have you received any coal or coke from your present (or a former) employer? **IF YES GIVE DETAILS BELOW** No...	X	X	SEE Q. 61	A247	A247

Per. No.	Quantity received in last 12 months (tons or cwt.)	If coke give brand	Free	Reduced price	Amount paid if not free including haulage costs £
.....	Coal	....	X	Y	....
.....	....	....	X	Y	....
.....	Coke	....	X	Y	....
.....	....	....	X	Y	....

 321 8 / 321 8; 322 8 / 322 8; A248 / A248; 323 8 / 323 8

TO A MARRIED WOMAN WHOSE HUSBAND IS TEMPORARILY NOT A MEMBER OF HOUSEHOLD

(i.e. CODED 2 IN ITEM 6 OF SCHEDULE A, PAGE 1) DNA....N ASK Q. 62 — 324 8 / 324 8

61. How much in total allowances have you received from your husband while he has been away? → 385 / 385

(a) How long a period does this amount cover? Period ....

NOW ASK Q. 62

12

TO ALL

62. Have you at any time during the last 12 months received any money by undertaking odd jobs, or any occasional fees for work or professional advice, which you have not yet mentioned?
EXCLUDE JOBS WHERE INFORMANT WAS WORKING AS AN EMPLOYEE FOR A WAGE OR SALARY

	Per. No.	Per. No.		Per. No.	Per. No.
				£	£
No. . .	X	X	ASK Q.63		

Per. No.	Description	Dates when job took place	Duration of job	Fees £		
					384 8	384 8
					381 8	381 8

TO ALL

63. Have you paid any tax direct to Inland Revenue during the last 12 months?
EXCLUDE TAX COLLECTED THROUGH PAYE DEDUCTIONS FROM WAGES OR SALARY OR DEDUCTED AT SOURCE FROM INCOME ON INVESTMENTS, PENSIONS AND ANNUITIES

No. . . X X ASK Q.64 — 392 8 — 392 8

IF YES

(a) How much did you pay direct in:

ENTER SOURCES OF INCOME BELOW

income tax? →		387 8	387 8
PROMPT			
surtax? →		389 8	389 8
capital gains tax? →			

SPECIMEN

TO ALL

64. Have you had any tax refunded directly by Inland Revenue during the last 12 months (other than PAYE tax, refunded in connection with a wage or salary)?

No. . . X X ASK Q.65

IF YES

(a) How much was refunded in . . . . income tax? → 390 8 — 390 8

PROMPT

surtax? → 391 8 — 391 8

ASK ABOUT EACH DEPENDANT UNDER 16

65. Have any of your children received an income from any source such as earnings from a spare time job, interest on a child's bank account or income from a trust fund within the past 12 months?
PROMPT FOR EACH CHILD

FRESH CARD FOR EACH PERSON

				Per. No.	Per. No.
Person number of each child					
(a) What kind of job or income?					
(b) Has he had this income throughout the past 12 months?	Yes. .	Y	Y		
IF NO For how many weeks has he had it?				£	£
		£	£	395 8	395 8
(c) How much did he get last time? →					
(d) How often does he get it?				396	396
(e) Does he usually:	dispose of it all himself?.	O	O		
	partly dispose of it and give the rest to you?.	X	X		
	give it all to you?.	Y	Y	397	397

W1511 11/74 OPCS

SOCIAL SURVEY DIVISION, OPCS,
ST. CATHERINES HOUSE, 10 KINGSWAY, LONDON WC2B 6JP.

OFFICE OF POPULATION CENSUSES AND SURVEYS,
TITCHFIELD,
FAREHAM,
HANTS.

Sample Survey of Incomes

SPECIMEN

I am writing to ask for your help in a sample survey we are doing in connection with the 1971 Population Census.

Good statistics about household incomes, related to such things as age, occupation, education and housing, are very much needed as background information in developing policies for many of the social and economic problems that face us.

Except for data on incomes all the other information that is needed was collected in the census taken about a year ago. This enquiry is therefore concerned only with incomes and is also addressed to only one out of every hundred persons up and down the country. This is a voluntary survey. You are one of those selected at random, as part of the sample.

The instructions given overleaf tell you what to do and how to send your form back. No one's answers will *in any circumstances* be passed to anyone or to any organization of any sort outside the Census organization. In particular, no other Government Department will see them. The information will be used only by the Census Office to produce tables of anonymous figures from which no one can be identified.

I hope that you will help.

Keith Joseph.

Secretary of State

This form is for..

TO COMPLETE THE FORM

1. Please answer all questions reading carefully any instructions included with the questions. Even if you have no income we would like you to tick the appropriate boxes.

2. Please write in ink or ball-point pen.

3. Where boxes are provided, please put a tick in the box against the answer which applies.
   For example, if the answer is 'Yes': ☑ YES ☐ NO

4. Do make use of any records that you have. If you are not sure of the answer please insert your best estimate.

SPECIMEN

WHEN YOU HAVE COMPLETED THE FORM, PLEASE:

1. Check your answers.

2. Detach the form from these instructions.

3. a) If you live alone or are resident in an hotel, hostel etc, post the form back to this office in the envelope provided—no stamp is required.

   b) If you are a member of a household, seal your form in the envelope and hand it to the head of your household so that he can return all the forms in one envelope. But you may, if you wish, post it yourself direct to this office—no stamp is needed.

INCOME SURVEY QUESTIONNAIRE
(Confidential)

EMPLOYMENT

A1 In the year ended 5th April 1972 did you at any time have a job in which you earned a wage, salary or commission? *Include odd jobs, casual work, full or part-time employment.* — ☐ YES ☐ NO
(If 'NO' go to question B1)

A2 For how many of the weeks during these 12 months did you receive pay from an employer? *Include paid holidays and other absences for which pay was received.* — .... weeks

A3 What was your total pay in these 12 months from all jobs before tax and other deductions? *Include payment for overtime, bonuses and tips.* If you have received your certificate of pay and tax (form P60) from your employer you should find it useful here. — £........................ in the year

OR, if that is not known, give an average figure for the weeks that you have worked. — £........................ per week

A4 a) Were deductions made from your pay under your employer's contributory pension scheme? *Do not include the National Insurance Pension Scheme.* — ☐ YES ☐ NO

b) Were you a member of an employer's non contributory pension scheme? — ☐ YES ☐ NO

SELF EMPLOYMENT

B1 In the year ended 5th April 1972 did you receive any money from self employment? *ie from your own business, professional practice or partnership or in payment for work done on your own account.* — ☐ YES ☐ NO
(If 'NO' go to question C1)

B2 What were your net earnings in the latest 12 months for which you have accounts, after deducting expenses and allowances for depreciation, but before any other deductions? *Include any sums drawn for your own use as well as sums left in the business. If you made a loss in the year enter the amount and write "Loss" after it.* — £..............

B3 Did you make any contributions to an insurance company to provide a pension when you retire? — ☐ YES ☐ NO

STUDENT'S INCOME

C1 During the 1971–72 academic year were you at any time a full time or "sandwich" student at a university or college? — ☐ YES ☐ NO
(If 'NO' go to question D1)

C2 Did you receive a maintenance grant from a local education authority, public body or private industry? — ☐ YES ☐ NO

C3 If 'YES' how much did you receive for the academic year? — £..............

PENSIONS OUTSIDE SOCIAL SECURITY SCHEMES

D1 In the year ended 5th April 1972 did you receive any pension from a former employer (*or husband's former employer*) or under a private pension scheme? — ☐ YES ☐ NO
(If 'NO' go to question E1)

D2 In how many weeks during these 12 months did you receive a pension? — .... weeks

D3 How much did you receive in total in this 12 month period before deductions for tax? — £..............

(Confidential)

SOCIAL SECURITY PENSIONS AND BENEFITS

E1 In the year ended 5th April 1972 did you receive any money from the following?

				If 'YES' for how many weeks during these 12 months did you receive this benefit?	How much did you receive a week? (Enter latest or final weekly rate. Give figures in decimal form e.g. £9.50.)
a)	Unemployment Benefit	☐ YES	☐ NO	..........weeks	£..............
b)	Family Allowances	☐ YES	☐ NO	..........weeks	£..............
c)	Sickness, Injury or Invalidity Benefit	☐ YES	☐ NO	..........weeks	£..............
d)	Family Income Supplement	☐ YES	☐ NO	..........weeks	£..............
e)	Attendance Allowance	☐ YES	☐ NO	..........weeks	£..............
f)	Retirement (old age) Pension	☐ YES	☐ NO	..........weeks	£..............
g)	Industrial or War Disability Pension	☐ YES	☐ NO	..........weeks	£..............
h)	Maternity Allowance	☐ YES	☐ NO	..........weeks	£..............
i)	Widow's or War Widow's Pension or Allowances	☐ YES	☐ NO	..........weeks	£..............
j)	Other Social Security or Supplementary benefit not included in the above	☐ YES	☐ NO	..........weeks	£..............

OTHER INCOME

F1 In the year ended 5th April 1972 did you receive income from one or more of the sources listed below?

Interest on money in a savings bank, or other kind of deposit account
Interest on money in a building society
Dividends and interest on shares, bonds, unit trusts, etc
Rent from property (after paying expenses)
Income from annuity, alimony, trust or separation allowances
Other sources not already mentioned

☐ YES ☐ NO

F2 If 'YES' what was your total income in these 12 months from these sources before tax? *If less than £50 write UNDER £50* £..........

FOR OFFICIAL USE

Processing No ....

Person No ....

Appendix F

NATIONAL BOARD FOR PRICES AND INCOMES

(Prior to April 1968, the National Board for Prices and Incomes Reports came under the Department of Economic Affairs)

REPORTS

1. (Interim) Road Haulage Rates. June, 1965. (Cmnd. 2695)
2. Wages, Costs and Prices in the Printing Industry. August, 1965. (Cmnd. 2750) (*Reprinted* 1970)
3. Prices of Bread and Flour. August, 1965. (Cmnd. 2760). (*Reprinted* 1970)
4. Prices of Household and Toilet Soaps, Soap Powder and Soap Flakes, and Soapless Detergents. October, 1965. (Cmnd. 2791)
6. Salaries of Midland Bank Staff. November, 1965. (Cmnd. 2389)
7. Electricity and Gas Tariffs: London Electricity Board and Scottish, South Western and Wales Gas Board. December, 1965. (Cmnd. 2862)
8. Pay and Conditions of Service of British Railways Staff (Conciliation, Salaried and Workshops Grades). January, 1966. (Cmnd. 2873)
9. (Interim) Wages in the Bakery Industry. January, 1966. (Cmnd. 2878)
10. Armed Forces Pay. January, 1966. (Cmnd. 2881)
11. Pay of the Higher Civil Service. January, 1966. (Cmnd. 2882)
12. Coal Prices. February, 1966. (Cmnd. 2919)
13. Costs, Prices and Profits in the Brewing Industry. April, 1966. (Cmnd. 2965)
14. Road Haulage Charges (Final Report). April, 1966. (Cmnd. 2968)
15. Scottish Teachers' Salaries. May, 1966. (Cmnd. 3005)
16. Pay and Conditions of Busmen. May, 1966. (Cmnd. 3012)
17. Wages in the Bakery Industry. June, 1966. (Cmnd. 3019)
18. Pay of Industrial Civil Servants. June, 1966. (Cmnd. 3034)
19. General Report April, 1965 to July, 1966. August, 1966. (Cmnd. 3087)
20. Laundry and Dry Cleaning Charges. September, 1966. (Cmnd. 3039)
21. Coal Distribution Costs. September, 1966. (Cmnd. 3094)
22. Rate of Interest on Building Society Mortgages. November, 1966. (Cmnd. 3136)
23. Productivity and Pay during the Period of Severe Restraint. December, 1966. (Cmnd. 3167)
24. Wages and Conditions in the Electrical Contracting Industry. December, 1966. (Cmnd. 3172)
25. Pay of Workers in Agriculture in England and Wales. January, 1967. (Cmnd. 3199)
26. Prices of Standard Newsprint. February, 1967. (Cmnd. 3210)
27. Pay of Workers in the Retail Drapery, Outfitting and Footwear Trades. March, 1967. (Cmnd. 3224)
27. (Supplement) Pay of Workers in the Retail Draper, Outfitting and Footwear Trades (Statistical Supplement). April, 1967. (Cmnd. 3224–1) (*Reprinted* 1969)
29. The Pay and Conditions of Manual Workers in Local Authorities, the National Health Service, Gas and Water Supply. March, 1967. (*Reprinted* 1968) (Cmnd. 3230)
29. (Supplement) The Pay and Conditions of Manual Workers in Local Authorities, the National Health Service, Gas and Water Supply. (Statistical Supplement). May, 1967. (*Reprinted* 1971) (Cmnd. 3230–1)
30. Pay and Conditions of Limbfitters Employed by J. E. Hanger and Company. April, 1967. (Cmnd. 3245)
31. Distribution costs of Fresh Fruit and Vegetables. April, 1967. (Cmnd. 3256)
32. Fire Service Pay. May, 1967. (Cmnd. 3287)

33. (Interim) The Remuneration of Milk Distributors. May, 1967. (Cmnd. 3294)
34. Bank Charges. May, 1967. (Cmnd. 3292)
35. Pay and Conditions of Merchant Navy Officers. June, 1967. (Cmnd. 3302)
36. Productivity Agreements. June, 1967. (Cmnd. 3311)
37. Costs and Charges in the Motor Repairing and Servicing Industry. August, 1967. (Cmnd. 3368)
38. Portland Cement Prices. August, 1967. (Cmnd. 3381)
39. Costs and Prices of Aluminium Semi-Manufacturers. August, 1967. (Cmnd. 3378)
40. Second General Report. July, 1966 to August, 1967. September, 1967. (Cmnd. 3394)
41. Salaries of Staff employed by the General Accident, Fire and Life Assurance Corporation Limited. September, 1967. (Cmnd. 3398)
42. Pay of Electricity Supply Workers. September, 1967. (*Reprinted* 1969, *revised price*) (Cmnd. 3405)
43. Costs and Revenue of National Daily Newspapers. October, 1967. (Cmnd. 3435)
44. London Weighting in the non-industrial Civil Service. November, 1967. (*Reprinted* 1968) (Cmnd. 3436)
45. Pay of Chief and Senior Officers in Local Government Service and in the Greater London Council. November, 1967. (Cmnd. 3473)
46. The Remuneration of Milk Distributors (Final Report). November, 1967. (Cmnd. 3477)
48. Charges, Costs and Wages in the Road Haulage Industry. December, 1967. (Cmnd. 3482)
48. (Supplement). Charges, Costs and Wages in the Road Haulage Industry. (Statistical Supplement). March, 1968. (Cmnd. 3482–1)
49. Pay and Conditions of Service of Engineering Workers. (1st Report on the Engineering Industry). December, 1967. (Cmnd. 3495)
49. (Supplement). Pay and Conditions of Service of Staff Workers in the Engineering Industry (Statistical Supplement). March, 1968. (Cmnd. 3495–1)
50. Productivity Agreement in the Bus Industry. December, 1967. (Cmnd. 3498)
51. Pay and Productivity of Industrial Employees of the United Kingdom Atomic Energy Authority. January. 1968. (Cmnd. 3499)
52. Costs and Charges in the Radio and Television Rental and Relay Industry. January, 1968. (Cmnd. 3520)
53. Flour Prices. February, 1968. (Cmnd. 3522)
54. Remuneration of Solicitors. February, 1968. (Cmnd. 3529)
55. Distributors' Margins in relation to Manufacturers' Recommended Prices. February, 1968. (Cmnd. 3456)
56. Proposals by the London Transport Board and British Railways Board for Fare Increases in the London Area. March, 1968. (Cmnd. 3561)
57. Gas Prices (1st Report). March, 1968. (Cmnd. 3567)
58. Post Office Charges. March, 1968. (Cmnd. 3574)
59. The Bulk Supply Tariff of the Central Electricity Generating Board. March, 1968. (Cmnd. 3575)
60. Pay of Nurses and Midwives in the National Health Service. March, 1968. (Cmnd. 3585)
61. Prices of Secondary Batteries. April, 1968. (Cmnd. 3597)
62. Increases in Rents of Local Authority Housing. April 1968. (Cmnd. 3604) (10 136040 1)
62. (Supplement). Increases in Rents of Local Authority Housing (Statistical Supplement). October, 1968. (Cmnd. 3604–1) (10 136041 X)
63. Pay of Municipal Busmen. April, 1968. (Cmnd. 3605) (10 136050 9)
64. Increase in Prices of Mercury Hearing-Aid Batteries manufactured by Mallory Batteries Limited. May, 1968. (Cmnd. 3625) (10 136250 1)
65. Payment by Results Systems. May, 1968. (*Reprinted* 1969) (Cmnd. 3627) (10 136270 6)
65. (Supplement). Payment by Results Systems. December, 1968. (Cmnd. 3627–1) (10 136271 4)
66. Price of Butyl Rubber. May, 1968. (Cmnd. 3626) (10 136250 9)
67. Passenger Fares and Freight Charges of the North of Scotland, Orkney and Shetland Shipping Company Limited. May, 1968. (Cmnd. 3631) (10 136310 9)

68. Agreement made between Certain Engineering Firms and the Draughtsmen's and Allied Technicians' Association. May, 1968. (Cmnd. 3632) (10 136320 6)
69. Pay and Conditions of Busmen employed by the Corporations of Belfast, Glasgow and Liverpool. May, 1968. (Cmnd. 3646) (10 136460 1)
70. Standing Reference on the Pay of the Armed Forces. 1st Report. June, 1968. (Cmnd. 3651) (10 136510 1)
71. Architects' Costs and Fees. May, 1968. (Cmnd. 3653) (10 136530 6)
72. Proposed Increases by British Railways Board in certain Country-Wide Fares and Charges. June, 1968. (Cmnd. 3656) (10 136560 8)
73. The Prices of Hoover Domestic Appliances. June, 1968. (Cmnd. 3671) (10 136710 4)
74. Agreements relating to Terms and Conditions of Employment of Staff employed by the Prudential Assurance Company Ltd., and the Pearl Assurance Company Ltd. June, 1968. (Cmnd. 3674) (10 136740 6)
75. Costs and Prices of the Chocolate and Sugar Confectionery Industry. July, 1968. (Cmnd. 3694) (10 136940 9)
76. Increase in Rented Charges for Equipment hired from IBM United Kingdom Limited. July, 1968. (Cmnd. 3699) (10 136990 5)
77. Third General Report. August, 1967–July, 1968. July, 1968. (Cmnd. 3715) (10 137150 0)
78. Award relating to Terms and Conditions of Employment in the Road Passenger Transport Department of Rochdale County Borough Council. (With Correction). July, 1968. (Cmnd. 3723) (10 137230 2)
79. Electricity Supply Industry National Guidelines Covering Productivity Payments. July, 1968. (Cmnd. 3726) (10 137260 4)
80. Distributors' Margins on Paint, Children's Clothing. Household Textiles and Proprietary Medicines. August, 1968. (Cmnd. 3737) (10 137370 8)
81. Pay Awards made by the City and County of Bristol to Staff employed in its Dock Undertaking. August, 1968. (Cmnd. 3752) (10 137520 4)
82. Report on an Agreement relating to the pay of Surveyors and Wood-cutting Machinists in the Saw Milling Industry. September, 1968. (Cmnd. 3768) (10 137680 4)
83. Job Evaluation. December, 1968. (Cmnd. 3772) (10 137720 7)
83. (Supplement). Job Evaluation. December, 1968. (Cmnd. 3772–1) (10 137721 5)
84. Report on a settlement relating to the pay of certain workers employed in the Thermal Insulation Contracting Industry. October, 1968. (Cmnd. 3784) (10 137840 8)
85. Pay and Conditions of Busmen employed by the Corporation of Dundee. October, 1968. (Cmnd. 3791) (10 137910 2)
86. Pay of Staff Workers in the Gas Industry. October, 1968. (Cmnd. 3795) (10 137950 1)
87. Proposed Increase in London Taxicab Fares. October, 1968. (Cmnd. 3796) (10 137960 9)
88. Pay of Pilots employed by the British Overseas Airways Corporations. October 1968.) Cmnd. 3789) (10 137890 4)
89. Office Staff Employment Agencies Charges and Salaries. November, 1968. (Cmnd. 3828) (10 138280 4)
90. Pay of Vehicle Maintenance Workers in British Road Services. December, 1968. (Cmnd. 3844) (10 138480 7)
91. Pay and Conditions in the Civil Engineering Industry. November, 1968. (Cmnd. 3826) (10 138360 6)
92. Pay and Conditions in the Building Industry. November, 1968. (Cmnd. 3827) (10 138370 3)
93. Pay and Conditions in the Construction Industry other than Building and Civil Engineering. November, 1969. (Cmnd. 3836) (10 138380 0)
94. Productivity Agreements in the Road Haulage Industry. December, 1968. (Cmnd. 3847) (10 138470 X)
95. Pay and Conditions of Busmen Employed by the Corporation of Wigan. December, 1968. (Cmnd. 3845) (10 138450 5)
96. Pay of Busmen Employed by the Corporation of Great Yarmouth. December, 1968. (Cmnd. 3844) (10 138440 8)
97. Distributors' Costs and Margins on Furniture, Domestic Electrical Appliances and Footwear, December, 1968. (Cmnd. 3858) (10 138580 3)
98. Standing Reference on the Pay of University Teachers in Great Britain. (1st Report). December, 1968. (Cmnd. 3866) (10 138660 5)

99. Pay of Maintenance Workers Employed by Bus Companies. January, 1969. (Cmnd. 3868) (10 138680 X)
100. Synthetic Organic Dystuffs and Organic Pigments Prices. January, 1969. (Cmnd. 3895) (10 138950 7)
101. Pay of Workers in Agriculture in England and Wales. February, 1969. (Cmnd. 3911) (10 139110 2)
102. Gas Prices (2nd Report). February, 1969. (Cmnd. 3924) (10 139240 0)
103. Pay and Productivity in the Car Delivery Industry. February, 1969. (Cmnd. 3929) (10 139290 7)
104. Pay and Conditions of Service of Engineering Workers (2nd Report on the Engineering Industry). February, 1969. (Cmnd. 3931) (10 139310 5)
105. Pay of General Workers and Craftsmen in Imperial Chemical Industries Ltd. February, 1969. (Cmnd. 3941) (10 139410 1)
106. Pay in the London Clearing Banks. March, 1969. (Cmnd. 3943) (10 139430 6)
107. Nationalized Industries. Top Salaries in the Private Sector. March, 1969. (Cmnd. 3970) (10 139700 3)
108. Pay and Conditions in the Electrical Contracting Industry in Scotland. March, 1969. (Cmnd. 3966) (10 139660 0)
109. Pay of Salaried Staff in Imperial Chemical Industries Ltd. March, 1969. (Cmnd. 3981) (10 139810 7)
110. Pay and Conditions in the Clothing Manufacturing Industries (With Correction). April, 1969. (Cmnd. 4002) (10 140020 9)
110. (Supplement). Conditions in the Clothing Manufacturing Industries. (Statistical Supplement). July, 1969. (Cmnd. 4002–I) (10 140021 7)
111. Steel Prices. June, 1969. (Cmnd. 4033) (10 140330 5)
113. Manufacturers' Prices of Toilet Preparations. June, 1969. (Cmnd. 4066) (10 140660 6)
115. Journalists' Pay. June, 1969. (Cmnd. 4077) (10 140770 X)
116. Standing Reference on the Pay of the Armed Forces. (2nd Report.) June, 1969. (Cmnd. 4079) (10 140790 4)
117. Pay and Conditions of Workers in the Exhibition Contracting Industry, June, 1969. (Cmnd. 4088) (10 140880 3)
118. Prices of Non-Alloy Bright Steel Bars. June, 1969. (Cmnd. 4093) (10 140930 3)
119. Man-Made Fibre and Cotton Yarn Prices. (1st Report.) June, 1969. (Cmnd. 4092 (10 140920 6)
120. Pay and Conditions in the Electrical Contracting Industry. June, 1969. (Cmnd. 4097) (10 140970 2)
121. Post Office Charges: Inland Parcel Post and Remittance Services. July, 1969. (Cmnd. 4115) (10 141150 2)
122. Fourth General Report July, 1968 to July, 1969. (Cmnd. 4130) (10 141300 9)
123. Productivity Agreements. (Cmnd. 4136) (10 141360 2)
124. Coal Prices. (Cmnd. 4149) (10 141490 0)
125. Pay of Staff in British Insulated Callenders' Cables Ltd. September, 1969. (Cmnd. 4168) (10 141680 6)
126. Smithfield Market. October, 1969. (Cmnd. 4171) (10 141710 1)
127. Man-made Fibre and Cotton Yarn Prices. (2nd Report). October, 1969. (Cmnd. 4180 (10 141800 0)
128. Pay of Ground Staff at Aerodromes. October, 1969. (Cmnd. 4182) (10 141820 5)
129. Pay of Pilots Employed by the British Overseas Airways Corporation. November, 1969. (Cmnd. 4197) (10 141970 8)
130. Plasterboard Prices. November, 1969. (Cmnd. 4184) (10 141840 X)
131. Pay of Certain Employees in the Film Processing Industry. November, 1969. (Cmnd. 4185) (10 141850 7)
132. Salary Structures. November, 1969. (Cmnd. 4187) (*Reprinted* 1971, *revised price*) (10 141870 1)
133. Portland Cement Prices. November, 1969. (Cmnd. 4215) (10 142150 8)
134. Standing Reference on the Remuneration of Solicitors. (1st Report.) November, 1969. (Cmnd. 4217) (10 142170 2)
135. Pay Structure within HM Stationery Office Presses and Binderies. November, 1969. (Cmnd. 4219) (10 142190 7)
137. Proposals by the British Railways Board for Fare Increases in the London Commuter Area. December, 1969. (Cmnd. 4250) (10 142500 7)
138. Coal Prices. (1st Report). January, 1970. (Cmnd. 4255) (10 142550 3)
139. Electric Motor Prices. January, 1970. (Cmnd. 4258) (10 142580 5)
140. Pay and Conditions of Workers in the Milk Industry. January, 1970. (Cmnd. 4267) (10 142670 4)
141. Costs and Revenue of National Newspapers. February, 1970. (Cmnd. 4277) (10 142770 0)
142. Pay of the Armed Forces. (3rd Report.) (Cmnd. 4291) (10 142910 X)

143. Hours and Overtime in the London Clearing Banks. (Cmnd. 4301) (10 143010 8)
144. Bread Prices and Pay in Baking. (Cmnd. 4329) (10 143290 9)
145. Pay of University Teachers in Great Britain. (Cmnd. 4334) (10 143340 9)
146. Pay and Conditions of Industrial Civil Servants. (Cmnd. 4351) (10 143510 X)
147. Margarine and Compound Cooking Fats. (Cmnd. 4368) (10 143680 7)
148. Prices of Primary Batteries proposed by the Ever Ready Company (Great Britain) Ltd. (Cmnd. 4370) (10 143700 5)
149. Pay and Other Terms and Conditions of Employment of Workers in the Pottery Industry. (Cmnd. 4411) (10 144110 X)
150. Pay and Other Terms and Conditions of Employment in the Fletton Brick Industry and Prices Charged by the London Brick Company. (Cmnd. 4422) (10 144220 3)
151. Bread Prices and Pay in the Baking Industry. (Cmnd. 4428) (10 144280 7)
152. Pay and Productivity in the Water Supply Industry. (Cmnd. 4434) (10 144240 4)
153. Coal Prices. (Cmnd. 4455) (10 144550 4)
    Supplement No. 1. (Cmnd. 4455–I) (10 144551 2)
    Supplement No. 2. (Cmnd. 4455–II) (10 144552 0)
154. Tea Prices. (Cmnd. 4456) (10 144560 1)
155. Costs and Efficiency in the Gas Industry. (Cmnd. 4458) (10 144580 6)
156. Costs and Revenues of Independent Television Companies. (Cmnd. 4524) (10 145240 3)
157. Standing Reference on the Pay of the Armed Forces. Pay of Senior Officers. (Cmnd. 4513) (10 145130 X)
158. Standing Reference on the Pay of the Armed Forces. Separate Allowance. (Cmnd. 4529) (10 145290 X)
159. London Transport Fares. (Cmnd. 4540) (10 145400 7)
160. Costs. Prices and Profitability in the Ice-Cream Manufacturing Industry. (Cmnd. 4548) (10 145480 5)
161. Hours of Work, Overtime and Shiftworking. (Cmnd. 4554) (10 145540 2)
    Supplement. (Cmnd. 4554–1) (10 145541 0)
162. Costs, Charges and Productivity of the National Freight Corporation. (Cmnd. 4569) (10 145690 5)
163. Costs and Charges in the Motor Repairing and Servicing Industry. (Cmnd. 459c) (10 145900 9)
164. Standing Reference on the Remuneration of Solicitors. (Cmnd. 4624) (10 146240 9)
165. Prices, Profits and Costs in Food Distribution. (Cmnd. 4645) (10 146540 9)
166. Pay and Conditions of Service of Ancillary Workers in the National Health Service. (Cmnd. 4644) (10 146440 1)
167. Pay and Conditions of Service of Workers in the Laundry and Dry Cleaning Industry. (Cmnd. 4647) (10 146470 3)
168. Pay and Conditions in the Contract Cleaning Trade. (Cmnd. 4637) (10 146370 7)
169. General Problems of Low Pay. (Cmnd. 4648) (10 146480 0)
170. Fifth and Final General Report. July 1969. March 1971. (Cmnd. 4649) (10 146490 8)
171. Supplement to Fifth and Final General Report. (Cmnd. 4649–I) (10 146491 6)

Appendix G

Review Body on Doctors' and Dentists' Remuneration
1st Report, 1971, Cmnd. 4825, HMSO
2nd Report, 1972, Cmnd. 5010, HMSO
3rd Report, 1973, Cmnd. 5353 HMSO
Supplement No. 1 to 3rd Report, 1973, Cmnd. 5377, HMSO
Supplement No. 2 to 3rd Report, 1973, Cmnd. 5517, HMSO
4th Report, 1974, Cmnd. 5644, HMSO
Supplement to 4th Report, 1974, Cmnd. 5849, HMSO
5th Report, 1975, Cmnd. 6032, HMSO

Review Body on Armed Forces' Pay
Report of the Review Body on Armed Forces' Pay, 1972, Cmnd. 4954, HMSO
2nd Report, 1973, Cmnd. 5336, HMSO
Supplement to 2nd Report, 1973, Cmnd. 5450, HMSO
3rd Report, 1974, Cmnd. 5631, HMSO
Supplement to 3rd Report, 1974, Cmnd. 5729, HMSO
4th Report, 1975, Cmnd. 6063, HMSO
Supplement to 4th Report, 1974, Cmnd. 6146, HMSO

Review Body on Top Salaries
1st Report: Ministers of the Crown and Members of Parliament, 1971, Cmnd. 4836, HMSO
2nd Report: Interim Report on Top Salaries, 1972, Cmnd. 5001, HMSO
3rd Report: 2nd Report on Top Salaries, 1973, Cmnd. 5372, HMSO
4th Report: 3rd Interim Report on Top Salaries, 1974, Cmnd. 5595, HMSO

Subject Index